Antique Trader™

ANSWERS TO QUESTIONS ABOUT

Antiques
&
Collectibles

KYLE HUSFLOEN

Antique Trader™ Editor-at-Large
and author of *"Kyle on Antiques"*

©2004 by Krause Publications
Published by

kp **krause publications**
An F+W Publications Company

700 East State Street • Iola, WI 54990-0001
715-445-2214 • 888-457-2873
www.krause.com

Our toll-free number to place an order or obtain
a free catalog is (800) 258-0929.

Library of Congress Catalog Number: 2004100729
ISBN: 0-87349-776-7

Edited by Kyle Husfloen
Designed by Sandra Morrison

Printed in the United States of America

Contents

A Word From The Author

One of the greatest pleasures for me as an editor, author and collector is learning all I can about the various antiques and collectibles that I encounter. Whether out on an antiquing foray or busy editing a price guide, I find real satisfaction in seeing, examining, reading about and researching a myriad of objects. This insatiable appetite to learn about the world around me began even before I started school in the mid-1950s, fed by gifts of colorful science and natural history books.

It was during my junior high school years that my study of true "antiques" began. I was fortunate enough to befriend an antiques dealer who opened my eyes to the wide world of vintage treasures. I soon had a growing library of popular reference books written by experts like the Kovels, the Warmans and Katharine Morrison McClinton.

Although my funds were limited, my earliest purchases included pattern glass, pewter and ceramics. For my high school graduation present I asked for and received from my parents a matched Victorian Eastlake armchair and platform rocker. Now, nearly forty years later, I have a diverse collection of these and many other objects. Although many collectors narrow their focus to a select category, I'm afraid the appeal of the unusual and beautiful has made me an eclectic shopper. But, again, I don't buy just to own but to study and learn about each piece I acquire.

I have been extremely lucky that my collecting avocation served as a basis for my vocation. I owe my situation to a combination of luck and good timing. My career with *The Antique Trader* began over 32 years ago when I sent my resume to the publisher, Edward Babka. To my utter surprise, within a year I found myself relocated to Dubuque, Iowa, and hard at work editing features and columns. Now, decades later, I still can hardly believe my luck. I have learned so much from collectors, dealers and experts in the collecting world and I always want to learn more.

It was in 1995 that I was asked to contribute a "question and answer" column to the *Antique Trader Collector Magazine and Price Guide*. My first one-page column appeared in the June 1995 issue. By 1997 "Kyle On Antiques" had expanded to four pages per issue. About that time *The Antique Trader* newspaper also began running it on a regular bases.

This new book presents a compilation of the best of the hundreds of letters I have received and researched over the years. I hope it will serve as a valuable research tool for collectors, dealers and appraisers alike. I have always striven to present the most accurate and up-to-date research possible and have always welcomed input from readers. They have provided some excellent updates and corrections to my replies and these are also included here

I hope you will find this new book interesting and educational. Although I've learned a lot in preparing my column there's so much more to know. May each of you also learn to appreciate the fun of researching your treasures.

I'm always interested in receiving your comments and suggestions. Of course, you're also welcome to address specific inquiries to "Kyle On Antiques," care of either *Collector Magazine and Price Guide* or the *Antique Trader Weekly*. Please keep in mind, however, I do have a large backlog of material awaiting publication, so please be patient. Remember if you write to include detailed descriptions with measurements, as well as clear color photographs (sorry, print-outs of color scans won't work).

Happy reading and best wishes for wonderful collecting experiences!

Kyle Husfloen

Tips on Collecting

Advertising Items

1. Watch out for modern soda pop advertising items. There are reproductions (close copies of original pieces) and "fantasy items" (brand new pieces with no old counterparts). Coca-Cola and Pepsi Cola items are especially abundant.

2. Collectors of advertising items always keep these points in mind: 1) Subject (company); 2) Rarity; 3) Condition; 4) Eye Appeal.

Artworks

A reverse-painted glass object, as the name implies, has the decoration sketched and then painte1. d in color on the back or inside. The most delicate examples are the tiny snuff bottles produced by the Chinese. Flat pictures were much easier to produce since the background design was sometimes stenciled on and then filled in with color. The Chinese did such painted pictures and, in the early 19th century, German artisans also produced such works, mainly as human portraits. Reverse-painted scenes were also quite often featured in the glass tablets above mirrors during the first half of the 19th century.

2. Currier & Ives prints are probably the most reproduced of any 19th century American lithographs. Read the inscription along the bottom edge with care. Many originals will have the date they were "Entered According to an Act of Congress," but some old ones are undated.

3. One test to help sort the originals from the copies is to use a 10X loupe and examine a small area. If you see tiny dashed lines, it is an original. If you see an overall design of tiny dots, it is a photographic copy. Also, if you can examine it out of the frame, you should be able to detect the watercolor paint on the surface. It will reflect light as it is turned at an angle.

Ceramics

1. Dogs are not the only old Staffordshire pottery pieces reproduced; other animals and even figural groups have been copied. Watch out for overall "crazing" of the glaze (early examples are seldom crazed). Also "firing holes" or vent holes on the bottom of originals are only about ¼" diameter. Modern pieces have much larger holes.

2. The "Wedgwood" Wares Confusion. Most people see the name "Wedgwood" on a piece of ceramic and assume it is a product of the famous Josiah Wedgwood firm that was established around 1769 and is still operating today. Several other English potteries, however, used markings that appear similar. Keep in mind the Josiah Wedgwood pottery uses only the word "Wedgwood" to indicate the firm (note: no middle "e" in "Wedgwood").

Confusing marks include "Wedgwood & Co." (1860 -), "H.F. Wedgwood & Co. Ltd. (ca. 1954-9), and "J. Wedgwood," the mark of John Wedge Wood (1841-60).

3. Ironstone china is a dense, heavy earthenware pottery that was the everyday tableware of most Americans from the 1840s until around 1910. First invented in England in the early 19th century, huge quantities were exported to the United States. In the 1850s all-white wares with embossed designs were popular, but patterns were also decorated with many transfer-printed designs in dark flow blue and, later, in lighter shades of blue, brown, green, etc. Copper luster trim and designs such as Tea Leaf were long popular as was the Moss Rose pattern.

Much ironstone carries company trademarks that may include other terms for the ware such as "Stone China," "White Granite," "Granite Ware," "Opaque China," "Parisian Granite" and others.

4. Watch out for "fake" R.S. Prussia marks. The new green and red mark has been available on decal sheets for a number of years and can be applied to any unmarked china.

5. Ceramics Primer. A "ceramic" is any object made from clay and fired in a kiln. There are two categories of "Ceramics": pottery and porcelain.

Pottery is usually heavier and denser than porcelain and can be made from several types of clay to produce redware (reddish ware), yellowware (pale yellow) and stoneware (dense grey body). These types were used for more common utilitarian items (crocks, bowls, jugs, etc.) A finer, whiter pottery clay produces earthenware used for better dinnerware and serving pieces. Most must be glazed to hold liquid.

Porcelain is made with special clays, one clay composed of kaolin (china clay), one petuntze (a fusible feldspathic rock). Porcelain is much finer and whiter than pottery and is also harder. Most pieces of porcelain will be translucent when held to a strong light. All pottery wares are opaque.

The Chinese developed porcelain in the 13th century, and it was rare and expensive in the West. The formula was finally "discovered" in Europe in the early 18th century and first produced by the Meissen factory in Germany. Porcelain can be glazed to give it a glossy finish or left unglazed, creating bisque. One type of all-white bisque is called Parian Ware for its resemblance to Parian marble.

6. "Nippon" is the Japanese name for their country. When the U.S. Congress enacted the McKinley Tariff Act in 1891, all countries had to mark the country of origin on their exports to the United States. (Markings could be paper labels and weren't limited to printed or stamped marks.) Pieces of ceramic marked "Nippon" date between 1891 and 1921. In 1921 the law was revised and the words "Made in" had to be added to marks. Also, the Japanese had to drop the name "Nippon" and replace it with the English name "Japan."

7. Many people don't realize that the W. Goebel factory made fine porcelain wares, including figural pieces, long before it introduced Hummel figurines in 1932. Watch for its printed or impressed early mark consisting of a crown over an entwined "W.G."

Clocks & Furniture

1. Don't be fooled by 20th century copies of 18th and early 19th century furniture. Early pieces will show hand craftsmanship with fine dovetailing, early tool marks and specific design features. More modern copies will generally not have dovetailing, will probably be made of thinner pieces of wood, and 20th century veneering is paper thin compared to early veneers, which can often be seen along drawer edges.

2. The "Morris chair" is named for William Morris, an English designer in Victorian England who invented the original version of this reclining armchair in about 1870.

3. "Mission" or "Mission Oak" are terms often used to describe the very simple, sturdy and angular furniture made during the peak of the American Arts & Crafts movement, ca. 1905-20. The name derives from the mistaken belief that it resembles the rare primitive furniture made for California missions of the 17th through 19th centuries.

4. The "Eastlake" style of late Victorian furniture takes its name from English author and tastemaker Charles Locke Eastlake, whose book *Hints on Household Taste* (1868) exerted a great influence in the United States. In fact, he was horrified to find his name associated with the often inexpensive, mass-produced furniture made in this country and sold as "Eastlake."

5. Federal "fancy chairs" remained popular into the 1830s. In 1829 Lambert Hitchcock of Connecticut was the first man to start a factory to mass-produce such chairs. "Hitchcock" chairs could be shipped unassembled or ready to use, and eventually reached markets in far corners of the globe.

Glass

1. Direct reproductions, as well as "adaptations" of Victorian Art Glass, are the bane of many beginning collectors. Keep in mind that, in general, 20th century copies will be heavier and more crudely finished than the originals. Check the base for a pontil scar. The best early Art Glass had a polished pontil that left a smooth shallow circle.

2. Even though the colorful iridescent glass from the early 20th century has been called "carnival" for some fifty years, there is no evidence that pieces were ever given away as prizes at old-time carnivals or fairs.

Jewelry

1. Be on the alert. A great deal of brand-new reproduction Art Nouveau style jewelry is on the market today, especially pieces in silver.

Advertising Items

Q. I inherited this cloth, measuring 22-1/2" square, from my mother-in-law. It was rolled in white paper but gradually became creased when other items were placed on top of it over the years. The colors are still quite bright. The only apparent damage is fading in the upper left corner where it originally had "Louisiana Purchase Exposition." Now only "Exposition" is clear. Can this be restored? What is its approximate value?

M.C.S., Yuma, AZ

World's Fair textile

A. Your textile is an interesting souvenir from the 1904 Louisiana Purchase Exposition, more commonly known as the St. Louis World's Fair. There was a huge volume of material produced to commemorate this event. Textiles are among the more fragile. I assume the two ladies in the portrait represent the United States and France, the parties to the original "sale" in 1804. It is too bad the wording is faded, but it helps that all the other colors are bright. The fabric appears to be in overall good condition. Old textiles require special care. A minimum of work should be done on the piece. After placing it under a towel, try ironing it on low heat. Too much heat could scorch the fabric. Do not use any steam as colors might run. Value might be in the $30-75 range.

Cream of Wheat ad

Q. I purchased this picture about 15 years ago at our neighbor's yard sale (for the frame actually). I'm not sure if it's worth anything, but I'm glad I kept it around without destroying what looks to be a painting. After looking at it closely, I noticed that it's painted over the paper or canvas right on to the backboard. The bottom reads: "Where the mail goes, Cream of Wheat goes." I hope you can help me with any information on it.

C.O.B., CA

A. Your picture is actually an early 20th century Cream of Wheat advertisement, which ran in magazines in the 1910-20 era. This scene of a cowboy using a Cream of Wheat crate as a mailbox was a classic. I believe the original artwork was done by James Montgomery Flagg, famous for his "I Want You" Uncle Sam World War I poster. It doesn't appear that the frame is as old as the picture and if the ad was trimmed to fit the frame it wouldn't have very much collector value. If full-sized, this ad in mint condition might be valued in the $25-40 range.

Promotional item

Q. Enclosed find a snapshot of a black-and-white humorous wedding picture of black people, evidently an advertising picture. It is over 100 years old. I have had it for many years and I know that the woman before me had it for a long time. I do not know anything about this or what it might be worth. It is in perfect condition with probably the original frame. I received it with the postcards at the bottom of the picture itself, but they do not pertain to the actual picture. I have gone to the library to try and find out some information, but found nothing, so hope you can tell me something. Picture is 16" by 20", titled "Honey Does Yo Lub Yo Man?"

C.M., NA

A. Your black comical photograph was produced as a promotional item by the Bernheim Distilling Co. of Louisville, KY, and would date right around the copyright date of 1897. During the "Jim Crow" era of the late 19th and 20th century, African-Americans were often depicted in ad materials in demeaning and stereotypical poses, often using what was considered their "race" dialect. Photographic poses are a bit more unusual than comic art but all such item are collectible today. For some, these items are painful reminders of our past, but for many others, including many African-Americans, they serve as important reminders of shared cultural experience. As noted historian and activist Julian Bond, himself a collector of these pieces, wrote in an introduction to *Antique Trader Books' Black Americana Price Guide*: "They have another worth— beyond scarcity and dollars—as well. They celebrate perseverance, endurance and success. They honor generations before mine for whom my collection was a daily reminder of their inferiority, their unfitness for civic life." Your staged wedding scene from the turn of the century captures a moment in time long past but not forgotten. Because of its large size and good condition, I would guess it might be valued in the $300-600 range.

Iced tea dispenser

Q. This teapot was found behind the Mason Café in Claremore, Okla. It had been thrown away and my husband and his father asked permission to keep it. We were in Claremore on vacation from California and visiting my husband's parents. The teapot is stoneware without any cracks or blemishes and is in three pieces as you can see by the pictures. The bottom piece is hollow and so is the top, which is the teapot. Total height is 20", cover 6" across, bottom 8" across, 6-1/2" tall, top 15" from spout to handle, 11" tall, the top is 34" around, bottom is 30" around, cover is 17" around. It's marked "Hall Made in USA."

A.L., Grove, OK

A. Your Hall China iced tea dispenser was produced in their famous high-fired pottery featuring the durable glaze they are famous for. The marking on the bottom of this piece indicates it is quite an early example of Hall, probably dating from the late teens through the early 1920s. I have not been able to find this exact piece listed in Hall reference books although a similar piece was reissued in their Autumn Leaf pattern about 1994. Because your piece is so unusual and would interest both Hall China collectors and collectors of advertising items, it's a bit difficult to pin down a value. I would think it might sell in the mid to upper $100s, but it depends on finding the right buyer.

Cigarette silk

Cigarette silk

Q. I'm sending you a lot of pictures. I hope you can help me. The pictures are of premiums from "Nebo Cigarettes." They are all silk. Are they collectible? Are they worth anything?

P.K., Jackson, MI

A. You have a nice collection of early cigarette silks, premiums used in packs of cigarettes in the first quarter of the 20th century. You have several different designs, with those featuring the American Indians probably the most desirable and those with birds and animals, the least. One group of your silks features pretty women representing various countries of the world and one with an early bathing beauty. The latter would be more desirable that the other ladies. Most of the ones you show appear to be in top condition without stains or damage. The rarer of these silks might be valued today in the $15-25 range each, while commoner ones might go for just a few dollars each.

Q. The toy truck in the enclosed photo belonged to a relative when he was a child in the early 1920s. It is 9-1/2" long, 5" high and 3-1/2" wide. One of the front fenders is missing, otherwise it is in good shape. Could it have been a container for Huntley & Palmers biscuits? I would appreciate any information you could give me.

Biscuit tin

E.H., Carle Place, NY

A. You have a nice example for figural metal packaging from the 1920s. The British Huntley & Palmers firm was famous for their cookie tins (English biscuit = American cookie) and they made them in a wide variety of shapes from the turn of the century onward. Your "Motor Van" originally had a white metal cover that overhung the cab. Since that and the fender are missing, that would lower the collector value. The rarest of the figural Huntley & Palmers tins can sell for thousands of dollars in perfect condition. Your van or truck is not as ornate or early as their choicest pieces and in its present condition (although the paint is in good condition), I'd say it might be valued in the upper $100s.

Q. Here are a few of the coasters my husband brought back from different countries he was in during World War II. Is there any value in them? They are in good shape.

A. These brewery coasters probably would find a ready market, but individual ones in perfect shape probably would sell for only a few dollars each to the right collector.

Brewery coasters

Q. I found this Pepsi Cola sign and would like to know what year it was made and what the value is. It is 21" by 17-1/2". It reads: "Pepsi-Cola, A Nickel Drink Worth A Dime."

A.N., Mountain, WI

Pepsi Cola sign

A. Your Pepsi Cola sign is pretty and appears to be reverse-printed on glass, but I suspect it is a newer promotional piece. The lady is based on the model used on Pepsi's 1909 serving trays and posters and this piece was probably made to look like something from the turn of the century. I think it most likely was made during the past 20 years and has decorative value but no real "antique" value.

Vault for a casket

Q. I am enclosing a picture of an old advertising vault for a casket. I found it in an old barn that was being torn down. It is metal with the exception of the front glass, which advertises the name of the funeral home in St. Joseph, Mo. I would say this piece dates from somewhere between 1933 and 1937. The miniature vault runs up and down the side tracks, or wire to be precise. It is powered by an electric motor attached to a pulley wheel by a small belt. It has the original neon tubing behind the glass with the funeral home name on it. All of the motor and lights are original and are in working condition. I would like to find the value and if there is any interest in this type of thing among collectors.

J.M., St. Joseph, MO

A. You have a very unique advertising piece and a mechanized item of that era would be quite rare. The subject of the product, however, might limit somewhat its general market appeal. It certainly could have good value but you would have to find just the right collector, perhaps someone involved in the undertaking trade today. Since it is so unique it is difficult to set any sort of exact price, but to that special collector, I would think a range in the low to mid-$100s would not be out of line.

Phone card

Q. I have a phone card that was given away in an English tabloid that was started and owned by Eddie Sha. This newspaper was discontinued after just a short run nearly 15 years a go. The card was brought out just after the introduction of phone card telephone service in the United Kingdom. The card is still enclosed in the sealed wrapper that it was dispatched in. The card is made of plastic and is 2-1/8" high and 3-1/2" wide. The card is in pristine condition as the seal on the packet has never been broken. Is it possible to tell me if this phone card is of any value, and if it is, how to go about getting a good price for it? Please find enclosed two scans of the front and the back of the phone card.

S.B., Cumbria, UK

A. It was a nice surprise to find a letter in my stack from a reader in Great Britain. I appreciate your writing and sending the color copies of your early British phone card. Since your example is some 15 years old I believe it pre-dates American examples by quite a few years. At present I'm not aware of any specific collectors of phone cards but I'm sure there are people out there who have been assembling collections of the many varieties which have appeared in recent years. A similar market has developed for early credit cards that first appeared on the American market in the late 1950s. Since the phone card market is so new it's hard to place any sort of value on your piece. It certainly is worth holding on to and could certainly excite collector interest in the future. Who knows, you may be a pioneer in a whole new field of collecting.

Q. I read your column the first thing every month. It has helped me on many an occasion and I thank you. Enclosed are pictures of a framed calendar I purchased from

Calendar

an antique shop. It is 8-1/2" by 11-3/4" and is (I believe) die-cut cardboard. The brownish background is the back of the frame it was mounted on, not the calendar itself. Where I have indicated there are indentations in the cardboard that mark where it might be folded; however, it has never been folded. I took a second close up of the bottom section, which tells you it is a two century calendar. The two boxes on either side give you a formula to determine which day fell on any given year between 1801-2000. I don't know what it is on the other side of this calendar as I am reluctant to disturb the framing. The identifying marks on the bottom are "Christian Herald Bible House, Established A.D. 1878 (date?) Louis Klopsch," and a few other words I can't read. I keep this piece in a dark room to prevent further fading and overall I would say it is in excellent to good condition (no wear on edges, just slight fading.)

K.H., Livonia, MI

A. The framed calendar looks like a typical advertising premium printed in lovely colors. Early calendars featuring pretty children were very popular in the late 19th and early 20th century and many companies had them made and given away. It is too bad it is mounted since there may be writing on the back of each section, which would give more history. Also, if it is glued down to old brown paper, that paper my eventually discolor the calendar. Overall the printing looks fresh and clean and "as is" it might be valued in the $40-80 range.

Q. I have 59 cigarette cards. All have lighthouses on them, and the back of the cards tell all about the lighthouse that's on the front of the card. The front is in color. Also on the back of the card it reads "Hassan Cork tip cigarettes The Oriental Smoke. The largest selling brand of Cigarettes in America." In small print it read "Factory No. 30 2nd Dist. N.Y." There are 50 of these. There also are nine others. Two are alike—"Factory No. 649 1st Dist. N.Y." I would appreciate knowing the age of them and approximate value, if possible.

E.B., Umatilla, FL

A. Small insert cards were very popular premiums in packs of cigarettes in the

Cigarette card

early 20th century. Many different designs were used including flowers, buildings, famous people and, especially sought after, baseball players. Your lighthouse series is a bit unusual, and there are collectors interested in that field. If each card is clean, bright and had no creases, rips or missing corners, I think a value in the $1-2 range might be about right, but you'll have to find just the right collector who'd like the whole set intact.

Pepsi Cola tray

Q. Can you advise me if there is any value to this tray? It is 14-1/2" long, has one small dent, some small rust on the back rim. The back of the rim is marked: (top) "Fab-craft, Inc. Frenchtown, N.J. Made in USA (lower) Pepsi-Cola" and "Pepsi are registered trademarks of Pepsico Inc. Purchase N.Y." The picture is of a Lillian-Russell-type woman in a restaurant/bar with the wording: "Drink Pepsi Cola Delicious—Healthful 5 cents." Thank you for your help.

J.P.M., Indian Head Park, IL

A. Your oval metal serving tray featuring Pepsi Cola advertising is a copy of a Pepsi tray originally produced around 1909. Since the 1970s such trays have been widely reproduced and the name "Pepsico, Inc." on this one indicates it is modern. It is a nice decorator piece but with the slight damage the value would be modest, perhaps in the $10-20 range.

Q. I really look forward to read-ing your interesting column in *Collector Magazine*. You really know your stuff! I have a photo of Abraham Lincoln as a young man. The print is in a gilt frame which measures 18" x 24". The bottom of the print reads: "Painting by Fletch-er Ronsom—Chicago & Illinois Mid-land RR Abraham Lincoln Onstott Cooper Shop, New Salem Illinois." I'm wondering if the print has any

Abraham Lincoln print

value and hoped you could give me any information on the piece. Thank you for your help.

L.Z., Barrington, IL

A. Your large print is a copy of a painting that was apparently done by artist Fletcher Ronsom. From the markings it might have been used as a premium for the Chicago & Illinois Midland Railroad. It apparently shows a scene from young Lincoln's life in New Salem, Ill. I would guess it dates about the 1930s. Since it would be of interest to both Lincoln collectors and people interested in railroad memorabilia I'd guess it might be valued in the $250-500 range.

Q. I hope you can help me with information on the Kewpies ice cream tray. It advertises "Hagan's" ice cream and is special to me.

E.R.H., Sugar Land, TX

A. Your ice cream advertising tray is especially appealing because it features the popular Kewpies. It probably dates from the 1915-30 era and may have been a design specially ordered by this ice cream maker. Kewpie items are always in demand. Your tray, however, appears to have quite a bit of surface wear and scratching. Unfortunately, that lowers its value to the most serious collectors. In this condition I'd guess it might be valued in the $75-150 range. In "near mint" condition it would bring considerably more.

Ice cream tray

Q. This advertising for the Gold Medal Flour is on canvas and has damage on the bottom. This hung in my grandfather's grocery around 1929. I'll be eagerly waiting for your answer.

L.H., Lakeville, IN

A. Early advertising items are an extremely popular field of collecting. The items that tend to bring the highest prices were made to promote popular products which are still well known today, such as Coca-Cola, some autos, beers,

Canvas banner

candies, etc. Gold Medal Flour, of course, is still on the market today so this is a vintage piece from that company. However, in addition to the brand name advertised, an advertising item needs to be especially colorful with unique, appealing graphics to draw the most attention. Today there not too many collectors of flour company items, with the exception of Old Sleepy Eye, so that would limit the market for this nice banner. The large piece does show an interesting cutaway view of any early flour mill, however, that's not as "eye-catching" as a pretty color land-scape scene or a lovely woman or cute child would be. Collectors love colorful pieces with eye-popping graphics. I'm sure there would be collectors interested in this canvas piece and I really can't accurately say what they might pay. My feeling is that somewhere in the $100-200 range might be about right.

Q. This can could possibly be silver or silver plated. It is etched all around with a picture of Blue Boar Inn. There is a carriage parked in front of the inn and another carriage from the oppo-site direction. Horses seem to be fright-ened as one man seems to be trying to hold them as people get off the carriage. Next to the inn appears to be a rooming house. The inside contains a tobacco can in very nice condition with the wording "Blue Boar Rough Cut." There is also a picture of a hunter and dogs that have caught a boar. The blue seal stamp has a date of 1910. U.S. Inter. Rev. A picture of John G. Adams is on

Tobacco tin

the stamp. This can sits in the outer can that has the maker's name of Reed & Barton on the bottom and an etching of the head of a boar on the side. I would appreciate any information you give me.

R.D., Paonia, CO

A. You have a very unique early tobacco tin. I don't recall seeing one like this before and it must have been a special order sort of piece. I don't quite understand how it might have worked, but the Reed & Barton company did make good silver plate wares in the late 19th and early 20th century. Since the two cans stack together I can only suggest that perhaps the lower can was perhaps meant to hold water that might have served to help humidify the tobacco in the upper container. Let's see if an experienced tobacciana collector can shed more light on this set. I'm sure it is very collectible and pretty scarce.

Reader Update

A.B.H. phoned to tell me more about the Blue Boar tobacco tin and liner featured in an earlier column. He has a similar 1-pound tin and the plain metal canister is supposed to fit inside the can and is held in place with the wire clip. There is also a ½ pound Blue Boar tin but it doesn't have the special liner. He suggests that the liner was probably a premium offered to special costumers.

Q. The print of a girl (16" by 20") was a give-away with the purchase of Iodent tooth-paste. There is some foxing on the upper right corner and about a 1" tear into the side of the picture. Any information would be appreciated.

J.K., Westchester, IL

A. This color print is a nice rendition of a Victorian painting, but with the foxing around the edges of the tear I'm afraid the value would be kept down. It could possibly be framed to hide these faults but I suspect it would not bring much over $25 on the market.

This Picture
NOT TO BE SOLD
This Fine Art Print is
Our 18th Anniversary
FREE GIFT TO YOU
when you purchase a Large Size
Tube of Iodent Tooth Paste

Toothpaste print

Airplane logos

Q. I would like to know if a collection of 1950s Wheaties airplane logos are worth anything.

S.G.W., Davenport, IO

A. There is a growing interest in items relating to commercial airline travel and airliners. I'm sure your logos or stickers would be of interest. The individual values may be modest but a nice collection should attract interest. I suggest you contact Bill Demarest of the World Airline Historical Society, P.O. Box 660583, Miami Springs, FL 33206. The group publishes a magazine, which might help you contact other interested collectors.

Q. Enclosed find pictures of a Dr. Scholl's Toe Flex advertising item. It's made of pure white porcelain. I has a print under the piece that reads "Genuine Doultonware The Scholl Mfg. Co. Ltd., London, W.C." It has the Royal Doulton lion logo and "Made in England." I purchased this item about 40 years ago and can't remember where. I can't find this item in any antique book under Royal Doulton or advertising books. I always remember seeing these feet made of plaster in a lot of drug store, but never saw one in porcelain. I would like to know if that have any value in the market today.

J.G., Statesboro, GA

Porcelain feet

A. You do have a unique advertising item. This must have been a special store display piece; and the fact that it was produced by the Royal Doulton firm would add to its appeal. It is likely that not many were produced so it is probably quite scarce. Although it is a fascinating piece the actual collector value may be limited somewhat due to its "display appeal." Not too many folks will find a pair of crooked feet appealing, however well done. What you need to find is a chiropodist or podiatrist collector

who loves advertising items or Royal Doulton wares. Maybe some reader has encountered this item and has a better feel of what the market demand might be. I would suggest, however, that the value would range anywhere from $75 into the lower hundreds.

Reader Update

Re: November 2002, response to question on Royal Doulton (Dr. Scholl). The question rang a bell with me. Several years ago I picked up a small Art Deco style sugar and creamer. They were marked with the usual lion mark but with the additional "Dr. Scholl's foot comfort service." It would appear that Royal Doulton made more than one advertising item for Scholl's. It would be interesting to find out if distribution was mainly in Great Britain or the States.

Jon Scarborough

Q. Help! I've been trying to find out if the Kellogg poster picture is a Harrison Fisher "girl". I wrote the Kellogg Company and found out that the poster was done in 1906 or 1907. A friend said he thought maybe the picture was done by Harrison Fisher. I am 81 years old and do not have a computer and this friend said might information on Fisher might be found at the Web site www.harrisonfisher.com. If you can help me, I would appreciate it.

A.F., Helpen, UT

A. Your advertising poster may feature the head of a Harrison Fisher girl, although I can't see his signature in the image. Of course, there were other artists in the early 20th century who drew very similar lovely women. There are some references on Fisher's work so you might try to track one down to verify if he did work for the Kellogg company. If it is an unsigned Fisher work it would be a bit more collect-

Kellogg poster

ible plus it appeals to collectors of Kellogg products. If it had been printed in full-color it would have a greater value but since it appears to be clean and undamaged I believe, due to its size (12" x 14") it could be valued in the $50-100 range.

Wooden sign

Q. I have an old wooden advertising sign for *Theatre Magazine.* It is made of five 6" slats of wood and measures 30" x 24". The frame is also wooden. A woman is pictured wearing a gauzy dress and a blue hat. The background is blue and the edges of the picture are white and uneven. It seems to be oil paint. In the bottom right corner is the name "Miss Blanche Sweet." The painting is signed "Hamilton King 1918." I know she was a silent film star and Hamilton King did work for Coca-Cola. I know there was a magazine called *Theatre Magazine.* Do you have any more information or possible value?

J.T., Independence, LA

A. I'm not sure exactly what you have here. Perhaps someone cut out and decoupaged an original magazine cover from the early 20th century on primitive wood boards. However, it is also possible that the magazine cover was just photocopied and glued down or printed on the wood in some other way. I don't have the feeling that this piece is terribly old and even if it is an early magazine cover the value would be very greatly reduced mounted in this manner. I think it would have only decorative value.

Q. I own this Coca-Cola pitcher and four glasses. The pitcher is 9" tall and 5-1/2" in diameter. On the front and on the back it says "Bacardi and Coke." The glasses are 5" tall with the logo "Enjoy Coca-Cola" on one side and "Enjoy Coke" on the other side. This is a promotional item I sent for many years ago. The items are still in the box and have never been used. Also enclosed was a page telling "The story behind the first rum and Coca-Cola" and "The first pitcher of Bacardi and Rum."

Pitcher and glasses

B.H., La Porte, IN

A. Most Coca-Cola items are collectibles, but the most sought items date before the 1960s. I checked several Coca-Cola price guides but couldn't locate this promotional pitcher. If it doesn't date before the mid-1960s I suspect the collector value is quite modest.

Q. Enclosed find a picture of a gasoline globe (Wadham's Mobil). I am interested in any information as to the value of the globe.

C.G., Menasha, WI

A. You have a nice example of a gas pump globe that probably dates from the 1930s. These are very collectible, but value depends a lot on the design on the lenses and the scarcity of the brand name. There are a great many "Mobilgas" globes still available and those with the flying red horse (Pegasus) logo tend to bring the best prices. If your example has the original paint and doesn't have any chips, cracks or serious wear I suspect it would be valued in the $300-500 range.

Gasoline globe

Budweiser girl

Q. I am enclosing a copy of an original "Budweiser Girl" I have had for about 56 years. It was given to me by an old gent who found it in a barn loft. The bottle she is holding states that the name "Budweiser" was owned by C. Conrad & Co. of Saint Louis. The frame is made of oak with the original paint and designs. At the top is "Anheuser-Busch" in raised letters. On the sides are stalks of grain. On the bottom of the frame is the date 1906. Overall size of the frame is 38-1/2" by 23-1/2". The picture without the matting is 28-1/2" by 14". Please let me know the approximate value of this picture.

J.B., Saint James, MO

A. You appear to have a wonderful example of early Anheuser-Busch advertising. Large poster-style advertising such as this piece featuring beautiful young women is very sought after. Your example even appears to be in the original marked Anheuser-Busch frame, an added bonus. From what I can see the print looks to be in truly excellent condition with no staining, fading or rips on the untrimmed print. I sent a copy of your photo to advertising expert Rich Penn of Pennyfields in Waterloo, Iowa, and he sent the additional information: He notes this print came in two versions, the girl in "short" sleeves and the girl in "long" sleeves. Yours is the "long-sleeved" version that isn't quite as rare as the other one. Rich couldn't be sure from your shot but thought perhaps the frame might have been repainted, which would lower the value just a bit. In top condition your large framed print could sell in the $1,500-2,500 range. The "short-sleeved" version could bring $300-500 more.

Q. Enclosed is a copy of the envelope and letter from the Coca-Cola Bottling Co., ca 1941. The original letter is in color but is a little faded. I would appreciate an estimate of value.

J.H., Wilmington, OH

A. Your "Letter from Santa" featuring the famous Coca-Cola Santa image is a nice memento but probably thousands of them were sent out to children each holiday season. Serious collectors of Coca-Cola items prefer much more colorful items that display well, such as signs, bottles, coolers, etc. I suspect your mass-produced letter would be valued at not much more than $10.

Santa letter

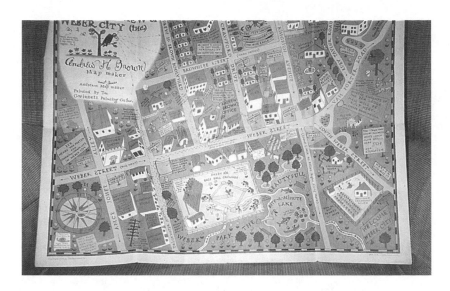

'Amos and Andy' premium

Q. I have several items relating to radio programs: The first is a map titled "Eagle's-Eye View of Weber City (inc.)," copyright 1935 by the Pepsodent Co. It seems to be related to the "Amos and Andy Show." The other items are scripts from: "Riders of the Purple Sage," Dec. 8, 1944, autographed by Cottonseed Clark and "The Jack Kirkwood Show," Dec. 8, 1944, autographed be Jeannie. Can you give me any information on these items (collectibility, value, etc.)?

E.N., Wayne, PA

A. Your color map of Weber City was a popular premium for the "Amos and Andy" radio show of the 1930s. If your piece is in "mint" condition and has the original mailing envelope it would be valued in the $25-50 range. I checked with an autograph expert regarding your autographed original radio show transcripts. Unfortunately, neither of these programs was one of the really "big" shows of the 1930s and '40s. Unlike "Amos and Andy" items there are probably few collectors looking for items related to these two shows. The "Riders of the Purple Sage" sounds like it might have a bigger following today than "The Jack Kirkwood Show," but our guess is that either of these might sell for under $50 unless you happened to find a really die-hard enthusiast.

Q. This cardboard sign for "O'Brien's Soap Liquid Lite" was found on the back of an old short wave radio.

V.H., Jonesville, WI

A. I'm not exactly sure what your "O'Brien's Liquid-Lite" piece is. It looks like it's just part of a sign, maybe originally part of a store display, and since it is in poor condition I don't believe it would have much collector value.

Cardboard sign

Q. I would like some information on this wooden box I have. It is 6" tall and 8" wide. I would like to know the age, type of wood, if it has any collector value and if so, how much.

V.S., Westfield, IN

A. You have an interesting commercial box from the early 20th century. I once again contacted my glass expert friend, Dean Six, of the West Virginia Museum of American Glass, about this company. The Saint-Gobain Glass Company of France and Corning Glass of

Commercial box

New York established the "Blue Ridge Glass Corporation" in 1925. They used a vacant Corning plant in Kingsport, Tennessee, and produced "flat" (i.e. window) glass. The company apparently changed its corporate structure sometime in the 1950s and I don't believe the factory is still producing. Your box is an interesting piece of American glassmaking history and makes a nice decorative accent piece. In the collecting market I think the value might be in the $45-90 range but perhaps a glass enthusiast might offer even more.

Artworks, Painting & Prints

Gurr painting

Q. About 15 years ago my wife purchased this painting by Lena Gurr at a Brooklyn auction. They gave us a paper listing her many awards and the museums that hold her works. I have no knowledge of her present values, but was told that they have gone up in price. Enclosed is a photo of a painting that we purchased for $300. It was painted in 1932. Any information would be appreciated.

E.M., Brooklyn, NY

A. The works of Lena Gurr (1897-1992) are highly collectible. She exhibited at the National academy of Design, 1939 World's Fair and Brooklyn Museum. She was a noted painter, lithographer and serigrapher. I would anticipate your painting has appreciated in value. Current oferings of her work include color serigraphs ranging in price from $550 to $800, with higher prices for larger pieces of work.

Q. Can you please give me any information on this picture? I don't know if it's a painting or charcoal. Overall, the whole painting is 41" by 37". The frame has been roughed up but it's the original. It was purchased at a flea market in 1981 for $30. Is there anything you can tell me about the artist or its value? Also bought at the same flea market was this portfolio of bouquets. There are four prints in the folder. The cover reads "Jean-Louis Prevost" and also says the pictures in this portfolio are etching toned prints by the Paris Etching Society. Each print has the name "J. L. Prevost," a small "r" in a circle, and the mark I've drawn for you. They are numbered 901, 902, 904 and 906 with copyright by Sidney Z. Lucas, New York City. Do you know anything about these?

R.A., Brockton, MA

Prevost portfolio cover

Color engraving

Prevost inspired prints

A. Your large color engraving of the two Classical maidens by a fountain appears to date from around 1900. I can see a name and perhaps a date in the lower left corner, but you don't mention these. It is likely a print based on a European painting of the period. The frame may well be original but the mat board looks later. The print appears to be in fine condition, however. I think it has discoloration from the old mat and that may have damaged the edge of the print because of the acid content. There also may be details on the engraver under the mat. In top condition, I'd say this piece might be valued in the $250-$450 range.

Jean-Louis Prevost was a French artist of flowers and still-lifes working in the late 18th and early 19th century. Your color prints are based on his original works and your set probably was made in the first quarter of the 20th century. As decorative pieces, they might be valued in the $50-100 range.

Q. I enjoy your column a great deal and am curious about these two pictures. One I got from my grandmother, the other someone threw away and I always liked it so I grabbed it. Picture information: W. Bovcvereav, 1896. Can you please tell me something about these? The one with the odd frame was my grandmother's so I figured the frame was old.

D.G., St. Croix Falls, WI

Damage limits value

A. You have two versions of the same color print of a pretty young girl. It appears to be based on a painting by a French artist and was likely released in the very late 19th century. I don't recognize the work it is based on but portraits of cute children and pretty ladies were especially popular during that time and many such prints were produced for the mass market. Unfortunately, I can see there is some serious water damage on your grandmother's print, which means it has little collector value. If the other print is clean and not faded, it might have some collector value, depending on the size.

Q. Enclosed is a photograph of a print I have. The bottom looks faded, but this is from the glare on the glass. I have been unable to find anything as to the artist, since it is not signed. It appears it might have been cropped along the sides so it would fit the frame. The print is 13" by 20". It is a beautiful print and the colors are very bright. We would appreciate any information

Circa 1895 print

you can give us as to the artist and value of the print.

B.C., Blountville, TN

A. Your charming color print of the late Victorian girl and her kitten has a lot of appeal. I suspect it was printed in quite large numbers and probably based on an artwork by a little known artist of the time. It is too bad that it appears to have been trimmed down to fit a later frame as the bottom border might have had information on the publisher and a copyright date. I'd say it might date around 1895-1910. Even trimmed, it is pretty and might be valued in the $50-100 range because of the topic, condition and nice size.

Q. I enjoy your column so much! Enclosed are photos of two items. I am interested in knowing what they might be worth as it is time to empty out my home and move to smaller quarters. Item 1 has a black frame with a silver border. Is it a print or lithograph? It is signed "J.O. Anderson" on bottom right and on top left in small print it says "Copyright 1892, Radthe Kauckner, (something) NY," as

Landscape engraving

close as I can make out. It's 2' by 3'. Item 2: Is it a print or original watercolor? It has a Stevan Dohanos signature (real), and is 18" by 27". The calendar shows Dec. and, the clock 5:00 (or 4) which says a lot.

B.O., Fairfield, CN

A. Your black and white landscape engraving is typical of the quality works produced in the late 19th century. I'm not familiar with the artist or the printmaker but it does appear to be in quite nice, clean condition and in the original frame. If it doesn't have any staining, foxing or

Dohanos print

water damage, I would guess it might be valued today in the $125-200 range. Your second color image is most likely a print. Stevan Dohanos was an artist noted for magazine cover art and did a number of *Saturday Evening Post* covers. He's not as well known as Norman Rockwell but did somewhat similar designs. This picture seems to show a young Chinese-American boy looking up at portraits of his ancestors and perhaps wishing he was old enough to join in the fight of the Chinese against the invading Japanese in their homeland. It probably was meant as a sort of propaganda piece and also would have helped show Anglo-Saxon Americans that they shouldn't confuse Chinese-Americans with Japanese. There was, of course, a serious backlash against Japanese-Americans after Pearl Harbor and their treatment by our government has been a topic of bitter discussion in recent decades.

Patriotic color print

Q. I just signed up to the Collector Magazine and enjoy your part of pricing guide and hope you will be of some help to me. Enclosed are three pictures of items I have not been able to find anything about. First, the school house picture is "The first raising of the American flag over a public school in Colerain, Mass." It is signed Percy Moran in white with "C" in a circle. It has a large margin. The size of artwork is 1'5" top to bottom, 2' 3/16" side to side. On bottom of picture it reads "made in USA. The Osborne Co. Newark N.J. &

Color print

Toronto, Ont. 1812." It looks like a thick paper-like canvas. The second picture is a woman with flower and under the picture it says "June." Also on the left hand side of picture it reads "Copyright 1909 by Bernhard Ulmann & Co., N.Y." It's on a cloth-type material. The Ulmann picture looks like it was done in oil but I am not sure. The third picture is of a cat and another cat perched on top of a fence. Under the picture it reads "Copyright 1907 by Bernhard Ulmann & Co." It is also on a cloth-type material. It also looks like it was done in oil but I'm not sure. Both the second and third pictures are 21 ¼" on the bottom and top and sides.

I.B., Traverse City, MI

A. You appear to have three nice old color prints in good condition. They don't appear to have any serious damage or staining so that adds a lot to their market appeal. The first print of the flag raising is based on an historical event and is a print copy of a painting by Percy Moran, a well-known Victorian artist who specialized in depicting scenes from American history. As

Color print

a nice sized print in an attractive early frame I'd guess it might be valued in the $125-250 range. Your other two pictures are color printed on fabric and would date right about the time of the copyright dates on them. The Bernhard Ullman (note spelling) company was a noted producer of postcards during the craze for them early in the 20th century and these images are similar to the sort of art they used on postcards. Themes such as lovely ladies and popular pets like cats are always in demand in the market. The lady is especially well done but cat lovers will like your garden scene with cats too. Since such fabric would be quite fragile it is nice these have survived in such good condition. They should be framed carefully using acid-free matting to insure they are preserved. Since they are a nice large size I would guess each might be valued in the $100-200 range unframed. The right collector might even go a bit higher.

Charcoal drawing

Q. When my mother-in-law died, she left us this picture and said it was handed down through the family and that C. Hoeber was Martha Washington's cousin. It's dated June 1, 1897; it's 21" by 27" and is in the frame it came in. Do you have any idea who C. Hoeber is or what the picture's value is? It looks like its done in charcoal.

J.S., Imperial, MO

A. I have not been able to find any artist with the name "C. Hoeber," although there was an American artist Arthur Hoeber, working in the 19th century. From your photos I would say your hunt scene is a hand-done charcoal copy of a German painting and the copyist signed it with his or her name. It is nicely done but not a theme that's greatly in demand these days. Since it's a large size in a nice turn-of-the-century frame, it might be valued in the low to mid-$100s.

Q. I am enclosing photos of two paintings that I purchased recently at an estate sale. The first painting (above) is a scene with trees and water in an ornate gold frame, measuring 35" by 17" inside the frame. The artist's signature is "M.W. 1940." The

Unknown artist

Print or painting?

other painting is a street scene in an off-white frame. I have enclosed a closeup of the artist's signature. It is difficult to read—it could be L. Kruse or Kiuse, I'm not really sure. I would appreciate any information you can give me about the paintings, and the value of each.

E.L., Georgetown, TX

A. Your long landscape with the river and autumn coloring appears to have been done by an amateur artist and it is nice that it is dated. The frame appears to be a generation or two earlier, perhaps dating around 1900. It may have been reused by the artist around 1940. It is pretty but such works by unknown artists are hard to value—it just depends on finding a buyer who likes it. The other work appears to be a Paris street scene, perhaps around Monmartre where hundreds of little-known artists worked over the decades. I could not find anything on this artist and I wonder if this actually is an original oil painting or just a print. If it is on cardboard rather than canvas, it is undoubtedly a mass-produced print. The cars in the scene would seem to date it to the late 1940s or early 1950s. Without further details that's about all I can say.

Q. Enclosed is a picture by L.F. Ferris. The frame measures 34" by 28" and the silk print measures 19" by 16 ½". It is in black and white. In the left hand corner is printed "Copyrighted and published 1887, by Fred Kaiser Co. of St. Louis and New York." I really hope you can tell me if it has any value. We purchased this many years ago. Love your "Kyle on Antiques."
L. McN., Sherman, TX

Silk print

A. Your charming picture is an interesting example of late Victorian printing techniques, with the image printed on a silk fabric background. There probably isn't much information available on the printer or the original art it is based on but at least you have the approximate date. Of course, color images are always more in demand and valued higher than black and white ones. Also, I can see that there appears to be mat burn and staining, probably caused by the backing material, which has damaged the fabric and would be nearly impossible to remedy. Any early print with matting or wood or cardboard back boards should be rematted with non-acid modern mat board which will lessen any further damage. It could then be remounted in what is likely the original frame. Your piece is a nice size but I'm afraid the general condition would lower the value to perhaps somewhere in the $75-150 range, including the frame.

Q. I recently purchased this original watercolor. It is titled "Red Hibiscus" by Tip Freeman of Tip Freeman Art Studios, Miami, Fla. I absolutely love it and I am interested in finding more by this artist. I looked him up on the Internet but didn't find anything. I would like to find out more about the artist, whether this painting has any value—but mostly where I could find other examples of his work.
K.B., Jacksonville, FL

Freeman Airbrush Work

A. Thanks for your letter. It has led me into some interesting research on the art and career of Tip Freeman. Through our library I was able to find information on a gallery in Miami that had been operated by Mr. Freeman and is now run by a former employee. I learned that Tip Freeman passed away some five years ago at age 87 after a long and eventful career. I was even able to visit on the phone with his widow who filled me in on much of his career. Tip Freeman was a trained artist who studied at The Chicago Art Institute during the Depression and then took a teaching position in Grand Forks, ND before moving on to California where he worked on scenic backdrops for Hollywood movies just before World War II. He was working on a film in Australia when the war started producing his airbrush artworks and continued working with this technique until the early 1960s. He specialized in pictures of tropical plants, birds and figures. Your "Red Hibiscus" work would have been produced later in his career when he moved to Miami. After giving up his airbrush work Mr. Freeman concentrated on working and his art is very collectible, especially in Hawaii. Not many works show up on the market today but Mrs. Freeman suggested you might go out on the Internet under "Hawaiiana" and locate other buyers and sellers of his art. They may give you a better idea of market values today.

Q. Enclosed is a photo of one of the three baby prints I own. One is titled "A Little Dream," two are titled "Heaven's Gift," all copyright N.B. 1932. Do you think collectors of baby things would be interested in something like this?

G.P.M., Hillside, NJ

A. The baby prints are charming and quite collectible. The baby prints of artist Bessie Pease Guttmann are most collectible today but these may be by one of her contemporaries. Depending on size and condition I'd guess they each might be valued in the $50-100 range.

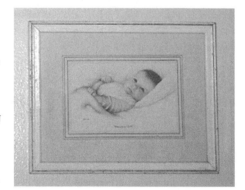

Baby print

ELECTRO TINT ENGRAVING CO., 1227-1229 Race St. Philadelphia, U.S.A.

2502—THE BUFFALO HUNT

Wholesale catalog

Q. I'm sending a few copy pages of an album that I have. There are over 100 beautiful color pictures in the book. Could you tell me what it was for? Also, does it have any value?

R.E., Empire, CO

A. Thanks for your color scan of the wholesale color catalog from the Electro-Tint Engraving Company. It appears to be in very fine condition, at least from what you show, and includes an interesting range of prints that apparently could be purchased by retailers for resale. The one shown is a nice buffalo hunting scene and is signed by R.A. Fox, a very popular print artist of the early 20th century. Other scenes include a Black comical and some animal and romantic-style prints. All the various topics included in this catalog would add greatly to its value. If all the pages are as fresh and clean as those you sent and if the binding is in top condition, it's a fine piece. Bill Butts, owner of Main Street Fine Books and Manuscripts, Galena, Illinois, and I agree it might retain in the $200-300 range.

Q. Enclosed are photos of two of what appear to be watercolors left to me by a great-aunt. I do not believe they are prints, but I have not removed the backing yet to be certain. One has an applied sticker on the back paper reading "At the Green Road/English/Artist J Mac Pherson/ painting dated 1850s." Can you give me any information on these and the value, if any.

English watercolors

A. I checked through art references and did find an English artist named John

Mac Pherson who worked in the period of 1865 to 1884. He did specialize in rural landscapes done in watercolor, so these could be works of his. Values seem to depend on the size and subject matter of each artwork. In general, pieces in the 10" by 12" size have sold in recent years in the $800-1,000 range. Larger pieces can bring more. These would be worth taking to an art gallery or auction house for further authentication.

Reims cathedral

Q. I acquired this church picture in the 1930s and have often wondered what its history is. In the lower right front the painting says: "ODY Right 1916 by Tabor Prang Art Co." Can you tell me what the picture represents, the age and value? Thank you so much for your most interesting articles.

M.B., Salem OR

A. Your print is a quality color print of the cathedral in Reims, France. It was probably sold within a year or so of the 1916 copyright date on the edge. It doesn't appear to have any staining, or other damage, so that would keep the value up. You don't give a size, but it appears to be fairly large. Perhaps in the right market it might be valued in the $75-150 range or perhaps a bit more if very large.

1910-20 print

Q. I am enclosing photos of a print my grandmother had for years. My own mother is 80 and can remember it when she was small. Can you tell me anything about the artist or if it's of any value? Thank you for any information you can give me.

Mrs. N. G., Grants, NM

A. I hope the photo of your charming print will show up here. The pretty blond toddler looking up at blossoming tree is lovely and would have great appeal today. I would guess it was printed around 1910-20. I am not familiar with the artist "Annie Benson Muller," but she was quite talented and her works would be worth collecting.

There appears to be some water or moisture staining around the edges of this print, and that does lower the market value. Since you don't give a size, it's hard to judge a value. Not knowing the complete condition is also a problem. For your own reference, if it is backed with old cardboard, I would have it rebacked with acid-free mat board to prevent further staining or deterioration.

Q. I have enclosed some copies of pictures that I obtained at Andres Alcove, a used book store that was part of the Carnegie Library in Pittsburgh. I was wondering if theses pictures that I purchased at 10 cents a piece held any value and if they were original. They are mounted on a thick paper stock and I think they were part of their photograph collection.

K.S.D., Pittsburgh, PA

Image of Egypt

A. Your large photos were probably part of a bound portfolio of late 19th century images taken in Egypt. The inscriptions, I can see are in French. They are interesting from the archaeological standpoint but were probably sold as a tourist souvenir type of volume. If they were quite widely printed and distributed, the value would not be terribly high, but I suspect you got a good buy at 10 cents each. Even at $1-20 each you'd make quite a profit, and each one could possibly sell for more than that.

Chariot Race Engraving

Landscape Watercolor

Q. We get a lot of antique magazines and my wife and I think your column is the best of all, and the rest of the magazine is good also. I cleaned an attic out in the 1950s, and these two pictures were in the mess of junk. I would like to know if they are old and worth anything. They are in good shape. The one has a year date that looks like 1815 and depicts a Roman Chariot race. The other is a country scene with two cows. The first is a 8 ½" wide, 22" long, and is signed "Wagner-Plinet" (on the right) and "R. Moran Ferris" (on the left). The names we're not sure of. The second is 8 ½" wide, 22 ½" long, and is signed "C.V. Atkinson." It was found in an old house attic on West North Avenue in Baltimore, Maryland.

J.W., Baltimore, MD

A. Your Roman Chariot Race scene looks like a nice quality engraving most likely produced in the early 20th century. I suspect the date noted is "1895" or "1915", not "1815". The names are those of the original artist and the engraver. It looks like it may be in the original frame with early mat board. I might suggest you have it rebacked and rematted with non-acid matting to help preserve it and reduce the chance of damage from acids in the old mat. If it is as clean and sharp as it appears, I think it would have collector value, though you don't note the overall size. If it is quite large, I think it might be valued in the $75-150 range, but again, condition is important. The rural landscape looks like it might be an original watercolor or perhaps a pastel. There were several artists named "Atkinson" working in the late 19th and early 20th century, when I suspect this piece was done, but none of them had the initials "C.V." Your piece may be the work of a talented amateur of that era, in which case setting a value would be harder. I would suggest you take this piece into an art gallery or art museum in your area and have it examined first hand.

Print or painting?

Q. I'm like many others; I look to see what is on your pages first. This picture is 17 ½" x 35 ½" and is painted by P.R. Kohler— N.Y. It is a pastoral scene with a lighthouse in the far background. I'd like to know about the painter, and also a price for it. It is from the turn of the century.

L.H., Hillsdale, WI

A. Your pretty landscape scene is possibly an original painting but more likely a color print. Is it mounted on stretchers and painted on canvas? It would have an open back then. If it is flat and has backing, it is less likely to be an original work but a copy. If you can carefully remove it from the frame, check along the bottom edges for any other markings. I have looked through several art references and there were several Kohlers working in the late 19th - early 20th century, but most were German and their initials were not "P.R." Even if it is a colorful landscape print with a nice frame, it could be valued in the $250-400 range.

20th Century lithograph

Q. My grandparents received this framed print or photo for a wedding gift in 1907. The artist is not named. The print measures 16" by 20". I would like to know the possible value and artist.

N.L., Walworth, WI

A. You have a lovely early 20th century color lithograph. Scenes of pretty women in romantic settings are always sought after, and your romantic scene was very appropriate as a wedding gift. I don't recognize this work, but perhaps in a corner of the print may be printed a name or the name of a publisher. If you can carefully remove it from what appears to be the original frame, you may find more information along the bottom edge. Also, if it has the original wood or cardboard backing, this should be removed and replaced with acid-free mat board to keep it from discoloring. It appears to be in fine condition and a nice size. As a decorative piece, I think it might be valued in the $250-400 range.

Q. I am enclosing a picture of Snow White and the Seven Dwarfs. This is a picture that I grew up with. My mother purchased this in Germany and had it framed in the United States years ago. It is 58" in width, and 37" in height. It is framed in a wooden gold frame. The picture of Snow White and the Seven Dwarfs is oil painted on the following: dark blue wool blanket background, brown wool blanket trees cut and hand stitched and then oil painted, potato sack roof and fine white linen room. This picture was created by A. Kaemmler in the time period of 1940-1945 in Sulzback A/Murr Stuttgardt Germany. Can you possibly give me an idea of its value since I have never seen anything like this anywhere?

M.H., Valley Stream, NY

German folk art

A. Your painted scene of Snow White and the Seven Dwarfs is a charming German folk art piece and nicely done. There is always an interest in fairy tale artwork, but the most sought-after objects relate to the Walt Disney animated feature made in the late 1930s. This work may have been done in Germany around that time period but does not directly relate to the Disney story. It is a rather one-of-a-kind piece, so is a bit difficult to evaluate as far as a current market range. The collector demand for it will basically set the value. Since it is a large size and in great condition, however, I wouldn't be surprised if it could sell in the $250 range.

Miniature watercolors

Q. These photos show a pair of pen and ink miniature portraits I purchased at a house sale in Bernardsville, N.J., back in about 1950. Inside, on the back is written "at 25 years" on the young man's portrait and "at 20 years" on the woman. I always thought they were worthy of better frames but never changed them. The smudged marks were on the glass not the portraits.

E.F.D., Bartonville, TX

A. Your miniature watercolor portraits appear to be of excellent quality, done by a well-trained artist. Without any signature along the edge it is difficult to attribute them to a specific artist although an Eastern auction house that handles this type of item might have an expert who could. I would date them, from the clothing, to the 1825-35 period. They may well be in original frames so it's good you didn't change those. As fine unsigned American miniatures I think the pair might be valued in the $800-1,200 range. If they could be attributed to a well-known artist the value would increase.

Q. We have done a small amount of research on the oil painting on ivory, but cannot find anything about the artist. The signature does not show in the picture, but it is signed over her left shoulder in white "HiL." She is absolutely beautiful.

M.R., Portland, OR

A. Your framed painting is very pretty. This type of ivory, or perhaps bone, frame was used to frame miniatures like this from the second half of the 19th century into the early 20th century. The portrait looks like it could date from the 1830-50 era but many copies of earlier works were made to be sold as decorative objects. Have you examined the

Oil painting on ivory

painting out of the frame to make sure it is actually hand-done? My guess is that it likely dates from the 1900-1930 era but is still a pretty decorative piece.

Q. I love reading your column. Keep up the good work! I'm enclosing two photos of pictures my mother had for many years. She gave them to me 43 years ago. I was wondering about their worth if any. Can you help? Thank you.

K.C., Cameron, WV

Popular design

Frame adds value

A. Your two black and white prints or engravings are designs that were very popular in the first quarter of the 20th century. The picture of the three horse heads appears to be a better quality engraving and may be marked along the border under the mat. I believe it is based on an original artwork called "The Pharaoh's Horses." It shows up on the market fairly often today, in top condition, without any tears, stains or other damage I think it might be valued in the $75-125 range.

The other picture appears to be a copy of another popular horse print of that era but the name of the original escapes me right now. It looks like it might have been a "hand-done" copy, perhaps in chalk. Condition again is of great importance but in this case it also comes with an attractive handcrafted late Victorian frame, which adds to its appeal. Size is also important. If it is around 8" x10" or a bit larger I'd guess it might be valued in the $75-150 range. Whenever I see older prints like these, which appear to be in old or original frames, I recommend that the owner have them rematted using acid-free mat board. It is important to remove the old wooden or cardboard backboards and front matting that are filled with pulp acid, which will stain the picture over time. The round opening on the first print would not be cheap to copy but it would help preserve the piece for the future.

Reader Update

It was a real pleasure for me to receive the following informative letter from my long time associate, Connie Morningstar. Connie is now retired but was the original "answer expert" for *The Antique Trader Weekly*, her column "Ask Connie" starting in 1972. She has written extensively over the years and has a special interest in decorative arts and American furniture. I was great to have her expert input on the following subject:

"Dear Kyle: Although it probably is stale news by now, I thought you might be interested in more about "Pharoah's Horses" from your columns of Oct. 2001 (page 27) and Dec. 2001 (page 37). The original painting, an oil on canvas, was offered for sale by the William Doyle Galleries, New York City, May 4, 1994. It was signed by John Frederick Herring Sr. and dated 1848. The painting is round, 24" in diameter and framed. Engraved prints of the work were listed in the 1902 Sears, Roebuck catalog for 75 cents—a bargain because they had been sold by dealers for $1.50 and by agents for as high as $2. "These also were round but only 10" in diameter and set in round, ornamental frames. Herring's "Pharoah's Horses" seems to have been a popular model for amateur artists of the late 19th century as well. I have a 27" square version in soft blues and grays done by a great aunt in the 1890s. I'm aware of several others".

Religious Lithograph

Q. I would like to know if you know anything about this item? It is a print on some form of oil cloth. It says "The Redeemer of the World. Printed in Germany."

D.S. Springfield, MO

A. Your large color lithographed picture of Jesus and the cross is typical of fine pieces produced in Germany in the late 19th century and early 20th centuries. It appears to be in good condition, but the market for such religious art is fairly limited. The print itself might sell alone in the $25-50 range, but it appears to be in a nice gilt plaster period frame, which might be worth $75-150 if in perfect condition.

ICKWOOD TECHNIQUE PLATE
Kalamazoo, Mich.

Art print

Q. Thank you so much for your help in the past. I have one more thing that I cannot find any information on. It's a green hard cover "folder" with 40 loose pictures in it. The pictures are of art techniques on how to draw nudes. I thought that maybe they came from an art school in Kalamazoo, Mich., that is no longer there. I would like to know how old they are and if they are worth anything? Thank you again for your help.

R.E., Empire, CO

A. Your folio of prints was sold to art students, probably in the late 19th or early 20th century. They could be mailed, I suppose, if a student couldn't travel to study. The prints are nicely done and may be copies of studies by known artists of that era. Not being in color or by an artist who is highly collectible today I would guess the set might be valued in the $75-150 range.

The French Village

The Mentor

Q. This print is titled "The French Village" by Plo Frangary. It is 12"x16". "The Mentor" is a folder containing different subjects of pictures dating to 1908 and earlier.

L.W., Cando, NV

A. The color print of a French village is hard to date. Many such works have been produced since the 1920s, and often the artists are not well known today. As a decorative piece in good, clean condition, I'd think it might be valued in the $75-150 range.

"The Mentor," a folio of reproductions of classic artworks, does have some collector value, but a surprising number of similar works still survive. Since the art is reproduced in black and white that keeps the value lower than comparable color prints of that era. I would guess each image and folder might be valued in the $20-40 range if perfect.

Q. This photo is of a painting that I realize is not
antique. There is a gold foil
seal on the back. It has a pillar
with vines in the center and
written in a circle around it is
"Fine Art Gallery—United
States Commemorative," all in
capital letters. The artist is
Dino Massaroni, © 1989. Is
this one of those starving artist
paintings or is it worth holding
on to? I paid $10 for it. I do
not have knowledge of paint-
ings so any information you can give me would be appreciated.

1989 print

L.W. Snohomish, WA

A. Without seeing the artwork firsthand it is a bit difficult to say, but from
your description of the sticker on the back I suspect this is an art print
based on an original by the artist. An original oil painting would generally be on
canvas mounted on a framework or perhaps on board. You would be able to see
brushstrokes on the front. If you look at the scene with a strong magnifying glass
you may be able to see a tiny overall dot design that means it's a photographi-
cally reproduced print. This appears to be a scene in Yosemite National Park and
is attractive. You could value it in the range of a new large color print of similar
size and quality.

Q. I own this Currier & Ives print,
about 10"x14". It is titled "Evening
Prayer. Hallowed Be Thy Name." In small
print it says 152 Nassau St. N.Y. It's not
listed in the books I have looked at.

A. I also checked references on Currier
& Ives prints but didn't find this
exact title, although there were other
"Evening Prayer" prints they did. Though
undated I'd guess this piece dates about
the 1860s-70s. It is in black and white,
which lowers its value. Also, I can't tell if
the design is meant to be there or not.
Perhaps it was printed that way. Although
cute, the value for such prints is still
modest, probably in the $50-90 range.

Modest value

1896 painting

Q. I have been reading your section in the Collector Magazine and really enjoy it. I hope you can help me regarding a painting I bought in Germany in the early '70s. I'm sending pictures. It was painted in 1896 by a J.V. Hirsch. I do not know anything about paintings or painters. It's painted on canvas and appears to be in the original gold frame. The measurements of the painting are 42" wide x 29" high. The frame is 52" wide x 39" high. I hope you can tell me about the painter and the value of the painting. The man's middle name may have been J. Van Hirsch..

C.E., Orange Park, FL

A. Your pretty autumn landscape does appear to be in an original late Victorian gilt plaster frame. Is the painting signed and dated on the front or is there just a sticker on the back? I've checked through several art price guides and found some artists named "Hirsch," both American and German. I couldn't locate any "Van Hirsch." I think it would be best to take this piece to a reputable auction house or gallery in your area. They would be able to evaluate it better and perhaps do more research. The value could depend quite a bit on how well known the artist is today and if there are records of recent sales of his work. Just as a guess, if it is a nice, large original oil from the 1890s I think it might fetch $1,500-3,000 in the right market. However, you should do more research to get a more detailed evaluation.

Q. I have enclosed pictures of two prints. I would like to know a value and information about them. The first one is by Cecil Golding and is an 18" x 24" image of a black angel and two children. The other is titled "33082 Campfire at Sundown" on the back. It is signed "Goodasson," we think. The signature is very difficult to make out. It measures 30" x 24" and has beautiful colors. Any information you can give us would be appreciated.

S.W.W., Madison, KS

Landscape picture

A. I am not familiar with the artist, Cecil Golding, but this charming print of black children and their guardian angel likely dates from the 1910-40 era. Because of the interest in Black Americana today I'm sure it would be very collectible. It appears to be in excellent condition in a nice old frame. I'd think a value in the $125-225 range might be about right.

The landscape may be an original pastel work by artist Andrew Gunderson and done in the early 20th century. It seems to be in fine condition in the original frame. Today similiar works can sell in the $350-450 range.

Golding print

Hand-tinted photograph

Q. When I purchased this picture I was told it is a Wallace Nutting but I do not see a signature so I am not sure. It measures 12"x15". Could you tell me if it is in fact a Wallace Nutting picture and its approximate value?
J.S., Signal Mountain, TN

A. Your pretty garden scene does appear to be a hand-tinted photograph such as those made so popular by Wallace Nutting in the early 20th century. However, every Nutting print that I am familiar with had a wide plain mat around the sides and was signed in pencil just below the picture on that mat. They were signed with the Nutting name but not by Nutting himself but by one of the staff decorators who worked on the picture. There were several other photographers of that era who copied the works of Nutting and some signed their works. You might carefully remove your piece from the frame and examine any border or the back for any mark. It is possible the picture was trimmed but the frame does appear to be a vintage frame, circa 1920. If it is an unsigned work, the value would be determined by the quality of the color tinting and the condition. Any dirt, fading or stains would reduce the value greatly. Since it is a nice sized piece in top condition it might still be valued in the $50-100 range. Any photographer's mark might up that value. Also note, if this happens to have the original old cardboard backing it would be best to have it rebacked with non-acid mat board which will keep it from deteriorating.

Silk paintings

Q. Enclosed are photos of antiques I inherited from my grandmother. These two are pictures of dancing girls bound in wood carved frames. The actual scene measures 11 ½"x15 ½" and the background material is silk. Originally, as noted in the one picture, all the dresses were painted in pastel colors, however, being exposed to the sunlight the colors faded. The pictures are not signed in one picture it is marked with the letters (I KAW) and since it is difficult to read without removing the picture from the frame, I am assuming that these letters are correct.

C.L.C., San Antonio, TX

A. You have some very nice late Victorian pieces. Your two pictures are most likely a pair. I gather from your description that the scenes are actually on silk fabric. If so, they would be extremely fragile and very susceptible to the fading you mention. Even in the basic black and white they are very pretty. I would say that these scenes were printed right on the fabric and then highlighted with pastel paints. The romantic scenes of dancing Grecian maidens were a popular theme with late Victorian artists, especially in France and I think these two are based on actual paintings done in the 1870-1900 era. Unfortunately I don't recognize exactly which works of art may have inspired them. They are also in wonderful gilt plaster frames of the period that have a very good value on their own. If there is no damage or staining, other than the fading, I feel their value should still be respectable. In the right market I believe this pair might sell in the $600-900 range.

German scene

Q. I purchased this oil painting at an estate sale. It is 23 ½" by 19 ½" and signed "H. Traypper."

E.G., Manhasset, NY

A. The oil painting is a nicely done German genre scene that may date from the late 19th or early 20th century. However, you don't provide any particular history on the piece so that's hard to judge. I have checked through art sales records and didn't find any artist with a name similar to this. There were dozens of lesser-known artists working in Germany in the late 19th and early 20th century. Similar paintings may still be available today. You might check with some of the larger auction houses that deal in fine art to see if they have any history on this artist. My guess would be that this painting might be valued in the $500-1,000 range, but again, it depends on the age, local market and overall quality of the work.

Q. I own this picture that measures 19" by 23". It is in good condition. It is signed "Tiffany Studios."

B.H., Mechanicsville, IA

A. Your color print of the two babies in charming but I have no idea what the significance of the "Tiffany Studios" mark in the corner is. The real Tiffany Studios never produced prints of this type—they specialized in fine leaded glass lamps and other bronze wares. Perhaps the name was pirated after the original studio closed down, otherwise I'm

Charming print

sure Louis Comfort Tiffany would have taken legal action. My guess is that the piece dates from the late 1930s or early 1940s. Collectors love cute baby prints so I would think, if it is clear and bright, it could be worth in the $50-75 range at least.

Modest value

Q. The enclosed photo shows a set of four prints (Ward, artist), each 15" by 6". They are marked "© Stapco, N.Y. Litho in U.S.A." Can you tell me who the girls are? What would you say the value is?

T.P., Miami FL

A. Your prints of the cute farm girls were probably printed in the 1970s or 1980s. I'm not familiar with the artist but cute children are always appealing subjects and these girls would accent a country American interior. They're slightly reminiscent of the very popular artworks of artist P. Buckley Moss who often features slender, stylized figures of Pennsylvania Amish. I think these were made to compete in the same market but I suspect their value is relatively modest.

Q. Could you advise me on the value of this chalk picture? It's quite large—5 to 6' by about 2'. Thank you

A.C., Clinton, IA

A. You have a lovely large picture and if it is an original hand-done chalk work it is quite

Chalk work

remarkable. Andrew Gunderson worked in the early 20th century. The detail and coloring of the long evening landscape is wonderful. It also appears to be in excellent condition, which is unusual. Chalk works are very fragile and have often deteriorated because of the moisture getting behind the glass or the glass rubbing on the surface.

Christmas Steps, Bristol

Q. First of all, I truly enjoy the magazine. I am not really a collector, but in my travels about town and checking out garage sales and not-for-profit organizations that sell a variety of things, I have come across some things that I took an interest in. I have taken pictures of three pictures. Could you possibly tell me if they are just great for looking at or are they worth a fair dollar amount (or maybe both)? I am not interested in selling but I am inquisitive enough to write to you. I truly enjoy your column—love looking at all the goodies. It's amazing when I think back to "the good old days" and I see things that my grandparents had and now they are collectors' items.

The first picture is actually a metal engraving on stainless steel. It's called "Christmas Steps, Bristol" and signed by Griffin, 74. It is made by Omicways Ltd., Bude, Cornwall, England. It is in pristine condition. Even the label is in excellent condition.

On the bottom of the second picture in the lower left is "MCH69," and in the center of the picture is "March, 1955." In the lower right corner is "The Francis Frith Collection, MC-MLXXXIII." On the back of the picture someone wrote: "To Donna and Bill with love." It is signed by Alice Bywate and Pat Bowes. 28A Station Road, Manea, March, Cambs PE150JL, England 035478556. Again

Reprint

the picture is in excellent condition.

The third picture is a sketch. It is black and white and in excellent condition. I am guessing at the signature. It is either "Ellyn" or "Emyn."

L.A., Holiday, FL

Sketch

A. You have some interesting decorative pictures but I'm not too sure about age. The first one, which you show the back label for, was apparently made in England and from the markings I would guess is not terribly old. The company appears to have specialized on pictures engraved on stainless steel but whether the work was done by hand is hard to tell. Being dated "74" (1974) would put it in the field of "collector's items" and it's difficult to track a value on such a piece.

The second photo of an English village scene is apparently a reprint from a negative taken in 1955. The copyright date indicates it was issued in 1983, so again, it's a collector's item.

The portrait of the woman may be an original but researching who the artist is or was could be difficult. If you acquired it in England, that would be the best place to try and track the artist. A work by a well-established modern artist can have value, but tracking the current market activity isn't always easy. Thanks for writing and enjoy these as attractive accent pieces.

Reproduction

Q. What can you tell me about this print? It is signed 1931 FBAR-RAVD. It is 18" x 22".

A. I did some checking in art references. I found several artists named "Barraud" listed. One Francois Emile Barraud (1899-1934) did apparently produce some portraits so perhaps this is a copy of one of his works. As a commercial reproduction, it would only have decorative value.

Original or copy?

Q. Is this little boy "Gavoche?" When I saw this canvas, it was so familiar I had to have it. I bought it but could never figure why it was so familiar until I went to France and showed a picture of it to my sister-in-law who said immediately, this is little Gavoche from "Les Miserables" and then I knew. Having grown up in France, as a child we all read "Les Miserables." It was on a daily or weekly paper or magazine with drawings if I remember correctly.

C.R., Central Islip, NY

A. Your cute portrait of the ragged boy could indeed be based on the character from "Les Miserables." You say this is done on canvas, but I wonder if it is an "original" work or a copy produced on a canvas-like material? During the 1960s and early 1970s there were several artists producing charming portraits of young children that were widely distributed in Europe and the U.S. Even if this is an original painting the value would depend a good deal on how well known and collectible the artist is today. I don't recognize the name in the corner but the style certainly reminds me of works done about 30 to 35 years ago. Tracking information on the artist could be a bit tricky since many have worked in the area of Montmartre in Paris and still produce oils on canvas for the tourist trade. Perhaps some other reader will recognize this artist's work but for now I'd just enjoy it as a memento of happy childhood memories.

Reader Update

C.T., Westbury, N.Y., sent in further information on the picture of the "ragged boy" shown in the June 2002 issue on page 48. She owns a few originals by the artist, Leighton Jones, and actually met him in person, at least 35 years ago, in London, England. Since then she has found posters of his work in New York and has seen a large original work by him in a Madison Avenue art gallery. With this additional background the owner of the piece shown in the column should be able to do further research on this artist and his career.

Q. This photo shows a picture I own. It measures about 10" by 10". It is a Coplex print, copyright 1901 by Cyans E. Cameron, and also marked "W.L. Taylor_98, copyright 1900 by Curtis Publishing Co."
D.H. Birnamood, WI

A. Your sepia tone print of the Native American couple is probably based on the legend of Hiawatha. These sorts of romantic scenes of American Indians and especially Indian maidens, were very popular in the first twenty years of the 20th century. Condition and size are important to value. If your print is clear and not faded, stained or ripped I think it could be valued in the $50-75 range, especially if it is in a nice period frame.

Sepia tone print

Q. This picture is titled "Making Friends." It is a picture of a girl and a dog. In the lower left corner on the bottom it says, "8019—Published and copyrighted 1907 by Hallen & Weiner, New York." We have had this for 40 years. It is in excellent condition with no marks of any kind on it but is not in the original frame.

1907 print

A. Your color print is typical of the cute pictures popular in the early 20th century. Dogs and children have always been appealing. Value depends on the condition since any fading, stains or rips will greatly diminish the collector interest. In top condition I suspect this print might be valued in the $50-75 range.

Carving

Q. I don't know if you will be able to help me with the enclosed picture of a carving but I thought I'd give it a try since I can't seem to locate any information on it, except for the information I received when I bought it. The dealer I bought it from informed me that he had gotten it from a woman who told him her husband had brought it back from the war. She didn't say which war, but I assume it was World War II. The dealer also told me that the wood the carving is made of was becoming extinct because of a disease that affects this type of wood and that smoking pipes had been made out of this same type of wood. I hope that you can identify the type of wood this carving is made of and if it has any value. There are no identification marks on it except on the back where there are two lines which are shaded lighter than the rest of the wood. There is also some evidence of glue, which seems to indicate that it was glued to something. The carving is made of one solid piece of wood which is 26" x 28" x 1-1/4" thick. Any information would be appreciated.

P.J.M., Fort Kent, ME

A. Your carved wood plaque may have been brought back from the South Pacific after World War II. The carved scene shows palm trees, huts and water buffalo, a typical landscape on islands of south Asia and the Philippines. Carvings such as this would have been carved for the tourist trade and similar pieces may still be available in that region. The value of such an item basically rests with its decorative appeal. For someone who enjoys exotic scenes it's a great accent piece. I have no way of verifying the dealer's story about the wood but I suspect this was carved from a wood that was quite readily available, at least 60 years ago. You note the carving is 26 x 28" and it is nicely framed for hanging. There are no set guidelines for valuing such pieces but my guess is it might sell in the $100-200 range to the right collector.

Q. I own this oil on canvas. The canvas size is 24" by 36" and there are seven faceless figures looking off the bridge. On the lower area is a woman and to the right of the creek is another woman. To the far right are two more women. None of the figures are detailed and are also faceless. The painting is signed "J. King." Could you tell me the value of this piece?

B.S., Carencro, LA

A. Your painting has a very stylized, modernistic look and I have not been able to find any information on who the artist might be. References list several artists by the name "King" but they generally worked in the 19th or early 20th century and I would date this work to the 1960s or later.

Modern painting

Copies of print

Q. Here are pictures of ships. I would like to know if they have any value. One is titled, "The New Excursion Steamer Columbia, the largest steam boat ever built for the excursion business," by Currier & Ives and the other is "Midnight Race on the Mississippi," also by Currier & Ives. Both are 9" x 12" in color. Thank you for your help.

J.H., Covington, GA

A. Your photos are a little small and although you mention the titles of the Currier & Ives prints there may be more details along the bottom of each one that would be helpful. A great many Currier & Ives prints have been reproduced in the past 80 years. Some are marked as such and many have a small notation along the border. Others copy more closely the original printing along the bottom of the print, however, the size of the image and type of paper will identify them as later copies. My guess is that your prints are later copies. In particular the bottom margin of each print is much wider than you usually see on an original. If the paper used is fairly heavy stock, almost like thin cardboard, then that also would indicate a 20th century date. As nice decorative pieces I think a value in the $25-50 range each might be about right. *See Artworks Tip #2.

Q. I need help. I own Japanese china with little paper labels imprinted in green, red, blue and black. What do these colors generally tell you? I have the dates for occupied Japan.

L.H., Lafitte, LA

A. As far as I know the colors used on the labels and printed marks for pieces marked "Japan" or "Made in Japan" are of no real significance. Most of these china novelties were mass-produced and meant to be sold cheaply in the U.S. Very few even carry a factory marking and a number of factories there were making the same type of item. The Noritake factory is the main exception to this rule since they usually did mark their wares and due to their better quality there are many collectors looking for them. References on the Noritake firm will discuss their markings and may indicate how the mark can help date an item.

Muller print

Q. In the June 2001 issue you reviewed a print by Annie Benson Muller. I, too, have a print by her. The colors are still very bright. The print hung above my parents' bed for as long as I can remember. It is in the original frame and does not have any damage that I can see. The brown paper backing the print has come loose in some places. The size is 15" x 19". I would like to know the value of the print and any other information concerning it.

D.K.B., Nashville TN

A. Your charming baby print is typical of the type so popular in the first decades of the 20th century. One of the most famous artists doing such works was Bessie Pease Gutmann and her prints can sell in the low to mid-$100s. However, there were a number of contemporary artists who did similar prints and Annie Benson Muller appears to be one of them. The prints of these lesser-known artists don't command nearly the prices of the Gutmann originals. If your picture is clean and undamaged I think it could be valued in the $50-75 range.

Q. I would appreciate any help you could give or advice about where to find information about these two prints that we have. The black and white print itself is 17" by 31" plus about a 3" border. Above the print in the border is "Copyright 1908 by Louis Wolff & Co. Ltd. 154 Tottenham Court Road London W. Painted in Vienna." At the bottom in the border is "Painted by E. Oberhauser." It also says "Lohengrin" and we were told that it is supposed to be Lohengrin's wedding. The print has the signature "Em. Oberhauser." I have been unable to learn anything about the artist at our local library.

Farm scene print

The farm scene print is supposed to be a Grandma Moses. My father won it as an attendance prize at a convention around 1967. It was professionally framed by Haley and Steele Art Dealers in Boston, Mass., but they have no

Lohengrin Print

record of it. I ordered a book that is supposed to contain all of Grandma Moses' paintings but it has still not arrived. I do not know whether to take the print out of the frame to look for further information in the border, considering the possibility that the mat may be covering the signature.

D.H., Cibolo, TX

A. Your large engraving of the scene from Lohengrin is a nice example of artwork popular in the early 20th century. It appears to be quite clean and in good condition. I don't detect any serious stains, tears or fading. Make sure you have it rebacked with non-acid mat board to keep it in top condition. Due to its large size I wouldn't be surprised if it was valued in the $250-450 range in the right market.

The color print does somewhat resemble works by Grandma Moses, however, her paintings were based on her childhood memories, which long predated the tractor I see in this print. I would carefully remove it from the frame and see if there is information on the artist or publisher. That may give you more information on who painted the original and if their works are collectible.

Drews original

Q. I am enclosing a photo I took of an oil painting I have. It is 19" by 27" and I have been unable to find any information on artist K. Drews. On the back of the photo are two stamps: "The Painters Exhibition, Copenhagen, Denmark," and "Malernes U Voldqadk Pa(?)" then 5929 after Pa. There was a Danish painter named Kai Drews (1884-1964). Could this be his work? The detail is exceptional. I have had it cleaned but not restored. It does have repairable damage. Any information would be appreciated including possible value.

M.H., Coupeville, WA

A. Thanks for your letter and photo. You've done some good homework on this artist and I believe this probably is an original by Kai Drews. The landscape does look like a winter scene in Denmark. The damages would keep the value down somewhat but I found a listing for a Drews oil on canvas landscape, which sold not too long ago for about $2,000. Your work might also be in that range depending on the local market and extent of damage.

Q. Perhaps you can give me an idea what the enclosed oil painting is worth. It has been in our family for over 80 years to the best of my knowledge. The Indian chief's name is Multonamah, chief of the Williamette tribe. The artists name is Mrs. Carrie M. Gilbert. She painted it in 1902. She evidently resided in Portland, Ore. This was written on the painting. I wrote to the Oregon Historical Society, which is located in Portland. Part of the information was that there was no real Chief Multnomah, a fictional creation of poet R.H. Balch in his work "Bride of the Gods." I have enclosed the information I received.

H.P., Apple River, IL

A. Thanks for your letter and the interesting background information on this intriguing portrait on deer hide. You have done some great background research on the artist, Carrie

Folk art

Monroe Gilbert, including having a copy of the feature story on her works from the 1902 Portland, Ore. publication. Since it appears that not even the Oregon Historical Society has much history on this woman and her art setting a value is difficult. In a sense this falls into the "folk art" category. Because of the age, quality and subject matter of the work I'm sure it would have a good value, especially in the Portland area, but there are probably few recorded recent sales of similar works. The value, therefore, will depend on what someone is willing to offer. You might see if you can contact a dealer in folk or regional art in the Portland area, who may be able to provide further insights.

Engravings

Q. These items were given to my husband's parents for wedding presents in the 1920s. They were married in Chicago and I have contacted the Art Institute of Chicago and they have no information. I have tried the Internet and haven't been very successful. The pictures are in their original frames and backing. My husband thinks they were done in Europe.

K.K., Garden City, KS

A. Your two engravings appear to be nice quality pieces and probably were made in Europe. I don't know if you've ever had them out of the frames, but there might be additional information on the back or lower edge of them. For prints of this age or older it is generally a good idea to have them rebacked with acid-free mat board and probably similar matting around them. Old cardboard and matting were full of acids that discolor the print. Each appears to be artist-signed in pencil in the corner, but without being able to read the name it will be hard to do further research. As nice decorative pieces in attractive frames I'd guess they each could be valued in the $100-250 range. If they can be attributed to a noted artist the value would increase.

Q. **What can you tell me about this oil on canvas in a beautiful old frame? The signature of the artist is "Kim O-Pao" (this is the way it is printed). The size is approximately 15" by 19".**
L.G., Ironton OH

A. I have tried to research an artist with the name you note but haven't found anything in recent art pricing guides. I also wonder if this is an original oil painting. If it is it will be mounted on a stretcher and have an open back showing this. My feeling is that even though the frame looks old that it is likely a modern copy of a Victorian frame. The artwork certainly has a cubist look to it but it will take more research to try and track down the painter if it is an original work.

Original?

Q. **This cow picture is of woven silk thread—there are no names or identifying marks anywhere. The overall picture is 15" by 19" and as you can see, the weaving itself, which measures 8" by 12", is removable from the shadow box frame.**
    The round print is 20" in diameter and is in a walnut frame. The label on the back lists the following information: Title: "Water Baby" by Draper, George Busse, 20 East 48th St., N.Y. I know there were at least four artists named Draper—could this be Herbert James Draper and didn't he work during the Art Nouveau period? Both these pictures were given to my grandmother by her sister back in the 1940s and I know she owned them for many years prior to that.
J.F., Graniteville, VT

Woven scene

A. Your silk cow picture is very interesting. It sounds from your description that the scene is actually all woven right in the silk. Such works have been done in Switzerland, as well as some in England, in the 19th and early 20th century. A woven scene in color would be of more value, but in top condition I'd guess this picture might be worth in the $200-500 range or perhaps more to the right collector. Your color print is very charming. It certainly has an "Art Nouveau" look, ca. 1900-1910 and it may be based on a work by Herbert J. Draper. It appears to be in excellent condition and I don't see any rips, stains or other damage. Since it is fairly large I believe it might sell in the $150-250 range in the right market.

Q. I am sending you a picture of a painting that I purchased at an estate sale. The painting is 11" by 14". It is in excellent condition. It is signed "JARVIS." I went to the library and found some information on the artist. His name was John Wesley Jarvis, American painter, 1780-1840. He painted many famous portraits signing them J.W. Jarvis, however, in his biography it says many of his smaller pictures were simply signed Jarvis. He lived in Baltimore for some time, where 1/10 of the population was Negro slaves. Somewhere between 1811 and 1814, Jarvis paintings were sold for $80-100. In 1816 and 1817 he was receiving $600-800 for portraits. In 1820 and 1821 he lived in New Orleans. Many of his canvases he painted there have not been located and

Which Jarvis?

are not dated. Good evidence that Jarvis spent the winter of 1828 and 1829 in New Orleans is provided by a document that shows that he had no scruples about keeping and trading slaves. Entering the state of Louisiana in December 1828, the painter is said to have brought with him a mulatto woman known as Margaret. Then on April 2, 1829, he exchanged this woman for a Negro girl named Maria, age about 9 or 10, who was an orphan and a slave for life. On this date the legal certificate recording these details was drawn up between Jarvis and Abner Robinson of Richmond. Jarvis was an American painter of the early 19th century standing in point of time between Gilbert Stuart and Thomas Sully. Jarvis left no register of his works. It is likely that a great many of his works remain to be identified. What more could you tell me about this and what is its approximate value?

B.N., Mapleton, IA

A. You did a good deal of research on an artist named "Jarvis," however, I'm afraid I don't feel that this portrait is a work by John Wesley Jarvis from the early 19th century. It has quite a contemporary look and I suspect was painted during the past 30-40 years. I checked some art references and there have been several other artists named "Jarvis," but this portrait doesn't sound like the type of work they produced either. You note that this is a painting, however, is it an oil painting on canvas? If so it would be mounted on wood stretchers. Some paintings were also done on artist board, which is still used today. The type of backing may help date the piece. Perhaps some reader will recognize similar portraits by an artist using this signature, however, a talented amateur whose works are not well documented may have done it.

Q. I am enclosing a photo of a colored print I've had since 1976—signed at the bottom right corner "M.J. Hummel." The print is 8" by 9" and the frame is 13" by 16".

L.D. Lakewood, CO

Hummel photo

A. Your photographic print shows a Hummel figurine. These were based on the artwork of Sister M.I. Hummel and have been produced by the Goebel Company of Germany since the 1930s. This is just a decorative accent piece and so the value would be fairly modest, likely under $50. A Hummel figurine enthusiast, however, might offer more.

Q. I own this piece that I assume to be a print by B.W. Leader; however, it is signed in pencil by him in the right hand margin. His name and the date 1887 are printed in the left hand corner of the print itself. At the top right it says: "London, Published May 1st 1888, by Messr. Arthur Tooth and Sons 5 & 6 Haymarket SW Copyright registered Mess. Shefbold and Co. Berlin. Entered according to the Act of Congress in the year 1888 by Mess. Max Knoedler and Co. New York in the office of the Librarian of Congress at Washington." It is approximately 29" x 17". Does this have any value?

P.K., Cincinnati, OH

Engraving

A. I researched your engraving and found that it is based on the work of the English artist Benjamin William Leader (1832-1923). He was a prolific painter of English landscape scenes and I found many listings for sales of his oil paintings, but few for the engravings. His original oils can range in value from the low thousands to over $100,000. The only engraving I found listed sold for only $60, but I don't know if he personally signed it. I think it would be worthwhile to check with an auction house or gallery that has more records of his work in order to determine if this piece is really signed by the artist. If it is as I suspect, it could be valued in the low $100s at least.

Q. I am 82 years old. I have no children and a house full of collectibles that I would like to sell but have no idea of value. The first item is a reverse painting in which some of the windows are lit with abalone shell. It is dated about 1904 but not signed. The second is a Bessie P. Gutmann print dated 1929 in its original frame.

M.M., El Paso, TX

A. Your oval reverse-painted picture of the U.S. Capitol is done on domed glass and this style was widely popular in the first quarter of the 20th century. You can find similar designs featuring the Statue of Liberty and other national sites. If the paint on the picture is in perfect shape and the frame is undamaged some of the pictures are selling today in the

Reverse painting

$100-200 range. * See artworks tip #1

The print of the pretty young woman is by the popular artist Bessie Pease Gutmann. She is best known for her pictures of cute babies and some of these can sell for hundreds of dollars, depending on the design and condition. Your print appears to be in excellent condition and in the original frame. According to sources I checked your image is titled "The Message of the Roses" and was originally published in 1925. In top condition it has a value in the $300-400 range.

Gutmann print

Q. This lithograph is 20" wide and 15" high. The design on the frame is raised. My parents purchased it at a house sale in 1946. On the bottom of the left it says: "Copyright 1907 The Gray Lith. Co. NY." On the right side on the bottom is "H.G. Plumb." What can you tell me about the value? There is a little foxing on the top border and bottom border. I was always kept out of direct sunlight.

L.W., Snohomish WA

Lithograph

A. I'm afraid I can't tell you much about the artist, H.G. Plumb. I suspect he or she was a commercial artist whose works were mainly reproduced as lithographs. The colorful scene of kittens would appeal to many cat collectors today and the frame appears to be original and in good condition. Any staining or damage to the print, however, would reduce the value today. In top condition I believe this framed print might sell in the $150-250 range. "As is" it would depend on how badly someone wanted it.

World War I era paintings

Q. I hope you can help an 80-year-old veteran. My Dad was in World War I and brought these paintings home. We never could identify it and the artist. I would greatly appreciate any information you can give me as to its value.

C.J., Park Ridge, IL

A. You appear to have a pair of very nice paintings. I am assuming they are oil on canvas and mounted on stretchers. Paintings with hunting scenes are always in demand, however, I haven't been able to determine who the artist may have been. We may be able to show an enlargement of the signature here and then maybe a reader can help us out. The first name appears to be "Muller," however I found that there are a couple of dozen German artists by that name working in the late 19th and early 20th century. Since these were brought back from Europe I suspect they were done in Germany.

The value will depend a great deal on the fame of the artist. If they are original oils on canvas and in top condition I would guess they might be valued in the $1,000-3,000 each range.

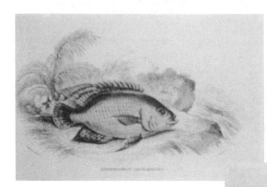

Hand-tinted engravings

Q. Enclosed is a picture of a "Centrachus Fish." I have a set of four. In the left corner is "Stewart delt.," in the right is "Lizars SC". The pictures look like a watercolor— very smooth with no dots or honeycombs. Do you have any idea of age or value?

S.P., Depoe Bay, OR

A. You appear to have a set of hand-tinted engravings of fish, perhaps dating from the first half of the 19th century. The original artist would have been "Stewart," but I haven't been able to track that person down. The "Lizars" probably stands for the engraving firm of W.H. Lizars of Edinburgh, Scotland. They are best known for producing the first 10 plates of John James Audubon's "Birds of America" in the 1820s. I don't believe these represent American fish species so they probably wouldn't be valued anywhere close to the original Audubons. If it can be verified that they are original 19th century prints and not later copies they would probably have a fair value, perhaps in the $50-100 range each or maybe more.

Q. My sister bought this picture for the frame many years ago and gave it to me to put my mother and father's picture in it. I never got the picture changed. I got it out where I had it stored and to my surprise there was the Statue of Liberty. The picture is painted on the back of curved glass. In the green area on the left it says: "Copyrighted 191(?), Chicago Portrait Co., Chicago." On the right side: "Goddess of Liberty." The frame is perfect but there is damage on the painting. Hope you can tell me about the painting and if it has any value.

Reverse painting

A. These reverse-painted pictures on domed glass were very popular just before and after World War I. Various American scenes such as the U.S. Capitol and the Statue of Liberty were popular designs. Your example is a bit more colorful than some I have seen, however, any damage to the paint will lower the value to serious collectors. The frame appears to be in nice shape and that is a plus. I would guess in the right market this picture might be valued in the $75-150 range.

Q. This picture is from Iran. I have been told that the frames on these pictures are made with tiny wires. It has a smooth finish and the picture is hand painted. Is the frame on this picture a type of cloisonné work? It is done on a wood frame. I paid $35 for it from a friend that visited his family in Iran. Can you give me a value for it? Thanks.

S.K., Kerrville, TX

Iranian painting

A. The Iranian painting may well have been produced for the tourist trade years ago. Most Islamic art forbids the use of human or animal figures. I suspect the frame has brass inlay in wood or plaster so it is not cloisonné. I think you paid a reasonable price for this artwork but it's hard to say what it might be valued at in the market today. There aren't a lot of collectors of Mideastern art of this type.

Picasso copy

Q. I recently purchased a print (?) at a church rummage sale and am wondering if you can help me determine if it is a true Picasso. The print is on canvas and from the dingy color of the canvas, I estimate it to be at least 40 years old. It has a plain black frame. The actual size of this print is 23" x 17". The curatorial assistant for the St. Louis Art Museum was kind enough to answer my inquiry to tell me that Picasso did execute several prints in 1959 that very closely resembles my piece, but she was unable to locate an exact match. She suggested I contact an art appraiser, but I would hate to pay an appraiser a large sum of money to find out my print is worthless.

D.D., Pleasant Plains, IL

A.   Although Picasso did produce a select number of limited edition prints I'm pretty sure some of his works were mass-produced and widely sold. The best editions would be carefully marked with the edition number, printer and other details. Anything with just the artist's name in the design is pretty certain to be a commercial copy with only some decorator value.

Watercolor

Q.   I own this watercolor on board. It really needs to be cleaned up. I love it, but it is a real mystery. My father seems to think it was a sketch an artist did before he did a mural somewhere for the government back in the 1920s or 1930s. No signature is on the front. It could be on the back but I did not want to take the paper off. The tag on the back reads "The Wallis Art Shop, 377 Fairfield Ave., Bridgeport, Conn." The shop is no longer in business and has not been in the last 40 years.

L.H.C., Lexington, SC

A.   I can't be certain from the photo but your rural scene does appear to be an original watercolor since I can see some wear on the surface. This indicates that it is very fragile condition so handle it with care. I would suggest you take it to an experienced framing company or art gallery and have the backing carefully removed. I don't recognize the art style so a name or some other information on the piece would be a great help. It should probably be reframed with non-acid matte board at any rate. There were many artists who worked on projects for the government during the Depression era, some of them famous, some of them little known today. Any name or further history on the origins of this piece would be important to evaluating it.

Q. This Oriental painting was purchased in 1965 from a used frame dealer for $25. It is on rice paper and the dealer said it was Japanese and old.

M.S., Stratford, CN

A. You have an attractive Japanese woodblock print, but I haven't been able to pin down exactly who the artist or printer are. I checked through a reference that lists all the major artists of the 19th and 20th century but couldn't

Woodblock print

quite find an exact match. I believe the three characters on the upper right side are probably the name of the artist and the character at the bottom center is the name of the publisher. It is framed in a narrow black wood frame that is typical of those used after World War II. If I had to guess I would say that this was a piece brought back from Japan by a G.I. during the Korean War. I suspect it was a new print at that time and although the works of some 20th century Japanese woodblock artists can be fairly valuable I believe this piece might be valued in the low to mid-$100s.

Q. I acquired all these items at house sales some years ago and would appreciate some information on them. The picture of the kitten in oil—scene is in the dump—signed "GIG." The puppy is also in a dump, bit is on paper board and has indentations—also by GIG. The large eyes are the highlight. They are 8" x 10". The wagon train scene is a salesman's

Decorative prints

Lithograph

sample, I think. It is a lithograph of picture done by F. Grayson Saynor. It has beautiful coloring and made by Newton Manufacturing in Newton, Iowa.

E.M.K., Omro, WI

A. Your cat and dog prints featuring big-eyed animals were probably produced in the late 1960s or early 1970s when this style was popular and often featured children. They would only have some decorative value. The Western wagon train print probably dates from the 1950s. For someone who likes the "Old West" appeal I would guess it might sell in the $35-65 range.

Commercial prints

Q. I own these two pictures. One, a painting or print, is signed by P. Rowier.

B.B., Devils Lake, ND

A. Both of your pictures are, I believe, commercial prints probably produced between the 1950s and the 1970s. I couldn't locate any information on either artist. Again, any value would be as decorator pieces, perhaps in the $25-50 range.

Q. Enclosed is a photo and information on a painting by James J. Allen, measuring 20" x 27" and framed, in excellent condition. It was probably painted between 1930 and 1950. I acquired this painting from an estate sale recently, along with the 5" x 7" photo of the painter and the article about him. I would really appreciate it if you could possibly give me some information on this artist and the value of this beautiful painting.

R.P., Port Richey, FL

A. You provided some good background information on this artist, but I have not been able to find any sales records for his works. Mr. Allen may have been fairly well known during his lifetime but it appears that his works don't show up on the art market much today.

Allen painting

The value of such works is usually reflected by the current popularity of the artist and if there is no great demand for the works of James J. Allen, I would guess the market value would be modest. I am assuming he died in New York City so you might check with galleries in that area for any details. This painting (apparently a watercolor) might be valued as little as the low $100s but perhaps in just the right market it might bring many times more.

Q. Enclosed is a photo of a "pastel" painting that was a wedding gift to a relative in 1911 in Spokane, Wash. It was signed "E. Carlsen." The picture measures 16" x 22" and with matting and frame it measures 26" x 32". The only thing written on the back of the wooden frame is #16319 in pencil. I would appreciate any information on the artist or painting and its approximate value.
E.R., Penn Valley, CA

Pastel

A. Your pastel artwork is very attractive. Such artist-signed pastels have become very collectible; however, I could not find "E. Carlsen" listed in the reference *The Power of Pastels* by June Rhode (self-published, 2000). Similar seascapes by unknown artists or unsigned works seem to be valued in the $350-450 range if in perfect condition. Having the original fame would add to the value also and it looks like you may have had it rematted, hopefully with acid-free matte board.

1923 print

Q. I purchased this print of Mary and the Christ Child at an auction for $10.
H.D., Harvey, ND

A. Your color print showing Mary and the Christ Child was produced about the time of the 1923 copyright. It is pretty, but religious art of this type doesn't have too strong a market today. Your scene is quite appealing, however, and in top condition with the frame, might be in the $40-80 range.

Watercolor

Q. I am interested in learning about a painting I have had for several years. My brother purchased it about 40-50 years ago at a yard sale, I believe. Originally it was in an old gold leaf plaster frame with green matting. I had it reframed a few years ago. The artist's name appears to be Len Hart. On the border of the painting is the word "England." It appears to be undated. The painting is on some sort of stiff board about ¼" thick.

S.D., Elijay, GA

A. Your watercolor landscape is very pretty and well done, but I have not been able to track down any information on an English artist named "Len Hart." References list quite a number of artists named "Hart" but I couldn't find any with a similar first name. I would guess that this was painted in the early years of the 20th century. I can only guess that it might be valued in the $500-1,000 range due to its appeal.

Q. Enclosed is an article (Chicago Historical Society) regarding Varin aquatints of Chicago. I have four in their original frames (listed below) and would appreciate any further information you can give me as to potential value. Aquatints: Michigan Avenue At Jackson Street (1889), 48/125, Randolph Street, Chicago (1864), 82/100; A Birds Eye View of Lake Shore Drive, Chicago (1889), 101/125; Michigan Avenue at the foot of Madison Street, Chicago (1864), 16/100.

R.N., IL

A. Thank you for the photos of your aquatint prints of early Chicago scenes and the copy of the 1948 feature put out by the Chicago Historical Society. As the story says, Ernest Byfield, in the late 1920s, contacted a French aquatint artist named Varin who was able to reproduce these scenes originally done in the 19th century

Aquatint

by the artists Jevne and Almini. These were produced in limited numbers around the early 1930s and are fine copies of the originals. I checked through a guide to pricing prints and a few years ago these "Varin" renditions were selling in the $150-300 range. I note yours may have some toning (darkening) and may have some mat burn from the original acid pulp mat board so you should have them reframed with acid-free matting. The condition will be a factor in valuing them but I'm sure they are still in demand with collectors in the Chicago area and you have excellent documentary background on them.

Q. This picture was given to me by an elderly woman years ago. She didn't tell me where it came from, but I do know she spent 13 years in Paris, France. This is a painting on canvas. It is about 21" x 31". The signature is G.A. Kinder or Kidder and the date either 1841 or 1844. I can't find anyone to appraise the picture for me.

M.M., WI

Painting

A. I've checked several references on American artists and have not been able to locate a G.A. Kinder or Kidder. Your work does remind me very much of paintings done around the turn of the century (perhaps your date is 1892) by the American artist Harry Roseland (1867-1950). Roseland painted a number of interior scenes featuring obviously well-heeled young white ladies visiting with poor black women, possibly their former "mammies." Today the works are considered overly sentimental, although they do give some good insights into what a poor African-American might have lived like around the turn of the century. Perhaps your artist was a student of Roseland or was influenced by his work. It would be worthwhile sending your photos and a close-up of the signature to one of the larger New York City auction houses for their opinion. Typical Roseland paintings today sell in the low to mid-thousands, but it's hard to say what a work by a lesser-known artist might bring.

Compton painting

Q. I purchased this watercolor approximately 30 years ago in an antique shop, as I liked the colors within the woodland scene. It is signed: "C.H. Compton" and I am hoping you know of this artist. Any information is greatly appreciated.

J.L., Salem, OR

A. I have checked several references on American artists and have not been able to find any listing for a C.H. Compton. It is very possible that this Compton was simply a talented amateur painter. Without a date on the painting it is difficult to say when it was done, but it could be from the late 19th or early 20th century when many people took up painting as a hobby. Value depends mainly on the decorative appeal and quality of the work, which looks quite good to me. You should probably check with an art gallery or a larger auction house in your area to see if they can find out anything more.

Q. I found this painting on canvas in a second-hand store and I was wondering approximately what is its value. I think it was painted in 1928 by Norman Rockwell. It measures 13" by 16" and has a gold frame that is cracking in spots and has red underneath the gold paint. Seems like a very old frame. Collector Magazine & Price Guide is a very informative guide to antiques and I can't wait to get my copy every month.

R.T., Glendale, CA

Rockwell print

A. Your framed Norman Rockwell print-on-canvas was probably produced about 20 years ago by the Donald Art Co. of Port Chester, N.Y. It is based on Rockwell's "Tea For Two" painting used on the cover of *The Saturday Evening Post* Oct. 22, 1927. Although it is appealing and has decorator value, it probably wouldn't be valued as highly as the original magazine cover. Enjoy it as a nice quality copy of Rockwell's work.

Appomattox engraving

Q. First I must tell you how much I enjoy your column in *Antique Trader's Collector Magazine*. It is always interesting to see and learn about items from our past. Recently my mom died and I am executrix of her estate. There were many items, but since my knowledge of antiques is only what I read in your column, I am turning to your for help. It is our hope to find a few items of value with which to finalize her accounts. We hope you can advise me on the picture enclosed. It appears to be a Civil War picture, possibly Appomattox as it seems there is a peace-signing taking place. On the bottom are signatures of Lee and Grant along with names of those present. The picture is edged with a gold-embossed design and around that is a black frame, which seems to be constructed of carved pyramids layered one upon another. There is a water mark on the upper part of the picture due to its storage in the garage. My neighbor says she thinks it could be restored but I need to know if it would be worth it or if anyone would be interested in it without restoration. Any advice you could give me would be greatly appreciated. The size of the picture is approximately 14" high by 24" long; with frame size is approximately 2' high by 2-1/2 to 3' wide by 2-1/2" deep.

R.F., Baldwin, NY

A. Your engraving does show the surrender scene at Appomattox that ended the Civil War. The printer's name is probably at the bottom and the signatures of Lee and Grant are only facsimiles. It would be difficult and expensive to try and restore this water-stained piece but someone might be interested in it "as is." I think the interesting carved "tramp art" frame probably has more collector value than the print. It is a fairly simple design but probably dates from the last quarter of the 19th century and could be valued in the low to mid-$100s at least due to its nice size. Good luck.

Charcoal drawing

Q. Enclosed is a photo of a carbon painting I purchased at a garage sale, size is 14" by 21 1/8". Written on the back is "The Faithful Watcher, Crayon by Prof. Webb." Any information on value and do you or any of your readers have a name for Prof. Webb? Also age? PS. I've been taking your *Price Guide to Antiques and Collectibles* since 1982. Love it.

C.F. Parishville, NY

A. Your charming charcoal drawing appears to be by an amateur artist of the late 19th century. I would guess it is based on another actual engraved print by another artist. Perhaps this "Prof. Webb" was an art instructor at some school. I doubt he is a listed artist. Because of its nice size and apparent good condition, plus the charming theme, I would say this piece might be valued in the $75-150 range today.

Farm scene

Q. I have these two paintings and would like any information you might be able to come up with. I became interested in my barn/farm scene when I saw a similar signature on a Grandma Moses and learned that there were other members of that family who painted. The barn/farm painting is oil on heavy texture canvas. Crude stretcher. The religious picture is in dark, strong colors. The white on bottom is from the flash. The canvas appears to be a heavy texture fabric. Signed in right corner "Del Vecchio." Size is 18" wide by 32" high.

V.DeP., Las Cruces, NM

A. The world of art and painting is very complex and many interesting works are difficult to attribute with any accuracy, especially "folk art" style pieces such as your snowy farm scene. A whole generation of artists were inspired by Grandma Moses in the 1940s and 1950s so only an expert might be able to say if your work was done by an artist whose work became collectible. You might send the photo and complete information on size, condition and back view to the Museum of American Folk Art, Columbus Ave. (between 65th and 66th streets), New York, NY 10023. The religious painting of Mary and the Christ Child appears to me to be a late 19th or early 20th century piece. It is nicely done but in fair condition and without a signature or historic background would be hard to trace. Sorry I can't tell you more.

Religious scene

Q. We live 12 miles from Iola, Wis. In 1962, our 90-year-old courthouse was demolished. I was able to rescue a picture of Lincoln on tin. It measures 20" by 24". I would appreciate information as to its age and value.

R.P., Weyauwega, WI

Tin picture

A. Your lithographed tin picture of Abraham Lincoln is typical of the wide variety of memorials to Lincoln that were widespread in this country from the late 19th century through World War I. Without any markings, it is difficult to date the piece exactly, but similar pieces were made in the 1890-1910 era and a variation of the Brady pose portrait was used as advertising early in this century. The centennial of Lincoln's birth in 1909 caused another explosion of Lincoln images, too. Overall your piece appears to be in nice clean condition without too much scratching, dirt, rust or dents. As a nice example of Lincoln memorabilia, I'd say it might be valued in the $300-600 range, perhaps more to the right collector.

Watercolor

Engraving

Q. Please help me with these two pictures my mother left me. The picture of the woman, 14 ½" by 8 ½" is signed "Dritton." Back has a magazine sheet advertising Old Overhold Straight Rye Whiskey, a picture of two men by a fireplace and "Many a pioneer neighbor said, "I don't know why—but Abe Overhold's whiskey is different." The other picture of the Arabian Garden is signed "Lambert, Arabian Garden," mainly black with a little green on some leaves and pink on some flowers, 17 ½" by 21 ½". It was purchased in the early 1920s. This frame was on it when I bought it.

P.C., Charlotte, NC

A. The picture of the young woman in Empire costume looks like it may be an original watercolor from early in the 20th century but I can't find any information on an artist named "Dritton" so he or she may have been an amateur. It is pretty but, again, damage in a corner reduces the value. The "Arabian Garden" print looks like it might be an engraving with some color highlighting. Many such pictures were produced in the 1920s and generally their value is for decorative purposes, perhaps in the $50-150 range without any stains or damage.

Chromolithograph

Q. I found the enclosed picture at a garage sale and am wondering if there is any value. On the back is a small piece of paper taped to the brown paper backing (which may not be original). It says on the back of picture: "Faith, hope & charity from P.O. Vichery & Co., Augusta, Maine. Publishers of Vichery's Fireside Visitor and Dealers in Jewelry, watches, books, games, etc., etc." On the front left side: "Strobridge & Co. Chromo Cin. O.;" middle: "Entered according to acts of Congress in the year 1875. By Strobridge & Co. in the office of the Library of Congress at Washington;" at right: "For exclusive use of P.O. Vishery." Love your column.

M.M., Clarkston, WA

A. Your print appears to be a nice quality of chromolithograph from the 1870s. There may be some discoloration due to an old wood backing board and that should be replaced with acid-free cardboard if you want to preserve this piece. The colors do appear to be nice and bright and I don't see other serious problems. As far as collectors go, however, the symbolic and semi-religious topic of the print would keep its value quite low. Collectors of Victoriana prefer landscape scenes, pretty ladies, animals or children. The size makes a difference also, so I'd say this piece might be valued in the $25-50 range.

Q. I really enjoy your section in the *Antique Trader's Collector Magazine*. I hope you can help me with my find. I found two old paintings in an aunt's attic. They are about 14" by 18", framed alike, perfect condition and they are under old glass (very wavy). The picture with the two figures standing has a signature, F. Andnealti or F. Andrealti or F. Andyealti. We couldn't be sure whether the letter was an "n," an "r" or a "y." There is a name on the back, "Say Yes." I didn't see a signature on the other picture. There had been a name on the back as you could see where it had been. Is it a print of an oil painting? What period was it painted in? I'd appreciate any information you can give me on age and value.

A.H., Crescent City, CA

Lithograph

A. I don't believe your two pictures are actual oil paintings. An original oil would not be framed under glass. The canvas would be open to the air and it would be mounted on an open stretcher at the back. You most likely have nice colored lithographs from the late 19th or early 20th century. I believe the scene of the couple in 17th century costume might be based on a work by Federico Andreotti, an Italian artist of romantic scenes (1847-1930). His original works can sell for thousands of dollars but your print, if in excellent condition, might be valued in the low hundreds. The artist of your other scene of the young musical couple in 18th century dress is not listed but the picture is probably from the same era and, if perfect, likely valued about the same as your other one.

Lithograph

Steel engraving

Q. I really enjoy your commentary in Collector Magazine. I am enclosing a snapshot of a steel engraving of the George Washington family that has been in our family for many years. This picture was given to my mother by her grandmother, and my mother (96 years old) gave it to me in 1995 on the occasion of my 50th wedding anniversary. I have been trying to find some information and history about this picture. I am enclosing copies of pictures similar to mine, but the two are credited to different artists. The Sargent picture is from an article in Grolier Encyclopedia and the Weaver picture from an art appreciation book. My picture has some different clothing and no world globe and also, Martha is seated on the left. The size of my picture is 24" by 16 ½" and the frame is 36" by 28 ½". The picture has never been out of the frame, which has a wooden backing. I would like to know who the artist is and the value of the picture and any additional information you can offer.

E.D., Gillette, WY

A. Your large engraving of George Washington and family is a variation based on the original painting done in the late 18th century. These fine engravings were popular during the mid-19th century. If your piece is matted and not trimmed you may find information on the engraver along the bottom edge. It appears to be in the original frame, however, you should have the wood backboard removed and replaced with acid-free mat board, as well as the mat around the print. The wood acid will damage the print if it hasn't already. In top condition, a print such as yours might sell in the mid- to upper $100s.

Reverse painting

Q. Enclosed is a photo of three paintings which are known as "reverse painting on glass." I haven't been able to locate information on these types of painting except that they were popular during the Victorian age. My mom has had these in her home for about 75 years. Can you tell me anything about them? Are they of any value? In the square painting, the center seems off.

Mrs. F.S., Plainview, NY

A. You are correct that these are reverse paintings on glass. These saw a revival in popularity right around the World War I and into the early 1920s. The oval ones (too dark to reproduce here) with the domed glass are typical of that era. You will find some examples featuring scenes of the Statue of Liberty or the U.S. Capitol, but yours are general land- and seascapes. The rectangular example may be a bit earlier but I don't recognize what scene it's supposed to represent, perhaps a castle in Europe. If there is no serious damage to the paint or frames, I'd say the oval ones might be valued in the $75-125 range and the rectangular one, because it appears more detailed, would be worth more.

Books & Paper Collectibles

Q. What can you tell me about this book? It measures 5 ½" by 7 ½". It is titled *Rip Van Winkle and The Legend of Sleepy Hollow* by Washington Irving, illustrated by George H. Boughton A.R.A., London, MacMillan and Co., and New York, 1893. It has gold embossing on the cover and binding and page edges.

B.E., Olympia, WA

1893 edition

A. This edition of *Rip Van Winkle and The Legend of Sleepy Hollow* is a nice late Victorian edition with a gold-stamped cover typical of that era. I'm not familiar with the illustrator but illustrated books do bring more than those without. Color pictures would add more to the value than just black and white ones. Book collectors are very fussy about condition so any damages to the cover or interior would hurt the value. Loose bindings or worn edges are among common problems. As just a nice example of late Victorian printing, I'd guess this volume in top condition might be valued in the $15-30 range.

DIE ABWEHR
Der Feindangriff zerbricht an der
zähen Abwehr der Infanterie

German poster

Q. I've had this poster for a long time. It looks like a German poster to me. I would be thankful if you could tell me what it says and anything you could about it, including the price range it would go for. There is no writing on the poster other than what you see. The poster's in mint condition and it's not faded. It is 16" by 20".

E.S., Sierra Madre, CA

A. Your German poster printed in black and white was undoubtedly issued during World War II for use in the homeland. From the format it appears that it might have been part of a series of such posters to bolster patriotism. The rough translation of this one reads "The Defense—The enemy aggression crushes on the tenacious defense of the infantry." Such World War II memorabilia is a very strong area of collecting today, so your piece should be desirable if it's in clean, good condition Since it's not in color, which adds to the value, I'd say it might be valued in the $50-75 range.

Q. What can you tell me about these two books? First, *The Wizard of Oz*, copyright 1899, copyright 1903, copyright 1903, by L. Frank Baum & W.W. Winslow. It is in good condition.

The Players Directory, Issue 37—year 1944 (First issue 1937) is a list of Hollywood players then in the armed forces of the United States. The list was furnished by the Screen Actors Guild. There is a little discoloration on the cover but otherwise it is in good condition. It is slightly curled a little on cover corner. I hope you can appraise these items for me.

H.L.J., Gordon, NB

Collectible books

A. You have a couple of collectible books, but age and condition are major factors in value. Your *New Wizard of Oz* book appears to be an early reprint of this children's classic with illustrations from the original book. Even though it is not a first edition, it should still be quite collectible. The cover appears to have some wear, but if there is no serious staining or damage or loose pages. I believe it might be valued in the $100-200 range.

I also checked with our in-house book expert, Bill Butts, about your directory of 1944 movie actors. From your information, it appears this edition only listed actors serving in the armed forces. Larger versions listing all the male and female members of the Screen Actors Guild might bring more; but this is collectible. The cover is a bit rough and might reduce the value, but it might still sell in the $40-80 range in the right market.

Q. Enclosed is a picture of a book written by Murat Halstead titled *Illustrious Life of William McKinley our Martyred President*. The book is copyright 1901. There is a hand written note on a forward page signed by Murat Halstead—printed I believe. The book is superbly illustrated with numerous engravings made from original photographs. The book is 10" x 7 ½" and has 464 pages of history. The cover is not mint condition but the book is complete and pages are in good condition. Does the book have any value other than as a history collectible? It is of interest to me as my dad and his mother got off the train in Gordon, Neb., the day President McKinley was as-

McKinley book

sassinated. They were met by my dad's father, driving a horse and buggy, and traveled north 12 miles to a ranch the family had purchased. It was home to my dad for the next 70 years. Your articles are great and I enjoy the magazine from cover to cover. Thank you.

H.L.J., Gordon, NB

A. Thank you for your letter and photos of the McKinley book. Your book has an interesting tie-in with your family, but I'm afraid the condition of the cover would keep the value to serious book collectors down. There probably were a number of books and publications published at the time President McKinley was assassinated, but today he isn't as well remembered as some presidents who died in office. The demand for such books is probably fairly low. I would guess in this condition it might be valued in the $25-50 range.

Q. I have an original of Alfred Dornett's book *It Was The Calm and Silent Night*, which was published in 1884. It is also called *A Christmas Hymn*. On the nameplate of the book are the words: "Illustrated, Boston, Lee and Shepard, 47 Franklin St., New York, Charles T. Dillingham, 678 Broadway, 1884." On the back of this page are the words: "Copyright, 1883, By Lee and Shepard, All Rights Reserved, Cambridge: Printed by John Wilson and Son, University Press." I have enclosed a scan of the cover, which is extremely thick and has some smudges on it from age. The edges of the pages are gold. The pages are very thick compared to books of today. There are etchings on every page along with the words of the

1884 book

story. The picture shows the exact size of the book. Can you tell me if this book has any value? If so, what would it be? Who, if anybody, would be interested in a book such as this? Thank you.

E.W., East Brunswick, NJ

A. I talked with our book expert Bill Butts about your interesting Christmas-theme book. In general anything Christmas-related does have collector value. Over the decades dozens of books have been published about this season. Today children's books in particular are in demand. I suspect your volume was meant more for the adult Victorian market. You note that it included etchings so I assume these are in black and white and most likely show religious Christmas themes. It would make a difference to collectors if the pictures were all in color and had whimsical scenes of Santa, toys and children. The cover is attractive but shows some wear. Bill feels that in the right market this volume might be valued in the $25-45 range.

Fire prevention poster

Q. I'm enclosing a lithograph signed picture by Charles Russell, "B???? to Breakfast." The picture measures 14" x 21". The entire picture is 17" x 21 1/2". It has a heading, "Prevent Range Fires," a small picture of Smokey Bear is in the upper left corner. It says, "Please be careful with Range Fires." At the bottom of the picture it says, "Reproduced by permission of and copyright." Please tell me if it has any value.

L.C., Mansfield, MO

A. This is an interesting old fire prevention poster and I would say it probably dates from the mid-1950s. Smokey the Bear became the American icon for fire prevention during those years and he usually appeared on these posters. This is a fascinating variation aimed at the folks in the wide-open West. I know older Smokey the Bear items have a collector following and this has the nice crossover Western appeal. It appears to be in very good condition with no serious tears, stains or fading. My guess is that in the right market it would be valued in the $75-150 range.

Fake bill

Q. My friend has a bill for $1,000 and it is only printed on one side. This is a copy of it. She says it was given to her by her grandmother in about 1940. It's cream in color, but over the years may have faded. I've never heard of a one-sided bill, but it looks great, if it's real. We would appreciate any information you might have.

L.D., Grayling, MI

A. I was a bit suspicious of this $1,000 bill so I contacted Dave Harper, editor of *Numismatic News*, another Krause Publications magazine. Dave confirms that this bill, always numbered "8894," is one of the oldest fakes in paper money that shows up on the market. He reports it first appeared in the late 1950s and into the 1960s when it became technically possible to widely copy paper documents. I'm afraid it only has curiosity value.

Q. A friend inherited a very handsome copy of *The Select Works of John Bunyan Containing the Pilgrim's Progress., etc.*, an "Illustrated Edition," the text on each page is surrounded by a blue or rose-colored ornate border. There are 668 pages. The book measures 7 1/8" wide by 10 ¾" long and 2 1/8" thick. The front and back covers are made, I suppose, of pressed cardboard and 3/8" thick. They are carved out to create an ornate brown, black and gold design. In the center appears the title "Bunyan's Select Works

Illustrated". The publishing information is: "Philadelphia, William W. Harding, No. 236 Chestnut Street, 1871." I wonder what the value of a book like this is. It is my understanding books such as these were popular during the last quarter of the 19th century. Enclosed are photos of the cover and two pages of the text with one of about a dozen illustrations.

C.H., El Paso, TX

Collectible
Bunyan book

A. You appear to have an attractive late Victorian edition of Bunyan's works. The cover is ornate and may be stamped leather, which would add to its collector appeal. You show one black and white illustration but don't note if there are others. Illustrated volumes such as this tend to have some interest to collectors. It is also important that the binding be tight and clean with all the pages intact with no staining or foxing. Even though it is a late edition of his works it appears to be a nicely produced edition of more value than a run-of-the-mill mass-produced version. I believe it might be valued in the $40-80 range as a nice decorative book if nothing else. The right collector might even offer more.

Reader Update

I received a helpful letter from George Theofiles of Miscellaneous Man, New Freedom, Pa. His firm specializes in retailing classic posters and other ephemera. George explained that the movie posters discussed in the December 2002 column are actually reproductions of authentic examples. A whole range of such repros was issued between 1975 and 1985 and included other examples for classic movies such as "King Kong" and "Gone With The Wind." The reproduction one-sheets are 20" x 29" while the originals are usually 24" x 41". Thanks for sending this important update.

German postcards

Q. **What is the value of these postcards? They are both in perfect shape. They were mailed from Gotha, Germany in 1904—the Czar had not been assassinated yet. Queen Wilhemina of the Netherlands is on both of the cards.**

D.D., Redmond, OR

A. You have a pair of interesting German postcards that would date between 1902 and 1910. One way to date them is by noting that one shows King Edward VII of England, the other his queen, Alexandra. They ruled between 1902 and 1910. I checked with an authority of early German cards of that era, and based on the cards being crisp and clean, without serious stains, creases or folds, they each might be valued in the $12-18 range to the right collector.

Q. **I am interested in the prices for these two comic books. They are 10" x 13". They are Vol. 5, No C-49, Oct.-Nov. 1976 (Superboy) and Vol 5. No. C-48, Oct.-Nov. 1976 (Superman).**

C.W., Midland, TX

A. I checked with John Miller, an editor of comic book price guides at Krause Publications, and he gave me the lowdown on your two comics. The "Superman vs The Flash" (C-48), is a "Limited Collector's Edition" of a comic first published in 1967. This version is from November 1976. Since the cover shows some wear and creasing this one would probably grade at about "good" to "very good" and have a value in the $4-6 range.

Grade affects price

Your "Superboy and the Legion of Super-Heroes" is another special Collectors' Edition from late 1976 and, again, would grade about "good" to "very good" with a value in the $5 area.

Q. I am interested in knowing if there is any value to these two photos. The first is of Ralph Waldo Emerson and the other is of Henry W. Longfellow. On the back is the following inscription: "COPYRIGHT, CHARLES TABLE 7 CO., New Bedford, Mass. 1882."

C.J.E., Carlsbad, CA

Mass-produced photos

A. You don't give a size for these photos but I'm guessing they are the larger "cabinet" size photos (about 4 x 6") popular in the 1880s onward. Although your photos are of famous American literary figures they are mass-produced copies made for the general public. Unless such a picture is actually inscribed by the person shown, which is quite rare, their value is quite modest. The signatures on these, of course, are just printed on. I would guess in the right market each shot might sell in the $10-20 range if it is clean and not faded.

Ceramics

Rookwood

Q. Many of the magazines I subscribe to have articles and pictures of Rookwood in them, but I haven't seen this particular vase. The colors are shades of rose, flowers are dark blue to black and the stems are deep green, but have no leaves. This vase belongs to my mother. I grew up with this vase in our house and I am 73. It is in mint condition. I hope you can help me to identify the flowers and information on the bottom and also an estimate of its value. (Symbol on the bottom looks like SP with XXII under it, and 1841 under it; also, L 19 l. It is in black paint.)

B.F., FL

A. Your Rookwood pottery vase appears to carry a matte glaze, a type popular in the early years of this century. The markings indicate it was produced in 1922 in the shape No. 1841. Although you did not give a size, I found in a reference book that this shape was 12" tall. The other markings are a little harder to decipher. There is usually the marking of the artist who painted the piece and perhaps letters denoting the type of clay. You have drawn what appears to be "L 19 L," which doesn't correspond to Rookwood markings I found combining letters and numbers. Could this perhaps be "L N L" Those were the initials used by Rookwood artist Elizabeth Lincoln, who was working there during this time period. Stylized floral designs were sometimes used on Rookwood so we probably won't know what blue flower these may represent. The uniqueness of the decorating and relative desirability of the artist, as well as the size and form of the piece, all help determine the value of Rookwood pieces. From what I can tell, I would guess this piece might have a collector value in the $600-$1,200 range. This could go higher if you determine for certain who the artist is and you find the right buyer.

Q. This cup and saucer set is deep blue and white with gold trim; 90 percent of the gold trim is still on the pieces. On the back stamped in red ink is "Made in Russia" and a mark. I know it has to be after 1920, but can you tell me any more about it?

G.B., TX

Made in Russia

A. This blue and white ceramic cup and saucer from Russia would probably date from the 1920s or 1930s and appears to be a takeoff on early 19th century designs. Although it is pretty, a single cup and saucer wouldn't have nearly as much value as a set. I would guess this piece was transfer decorated, but if it is hand-painted that could raise the value. As a nice transfer-decorated cup and saucer, I think a collector might find it appealing in the $30-$60 range.

Q. Enclosed are several photos of a jardinière labeled "Doulton Lambeth England #9803." It measures 9" in diameter, 7" high. The design is of real leaves that have been embossed with hand sculpting in between. I have never seen one like it. Can you place a value on it?

E.N., NY

Doulton ware

A. You appear to have a nice example of an early Doulton ware known as "Natural Foliage Ware," produced between 1886 and 1914. Actual leaves were impressed into the damp clay to leave the design that was later glazed shades of brown. The mark you show dates this pot between 1891 and 1902. The scratched-in initials "EP" are probably those of the decorator whose name I haven't been able to pin down. I would imagine this form of early Doulton pottery is quite scarce and collectors of Doulton and Royal Doulton wares would fine it quite desirable. Since it's a scarce ware, a value is hard to pin down. Just guessing, due to its size and attractive design, I think a figure in the $500-$1,000 range wouldn't be out of line. Perhaps a serious collector might pay more.

Q. Enclosed are two photos of a cookie jar I bought at auction two years ago. It is about 8 ½" wide at the handles and also top to base. It's 5 ½" at top and base. On the bottom are the letters: "R.R.P. Co. Roseville Ohio 312." I have looked through all old *Trader* magazines back to 1984. Can you give me value and date it was made?

L.G.P., Regina, Sask., Canada

1930s era cookie jar

A. Your cookie jar with the embossed apples and leaves on the sides was a product of the Robinson-Ransbottom company and probably produced around the 1930s or '40s. They were a major producer of cookie jars but the figural jars they made seem to be in most demand today. Your piece with the simple round form might be valued in the $50-$150 range, depending on condition and local demand.

Roseville pottery

Q. Enclosed is a photo of a ceramic piece I have that I believe is Roseville Morning Glory pattern. I do not know what this piece is called. Is it a console? What value might be placed on it? The piece belonged to my mother-in-law. It is also in perfect condition. (Dimensions 11" by 5 ½" by 5 ¼" high. #271 on bottom.)

Mrs. E.C., Duncanville, TX

A. You are exactly right about your piece being the Morning Glory pattern produced by the Roseville Pottery and introduced in 1935. The piece of this form is usually referred to as a planter or "jardinière," French for large planter. The number "271" on the bottom is the pattern number and this piece should be about 10" long. Many lines of Roseville are very collectible today and larger pieces in perfect condition are always sought. According to recent price listings I checked, your piece would be valued in the $400-$600 range.

Q. Please find enclosed photos of a meat platter that I bought at a yard sale. The woman I bought it from had no information on it. The platter is in excellent shape and has no damage. There are two marks on the back; the blue mark reads "Royal Hunters," under that is the name "Davenport." The other mark is indented with the number 21 and under that "Davenport" with a drawing of an anchor. It is 18 ¾" long, 15" wide. It sits up about 2" to 2 1/2" off the counter because

Staffordshire platter

of a broth drain at one end. I hope this rough drawing of the platter showing the drain helps.

B.S. Lantana, FL

A. You made a very nice purchase at the yard sale, one that many collectors would envy. Your large earthenware pottery "well & tree" style meat platter is Staffordshire transfer-printed ware, and from the style and design I'd date it around 1830-40s. The blue and white color is always popular and Davenport was one of the best-known makers in England's Staffordshire pottery region. "Royal Hunters" would be the pattern name. These quality early Staffordshire wares have really been increasing in value in recent years and I wouldn't be surprised if a very large platter like yours, with no chips, crazing or staining might sell in the $250-$500 range today.

Q. Enclosed you will find a picture of a porcelain figurine. It is 9" tall, 12" wide and 8" deep. The markings underneath crossed arrows are "Germany Dresden" in gold lettering. I know this was purchased in Germany quite a number of years ago. The cello's bow is missing but everything else is in mint condition. Could you please tell me the age and value of this piece?

N.H., Sturgis, SD

German figurine

A. Your porcelain figure group is typical of the decorative type produced by German factories for nearly 200 years. These groups were especially popular in the late 19th and early 20th century and have continued in production from the 1920s onward. One firm that used blue crossed arrows was the Christian Fischer factory, which operated between 1875 and 1929. I suspect your piece may be somewhat newer since gold markings are more common pieces from the 1930s and then continuing into the 1950s and 1960s. Even if your grouping is not a true antique, it has great appeal because of the fine lacy trim and careful painted decoration. I would guess today it might be valued in the mid to upper $100s and perhaps more to the right collector.

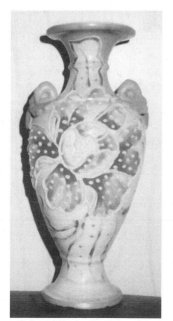

Q. There are no identifying marks on this 9 ½" vase. The handles on each side are crudely applied. There is a yellowing on the inside and bottom. The dots in the flowers are raised like French knots in embroidery, or tiny rosettes. The pattern is the same on the other side. My mother found this in an antique shop during World War II. Can you tell me what it is and its value?

L.L.C., Taft, CA

Vase

A. Your decorative vase with the large rose-colored blossom outlined with raised slip banding appears to me to be an early 20th century example of Japanese pottery or porcelain. The raised beaded decoration is referred to as "moriage." Vast amounts of similar vases and other decorative wares were imported from Japan in the first quarter of this century and not all carried permanent markings. If this piece were marked with a "Hand Painted Nippon" mark we'd know it was decorated porcelain from that era and Nippon has a good collector following. As just an unmarked colorful vase, however, I'd guess it might be valued today in the $75-$150 range.

Earthenware pottery

Q. Enclosed please find a picture of two items. The pitcher is octagonal, marked on the bottom "Foliage." It is over 100 years old, been in the family that long. It is 8 ¼" high at the spout and 8 ¾" high on the handle side. I would like to know the origin, design name and approximate value. Condition is fine. The shaving mug is 3 ¾" high marked "Ironstone" with a crest with two upright lions on either side, with "Victoria" inside the top of the crest. Condition is fine. The handle is pierced with three holes. Is there a design name other than Ironstone? Age and value, too, please.

M.B., Belleville, IL

A. You have two interesting pieces of earthenware pottery. The "scuttle" shaped shaving mug with the dark blue landscape decoration I believe is a modern copy of a Victorian style design. Many such items have been exported from England in the past 30 years or so and most only have a generic mark with words like "Ironstone," "Staffordshire" or supposed pattern name like your "Victoria." Nearly all old flow blue or dark blue transfer-decorated English wares would have carried a maker's mark and name with a special trademark. Some of these newer pieces are attractive decorator items but rarely have very much collector value. By contrast, your octagonal pitcher is a nice early example of "Flow Mulberry" ironstone ware with the "Foliage" pattern, produced by the Edward Walley firm around 1850. Flow Mulberry wares, though not quite as expensive as Flow Blue, are increasing steadily in value today. A nice pitcher such as yours, if in perfect condition, might be valued in the $200-$300 range.

Q. I recently acquired a set of china, over 100 pieces, in the enclosed pattern. I have been told it is a type of flow blue and that it was made by Mason. Any help you can give as to age and manufacturer would be appreciated.

M.S., Ft. Payne, AL

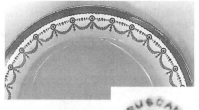
Jones earthenware

A. I hope the photocopy of your blue and white plate pattern will reproduce well, but we also will show t he marking on the back. The initials above the crescent are "GJ" for the George Jones firm and in the crescent are the words "& Sons," not "Mason" as you thought. This marking was used by the Jones firm from 1893 into the early 20th century. Today George Jones earthenwares are becoming very collectible, especially the fine majolica wares. They also produced many blue and white patterns, the most popular being their "Abbey" design. Your pattern is "Truscan,' as shown on the base. I couldn't find it listed among true "flow blue" patterns, but it is attractive nonetheless. Value would depend on what types of pieces were in your set since cups and saucers and covered serving pieces can add greatly to the overall appeal of the set. Also, some early patterns are not easy to replace today which sometimes makes it a little harder to sell them. Without knowing more, I'd guess your nice George Jones set might be valued in the mid- to upper-hundreds and perhaps more to the right person.

Red stoneware

Q. I have this container that I have not been able to find information on. It is some kind of glass, but I'm not sure. There is a chip on the bottom of the lid and it looks kind of like red pottery. There is a #3 on the lid and bottom. There is also a distinctive mark on the bottom. I'd appreciate your help.

A.F., Emmett, ID

A. Your interesting bottle and stopper is made of fine red stoneware pottery and the stamped mark on the bottom, featuring a small bottle enclosing the initials "EH," indicates this was produced by the Eugan Hulsmann Pottery of Altenbach, Germany. The company opened in 1881 and operated until after 1932. This sort of ware with a design reminiscent of Mideastern pottery was probably produced in England and other countries. The pottery of the Hulsmann firm is not well known to collectors today but because this piece appears to be of fine quality and a nice size (not given), I'd say it might be valued in the $75 to $150 range. * See Ceramics Tip #5.

Canova platter

Q. The picture enclosed is of a platter that came with my mother's family from England in the 1870s. It is in perfect shape, 12 ¾" by 15 ¾", on the back is "Canova, T. Mayer., Stoke upon Trent," indented with the number "14." It is black and gray and white. Can you please tell me of its value? My mother was offered $100 for it many years ago. The trouble is, with antiques such as this, where is it possible to sell them for what they are worth? Any information you give me would be gratefully appreciated.

Mrs. E.B., West Shokan, NY

A. Your nice earthenware platter is a fine example of the transfer-printed wares produced in the Staffordshire region of England in the 19th century. The Thomas Mayer pottery used a mark similar to the one you describe in the 1830s so this piece could be antique indeed. "Canova" is the pattern name and this pattern was produced over a long period of time and in several colors. Your dark purplish color could be referred to as mulberry, though this piece is not the "flow mulberry" ware so popular with collectors today. To have a large piece such as this without any serious damage, stains or crazing is quite a find. Such wares have been increasing greatly in value in recent years and your large platter might be valued in the $300-$500 range in the right market.

Q. The picture of the plate I am sending you is a favorite of mine. I have a lot of antique books but cannot find this plate. I love your articles and look forward to them. You have shown a lot of what I have collected over the years.

P.K., Jackson, MI

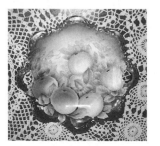

Bavarian plate

A. Your porcelain piece has a colorful transfer design of fruit on a green ground. The mark on the back, a shield and crown flanked by "P" and "T" is the mark for the Porcelain Factory Tischenreuth of Tischenreuth, Bavaria. The firm was founded in 1903 and I'd guess this cake plate was produced before World War I. If it does not show wear or have any chips or cracks, and depending on size, I'd think it could be valued in the $35-$55 range.

Q. I have also been trying for years to find out the identity of the pottery that made the "Avenue of Trees" pitcher, and its current value. Everyone knows it is the "Avenue of Trees" but nobody knows who made it! As the picture shows, it is cinnamon glaze, 9" tall, 6" diameter, no mark, weighs about 5 pounds. The design is not sharp and is hard to photograph. Can you help?

R.B., St. Louis, MO

A. Your "Avenue of Trees" pottery pitcher features a dark brown Rockingham-type glaze. Pottery expert Steve Stone of the Blue & White Pottery Club gave me the background on this piece. It was produced by the Brush-McCoy Pottery between about 1911 and 1923 as part of what they called their "Woodland Line." This piece was produced with several different glazes including the dark brown, green, yellow, and solid blue as well as the shaded blue and white. The solid color examples such as yours only demand about $50-$75 on the market while choice examples in the blue and white can sell for around $200.

Brush-McCoy Pottery

Q. Enclosed is a photo of a recently acquired old Weller vase. I need your expert opinion as to age, value, and whatever else you can tell me. The vase is 14" tall and 8" wide at widest part of handles. Color is dull pink and green, flower is pink-tinged, creamy white. There is some crazing on and around flower. No design on back. Only marks on bottom are "Weller" and the letter "A." I enjoy your column immensely and welcome the chance to participate.

G.L., W. Bloomfield, MI

A. Your vase is in the "Wild Rose" pattern by Weller, produced in the 1930s. Although attractive, this line is not one of the most sought-after of Weller's products. However, since it is a large size and appears to be in excellent condition, I'd say it might be valued in the $100-$200 range.

Wild Rose pattern

Q. Enclosed are two pictures and a tracing of a mark. I believe my pottery piece is Marblehead Pottery. It is a lovely blue with brown glaze inside, top opening 3 ¼" around, 5" wide and about 3 ½" tall. It has a couple of minor "scratches" on it. I love my 25-cent garage sale "find" and hope you can advise its true worth.

K.T., Fairfield, OH

Marblehead pottery

A. You are correct, your bowl/vase is a nice example of Marblehead Pottery and features its sailing ship flanked by "M" and "P" mark. This pottery was founded in 1904 in Marblehead, MA by Dr. Herbert J. Hall and was set up to be a therapeutic outlet for patients in a sanitarium he ran.

It was later separated from the sanitarium and continued to operate until 1936. Most pieces were in the Arts & Crafts style popular at that time and some featured simple stylized designs. Those examples tend to be rarer and more valuable. Your simple piece with the nice dark blue glaze might be valued in the $200-$250 range if in perfect condition. You made a great buy!

Q. I am again writing to the person who writes my favorite feature in *Antique Trader's Collector Magazine!* Referring to a Collector Club listing in your magazine, I wrote to them but didn't receive a reply, so I am turning to you for your help. I am enclosing a photo of the Red Wing pitcher in question. Could you be kind enough to identify the pattern and tell me what a fair price might be for it? My only interest is in selling it and turning funds over to the local charity.

E.N., Wayne, PA

Red Wing pitcher

A. Your water pitcher is in the Concord shape introduced by Red Wing in 1941. The pattern with the large roses is "Lexington." According to sources I checked, this piece might be valued in the $25-$50 range or more to the right collector.

Q. Enclosed are photos of an oyster plate I purchased at a yard sale. It is ceramic, 11" in diameter and nicely decorated with gold trim. There is slight crazing on the back of the plate, no mark. I wondered about what age and value it has. The plate is in excellent condition, no chips or cracks.

J.H., Lake Isabella, CA

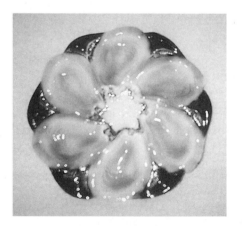

Oyster plate

A. Your attractive porcelain oyster plate was likely produced at a German or Austrian factory around the turn of the century. The French also produced these in large numbers and they were made in majolica in England as well as china. Even some scarce examples were made in this country. Right now there is a big demand for oyster plates and they're seen at top quality antiques shows with high prices. A few years ago you could purchase nice examples in the $75-$100 range. Today many examples have doubled in value with the rarest

selling for hundreds of dollars. You note there is "slight crazing" on the back, but I can't see it in the photo. Depending on how serious it is, I'd say your piece might be valued in the $100-$200 range.

Q. Enclosed is a picture of a vase that I received from my aunt's estate. It is 8" high and the dress is off-white with green trim. The hair is a real light yellow and the rose and her lips are red. The vase part is the basket she is holding in her right hand. In her left hand she is holding a rose to her head. On the base under the glaze is painted "357 Kaye" in script numbers and letters. Directly under the "e" in "Kaye" is a capital "R." After the glaze material was applied and before it was fired just to the right of this lettering a second letter is scratched, a big capital "R" which shows rough on this glazed surface. Can you tell us anything about this piece and what the value is?

L. & S.C., Rockford, IL

California pottery

A. When I first saw your figural girl planter with the name "Kaye" I thought it might relate to the works of California potter Kay Finch, but she didn't spell her name with an "e." In checking through references on other California potters of the 1940s and 1950s who did similar figures I saw pieces by designer Hedi Schoop and, finally, I think I found who made your piece. Kaye of Hollywood was a firm run by Katherine Schueftan, a former decorator for Hedi Schoop, hence the similarity in design. I don't believe much information is available as yet on this maker or her wares but collectors of California pottery would find it interesting. If perfect, I'd say it might be valued in the $25-$50 range.

Q. Here is a picture of a vase we have. It was brought back after World War II. It is 12 ½" high. It has what we believe is the story of the Prodigal Son on it. The mark on the bottom is an "L" in red. No name on it. Maybe you can tell me something about it and what it's worth, also how old it might be.

L.H. Taconite, MN

A. Your vase is an example of 20th century Japanese Satsuma pottery. It may date from between the wars or may have been fairly new when bought. The embossed scenes are a bit unusual but the bright colors and heavy gold trim are typical of 20th century pieces

Satsuma pottery

made for the Western market. Even though it is a nice size, such examples don't have nearly the value of the more finely painted Satsuma pottery produced in Japan in the 19ᵗʰ and early 20ᵗʰ century. If there are no chips or other damage or wear, I'd say it might be valued today in the low $100s.

Q. This pair of Imari vases has been in my family since about 1900, probably a wedding gift to my great aunt who died in 1919. They are 18" tall, very heavy and unmarked. Due to the thickness, I think they are Japanese. There are two small holes on the insides of the tassels where there might have been brass fittings. The gold, red and blue are still very bright; a small piece is missing from the lip of one vase.

R.S., Childress, TX

A. You appear to have a nice pair of large Imari vases produced in the late 19ᵗʰ or early 20ᵗʰ century. A professional china restorer should be used to repair the rim damage. But even with that, I'd say the pair might be valued in the $1,500-$3,000 range because of their size and decoration.

Imari vase

Q. I recently came across this birdhouse by the Roseville Pottery. It is in good condition and very well marked. It has three holes for hanging by a wire or string and/or also a hole for hanging by a nail. Has a hole for a bird to enter plus a little hole for a stick so a bird can sit on it. The lid in photo is marked "patent pending" on top. The other mark is "Roseville/National." Would appreciate any information and what you might think it is worth. I have been through all the Roseville Pottery books I could find and found no information.

B.B., Lancaster, OH

A. You couldn't find this birdhouse in a Roseville Pottery book because it was not made by that firm but by the National Pottery firm, also of Roseville, OH. They produced utilitarian

National Pottery birdhouse

This Art Deco period novelty lamp is composed of a bronzed cast-metal base featuring a scantily clad lady and a blossom-shaped frosted glass shade. Similar lamps today can sell in the **$150-250** range. *Photo courtesy of Mark Moran and J. Kruese.*

A number of patented Art Glass lines were introduced in the U.S. during the late 1880s. One of the scarcest varieties is "Agata," produced by the New England Glass Company. The shaded pink ground features an overall "oil spot" decoration. This 3 3/4" tall tumbler is valued in the **$550-750** range. *Photo courtesy of Brookside Antiques, New Bedford, Massachusetts.*

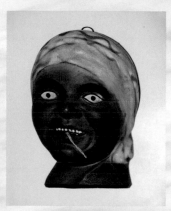

Black Americana is a popular collecting area today. In the past many kitchen accessories featured exaggerated portraits of blacks. The chalkware "Mammy" head string holder, circa 1950, might sell for about **$225**. *Photo courtesy of Ellen Bercovici.*

The prints produced by the firm of Currier & Ives were probably the most widely popular decorative images in America during the second half of the 19th century. Many originals are still available on the market today and "common" ones can sell for under $100. However, rare "large folio" designs such as "The Road - Winter" are much rarer and very costly. Introduced in 1853, this sleighing scene has been widely popular ever since. However, this is also one of the most rampantly reproduced Currier & Ives prints found today. An original in top condition, such as this example, might sell for over **$50,000!** The 20th century copies should sell for well under $100. *Photo courtesy of Skinner, Inc., Bolton, Massachusetts.*

In the late 19th century elegant fireplace mantel garniture sets were very popular in the homes of the wealthy. This French set includes an ornate gilt-bronze clock with enameled panels flanked by matching urn-shaped candelabra. Expect to pay in the $1,500-2,500 range for such a grouping today. *Photo courtesy of Copake Auctions, Copake, New York.*

A great many fine wall "Regulator" clocks were imported from Austria and Germany in the late 19th and early 20th century. This Austrian example, circa 1880, features a walnut case 46" tall. Comparable examples can sell today in the $800-$1,200 range. *Photo courtesy of Charlton Hall Galleries, Columbia, South Carolina.*

The Ansonia Clock Company, Ansonia, Connecticut, was one of the largest manufacturers of quality clocks in the late 19th and early 20th centuries. This clock, with a gilded cast-metal case, features a seated figure beside the upright dial. Today this clock is valued in the $600-700 range. *Photo courtesy of Elden and Jenny Schroeder, Onalaska, Wisconsin.*

Shirley Temple was undoubtedly the most famous American child star of the 20th century. A wide range of items was produced featuring her image during the 1930s and the composition dolls, made by Ideal, are certainly among the choicest collectibles. This 20" tall Ideal Shirley is all-original and complete with her box and photo. This rare grouping could sell today for over **$1,700**.

Some of the finest bisque head dolls of the late 19th and early 20th century were manufactured by the German firm of Armand Marseille. This 42" tall bisque head girl features blue "sleep" eyes and a brown human hair wig. She is marked on the back of the head "A 20 M - Germany." In top condition this pretty young lady could sell in the **$800-900** range. *Photo courtesy of McMasters Doll Auctions, Cambridge, Ohio.*

The Effanbee Doll Company produced a whole "family" of composition "Patsy" dolls during the 1930s. This 26" tall "Patsy Ruth" is in excellent condition and redressed in a nice outfit. She has sold at auction for **$900**. *Photo courtesy of McMasters Doll Auctions, Cambridge, Ohio.*

In the first decades of the 20th century inexpensive "costume jewelry" became the rage. Some designs used very modern designs while others, such as this necklace, reflected a renewed interest in Victorian era designs. Composed of a gold-plated double chain suspending seven squared panels decorated with enameled flowers and black oval stones framed by seed pearls, this piece is signed "Hobé." At 15" long, it could sell today in the $200-250 range. *Photo courtesy of Marion Cohen, Albertson, New York.*

This costume jewelry brooch-pin reflects the Victorian Revival designs popular in the 1930s and early 1940s. It is made of gold-plated metal with an antique finish and is centered by a large red stone framed by small grey and red accent stones. Signed "Sandor," this 4" long piece is valued today in the $65-85 range. *Photo courtesy of Marion Cohen, Albertson, New York.*

In the late 19th and early 20th centuries, fancy glass bowls on silver plated stands were popular wedding gifts, hence the name "Bride's Baskets." This fine example with a shaded pink interior decorated with enameled leaves and flowers could sell in the $450-550 range today. *Photo courtesy of Temples Antiques, Eden Prairie, Minnesota.*

In the early 20th century a new colorful glassware was introduced as an inexpensive counterpart to the very expensive iridescent art glass produced by makers such as Louis Tiffany. Today known as "Carnival Glass," it was made in dozens of patterns, colors and forms. This punch set in deep purple is in the popular "Grape and Cable" pattern produced by Northwood. In top condition a seven-piece set like this could sell for over $1,400 today. *Photo courtesy of Parker-Braden Auctions, Carlsbad, New Mexico.*

▶ Many late Victorian parlors and dining rooms featured fancy hanging kerosene lamps. This one, with a rare mother-of-pearl satin glass shade and font and fancy brass frame, sold for nearly $4,500. Other nice examples are still available for under $1,000. *Photo courtesy of Jackson's Auctioneers, Cedar Falls, Iowa.*

▶ In the late 19th century kerosene was the fuel of choice for home lighting. This fancy parlor table lamp features a hand-painted ball shade and matching glass base with scenes of monks and a keg of spirits. The fancy metal fittings are gilt-metal and this piece probably dates from the 1890s. Because of its large size and unusual painted decoration this lamp could sell for well over $1,000. Many other similar, but smaller, lamps of that era, today called "Gone-with-the-Wind" lamps, can sell in the $200-600 range. *Photo courtesy of the Gene Harris Antique Auction Center, Marshalltown, Iowa.*

▶ The Haviland china company of Limoges, France, manufactured some of the finest and most popular dinnerwares of the late 19th and early 20th century. This 6 1/2" diameter bread and butter plate is in the "Paisley" pattern. Today this plate would sell for around $26. *Photo courtesy of Nora Travis, Cerritos, California.*

▶ Early electric table lamps with leaded glass shades are extremely collectible. The rarest examples were produced by firms such as Tiffany and Handel, however, nice examples by lesser-known firms are also increasing in value. This fancy Duffner & Kimberly lamp features a 21" wide shade and stands 24" high. It could sell in the $4,000-5,000 range due to its fine workmanship. *Photo courtesy of Skinner, Inc., Bolton, Massachusetts.*

The fine "Nippon" porcelain, produced in Japan between 1891 and 1921, is very popular with collectors today. Large numbers of vases and tablewares were produced but large molded-in-relief plaques, such as this example featuring a pair of lions, are quite scarce. This piece, 10 1/2" in diameter, is valued at about $575. *Photo courtesy of Jackson's Auctioneers, Cedar Falls, Iowa.*

"Head vases" were originally inexpensive ceramic novelties often used by florist shops in the 1950s and 1960s. Today they have become hot collectibles. This graceful lady, known as the "Mitzie Gaynor" model, was the No. E2968 style produced in Japan for Inarco. On today's market she could sell for $650. *Photo courtesy of Maddy Gordon, Scarsdale, New York.*

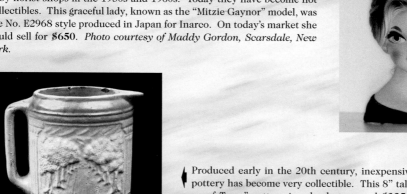

Produced early in the 20th century, inexpensive "blue and white" pottery has become very collectible. This 8" tall pitcher in the "Avenue of Trees" pattern is valued at around $325. *Photo courtesy of Susan Cox, El Cajon, California.*

During the 1940s and 1950s the "Little Red Riding Hood" line of kitchenwares was very popular. A wide variety of figural pieces, such as cookie jars and salt and pepper shakers, were produced by the Hull Pottery and Regal China. This rare advertising display sign was used in a store that sold these wares. Only six of these 11 3/4" long pieces are known to exist today, which helps explain the estimated value of around $20,000. The actual "Red Riding Hood" pieces themselves can be found for much, much less, with cookie jars selling in the $300-1,000 range while salt and pepper shakers can be found for under $50. *Photo courtesy of Susan Cox, El Cajon, California.*

Delicate bisque figurines were extremely popular in the late 19th and early 20th century. Some of the finest examples were produced in Germany and France and large pieces are in great demand. This charming Victorian boy with basket was probably made in France, ca. 1890. He stands 13 1/2" tall and could easily sell in the **$200-300** range. Collectors need to be aware, however, that many bisque figures have been reproduced during the past sixty years. *Photo courtesy of Temples Antiques, Eden Prairie, Minnesota.*

One of the hottest areas of collecting today is Roseville Pottery. There are dozens of patterns available to collect and prices vary according to the demand for a specific line and the rarity of the piece. This seven-piece beverage set in the "Bushberry" pattern is quite rare. In top condition it could sell for over **$1,000**. *Photo courtesy of Cincinnati Art Galleries, Cincinnati, Ohio.*

In the past decade, colorful Victorian majolica pottery has become extremely collectible. The best examples were made in England, France, Germany and, in the United States, by the firm of Griffen, Smith & Hill of Phoenixville, Pennsylvania. This rare punch set was part of their "Etruscan" line and features a water lily pattern. It has sold for nearly **$3,000**. *Photo courtesy of Michael Strawser, Wolcottvile, Indiana.*

Produced in an American factory around the 1890s, this Golden Oak style platform rocking chair features nice leafy scroll carving on the crestrail and pierced scrolls in the lower rail of the back. Today this rocker could sell for around **$350**. *Photo courtesy of Mark Moran, Rochester, Minnesota.*

Large, heavily-carved pieces of dining room furniture were quite popular in the homes of the wealthy during the last decades of the 19th century. Often made of solid oak or another hardwood, some of the fanciest examples were imported from Europe. This extremely large two-part sideboard features its original hardware and dark ebonized finish on the oak. It dates around 1890 and stands 96" tall overall. In today's market the collector with the right home could purchase such a piece for around **$3,200**. *Photo courtesy of Mark Moran, Rochester, Minnesota.*

This style of country-made desk is often referred to as a "plantation desk," based on the belief that similar types were used in the offices of plantations in the South. Actually, they were used in offices all over the U.S. This type of desk features a tall upper section, often fitted with solid doors, above a projecting lower section. The example shown here is made of butternut and does not have doors enclosing the upper section. Dating about 1850-1870, this piece is valued around **$750**. *Photo courtesy of Greg Kowles, Winona, Minnesota.*

This high-backed bed is a fine example of the Victorian Renaissance Revival style. It is made of solid walnut and burl walnut panels, all highlighted by fine carving. Made in the U.S.A. around 1875, this piece is valued at **$3,500**. *Photo courtesy of Mark Moran, Rochester, Minnesota.*

pottery wares beginning in the first quarter of the 20th century. The company's other raised mark features a profile of an Indian chief with the word "National." As an interesting early pottery piece, I'd say your birdhouse might be valued in the $50-$100 range. The value should increase in the coming years.

Q. Could you please tell me anything you know about this vase? I thought it could be a piece of Boch Freres pottery that was made in Belgium. I looked it up in the *Antique Trader Books' American & European Art Pottery Price Guide* but the pottery mark is a lot different. Then what's on my vase? If it is a Boch Freres piece, what would it sell for? The vase is 7" high. The circular mark on the bottom of the vase states: "Made in Belgium, Fabrication belge. BochF. La Louviere. K-612."

E.S., Sierra Madre, CA

Boch Freres vase

A. Your pottery vase was produced by the well known Boch Freres works of La Louviere, Belgium, probably between the wars. They continued production after the war, so it could be a bit later. It has a nice streaky glaze, however, it doesn't fall into the range of their wonderful Art Deco design pieces designed by Charles Catteau. Those pieces are very desirable today and sell in the mid- to upper hundreds or more. I think your piece might be valued in the $150-$300 range, if perfect.

Q. I was given the following vase (?) about 21 years ago. It came from an elderly woman who lived in Cape Cod, MA. I find it to have an interesting shape. It weighs about four pounds. It is 10 ½" high and 6" wide. The top lid of the vase is 2" wide with a ½" pouring hole. The glaze is shiny. The colors are well represented in the enclosed photos. I have enclosed a hand sketch of the markings on the bottom. I have tried to find the identification of the mark, to no avail. Perhaps it is from a private collection. I call it a vase, but I think it was used to store a liquid, perhaps water or wine. Any information you can provide is appreciated. I look forward to your publication each month.

J.C., Revere, MA

A. Your interesting bottle-form pottery vase is a bit of a mystery to me. The conjoined "AA" mark at the first resembles that used by the famous Van Briggle Pottery of Colorado Springs, CO. However, that marking has always been within a circle and included the name of the pottery. Also, this is not a

Danish pottery

form typical of their wares, which nearly always have a matte glaze. Your piece may well be hand-made by a more modern studio potter who isn't well known. The style and glaze remind me of pieces from the 1950s and 1960s. Anyone else have any clues?

Reader Update

"Regarding your May 2000 issue and the query on page16 regarding the "bottle-form" pottery vase, I may have an answer for you! If the mark, which you describe as conjoined "AA," looks like the one I've shown, it is the work of Bode Willumsen, a Danish potter who worked from the mid-1920s to at least the late 1940s as a studio potter and from 1925 to 1930 and later at Royal Copenhagen. The glaze, as best I can tell from the black-and-white picture, further suggests his work. I hope this is helpful."

Dr. S.O., Shaker Heights, OH

German heirloom

Q. Enclosed are photos of a cup and saucer brought to Texas in the 1840s by one of my great-great-great-grandmother when she emigrated from Germany. It has been passed from mother to daughter ever since, and probably before also. Could you please advise as to origin and also valuation? I think the scene is poetic!

P.V.M., St. Augustine, FL

A. You have nice family heirloom. The scrolled "F" mark on your saucer indicates that this was a product of the Ducal Brunswick Porcelain Manufactory and Furstenberg Porcelain Factory of Fustenberg, Germany. Several variations of this letter have been used over the years but your set could date from the 1840s era. It has a nice hand-painted scene with German inscription. The painting is well done but not quite the finest of the fine German landscapes on porcelain. Still, I think if the set has no chips, cracks or serious wear, it might be valued in the $100-$200 range. Of course, as a family heirloom, it's priceless.

Bisque figures

Pottery stein

Q. When I receive my copy of the *Collector Magazine* I always read your column first and enjoy it very much. The enclosed picture is of a pair of figures that have been in our family for a long time. I hope you can tell me about them and give me an idea of their value. They have oval bases that are 5" across and 13" tall. There are no marks on them.

The stein is 12" tall, ivory in color with dark green at the top. The "picture" is in relief showing two men, a woman and two children at a table, also a dog and jug below. The proud hunter has brought in a deer. The words are printed on the side: "Ein Leiter Sinn der lueste Gewim. Der erste Rehbock." "Germany" is written on the bottom. What is the value?

L.R., Fredericksburg, VA

A. Your pair of Parian bisque figurines probably dates from the 1855-75 era when such wares were especially popular. Such pieces were widely produced in Germany and England, so without any marking it's difficult to say where yours originated. They probably represent "Rebecca at the Well" and "Ruth, the Gleaner" popular Biblical themes. If perfect I think the pair might be valued in the $150-300 range.

Your pottery stein probably dates from the first quarter of the 20th century. This style is not as popular as the first Mettlach pottery steins and ones like yours were much less expensive originally. Today, because of its size, it might be valued in the $75-$150 range, if perfect.

Pottery Queen creamer

Q. Enclosed is a photo of a creamer I have. It has a stamped mark on the bottom, "Queen Pottery," in a circle. Any information and value on this piece would be appreciated.

V.S., Westfield, IN

A. According to Lois Lehner's *Lehner's Encyclopedia of U.S. Mark on Pottery, Porcelain & Clay*, the mark "Queen Pottery" was actually used by a pottery outlet called "Pottery Queen" in Zanesville, Ohio. Mark Heatwole owned the firm and they set up a pottery decorating department in the mid-1960s; the firm was sold in 1973, so your piece would date from that period. They bought pottery blanks from various firms but developed some interesting glazes, such as on your piece. Since this firm is not well known and pieces are fairly modern, I think the collector value would be modest, perhaps in the $20-$40 range.

Hand-painted tea set

Q. Enclosed are pictures of a tea set I acquired at a flea market. The set consists of one 2-3 cup teapot, a regular size creamer and sugar, cup and saucer, and tray, the tray is a little heavier porcelain than the rest of the group. It appears to be an Oriental motif, completely hand-painted and in near mint condition with slight wear to the gold trim. The marks on the bottom were impressed (not colored) so I was unable to photograph them, but have enclosed drawings. The teapot, creamer and sugar have similar marks but not exactly the same. The tray and cup and saucer have no marks. Could you give me any idea of age and value? I read your column first when I get my *Collector Magazine* and love it!

S.H., Aloha, OR

A. Your pretty little breakfast tea set appears to be hand-painted in an Oriental-inspired design of the type popular in the 1880-1900 era. I have been unable to track down the impressed "L&C" mark, but such impressed markings are usually from German firms and there were many operating at that time. It might possibly be French, but their marks on china were generally printed rather than incised. Your set appears to be in overall excellent condition. As a decorative set, I would value it in the $150-$250 range.

Q. Enclosed are pictures of an Oriental vase that was left to me by my mother. It is in perfect condition. I have looked in several books to try and identify it and could not find anything similar. The height of the vase is 13 ¾", base is 4 ¾" across center. It has a crackle glaze and an Oriental inscription on the bottom. I enjoy your column very much and look forward to getting some information on its age and value.

A. Your large crackle glazed vase was produced in China, probably around the turn of the 20th century. A great deal of colorful porcelain was exported to the West at that time, including crackle glazed wares. Your piece features colorful scenes of warriors but the painting is not of the finest quality so it was probably a more

Chinese vase

commercial piece rather than fine art. Such pieces are collectible today and appeal to those who enjoy Oriental motifs in decoration. Because of its size and apparent fine condition, I would say it might be valued in the $200-$400 range in the right market.

Q. I am hoping you can help me determine what this is, how old and its value. It was in my grandmother's home for many years. I am told by a friend that it is a jardiniere, but that is all I know. It is about 14" by 7 ½" high, bottom base is 7" long. The front is rose, seafoam green and metallic gold around the flowers. The back is solid rose color. It has an embossed design. On the bottom is embossed "808," and either "XI" or LX" is written on the bottom. Your column helps so many and we love it.

Earthenware planter

R.F., Baldwin, NY

A. You have an earthenware jardinière (planter) that would date from the late 19th or early 20th century. The colorful glazes would probably place it in the category of "majolica," which is very collectible today. Although not directly marked, I think this piece was likely produced in Germany. If there are no chips or cracks, which are common on such utilitarian pieces, I think it might be valued in the $250-$450 range.

Satsuma vase

Ironstone mug

Q. I have enclosed pictures of two items that I have wondered about since purchasing them in the UK several years ago. We believe we've verified the mug's date as ca.1820, according to the Mason mark on the bottom. However, we have no idea of its value, if our "dating" is correct. It's in very good condition, no chip's, etc. It is 4" tall, 4 ¾" across the top, 5 ½" across the bottom; the handle looks like luster and ends in a snake (?) head where it attaches to the mug. The vase has defied our attempts to identify it. We bought it because it's so pretty and because the workmanship looks so good. We turned it into a lamp without affecting the vase in any way and it is always admired by others. We find no marks on it to identify a source. We're guessing it is Japanese because of the cherry blossoms and butterflies and from the shape and color. It is

17" tall and the base is 6 ½" in diameter. As you can see from the close-up pictures the tree limbs and blossoms are very well done. The vase has one chip on the base (see picture). I will greatly appreciate your comments as to the origin of the vase and the potential value of both.

Mrs. J.W., Hilton Head Island, SC

A. Your ironstone mug is a nice example from the Mason's factory, however, according to Geoffrey Godden's mark book, this version of the mark with crown would date it around 1845. The Oriental Imari-style colorful decoration was long popular with English collectors and used a great deal on Mason wares. Without any serious chips, cracks or staining, I would say it might be valued in the $150-$250 range.

The tall vase appears to be a very nice example of highly decorated Japanese Satsuma pottery. The close-up of the bottom rim shows the fine crackle glaze typical of Satsuma wares. It does have a chip on the foot but a professional restoration could help recover more of the value. I would say it might date from the late 19th or early 20th century. Because it is large and finely decorated I think, even with the slight damage, it might be valued in the $250-$600 range.

Q. Thank you for a wonderful column. My wife and I have learned much from it, and we have grown to love antiques. It is our hope that you can tell us something about this footed bowl. It was my wife's mother's. It has a peony design in pink with the rim being somewhat iridescent. It has two handles and is in excellent condition. Can you tell us who made it, when and what is its value?

E.F., Baldwin, NY

Unmarked bowl

A. Your footed bowl appears to be porcelain with a lightly iridized blue rim and hand-painted pink roses. The overall design would date it in the 1920-30 era but without any marking on the base it is difficult to determine exactly where it was made since factories in Japan, Germany and Czechoslovakia were turning out similar wares during that time. As a pretty unmarked bowl, I think it might be valued in the $45-$65 range.

Q. I have enclosed two pictures. #1: Large vase, marked (as close as I can decipher it), "H&C Seth, Bavaria, Hieyrield, KS Roue." This as near as I can make out. It is 11" tall, 8 ½" across, with handpainted cherry blossoms. #2: Large vase, Imperial Nippon, handpainted, 12" tall, 6 ½" across, cherry blossoms, gold on the handles, gold dots ½" below the top, design is raised.

F.T., Alexandria, LA   *Bavarian vase*

A. You have two nice pieces. Your large bulbous porcelain vase was produced by the German firm of Hertel, Jacob & Co. of Rehau, Bavaria, and they used the mark you drew between 1892 and 1969. If the mark does not include "West Germany," I would say the vase was produced before World War II. It has a pretty Oriental-style decoration and is a nice large size. A possible value range: $75-$150.

Your other vase is a pretty example of Nippon porcelain from Japan, probably made just before World War I. It has a nice floral decoration and gold trim and is a nice size. If perfect, a value in the $125-$225 range might be about right. * See Ceramics Tip #6.

Nippon vase

Weller jar

Roseville ewer

Q. I really enjoy your magazine. I find it very helpful with what few antiques I have. I do have two items that I would like you to tell me about. The Roseville ewer is marked "Roseville USA 13-6." The colors are still very vivid. It was given to me by my sister, who had a lot of antiques. She also gave me this Weller jar or vase with a lid. I haven't been able to find it in the Weller books. It is marked "Weller" and it also has a black "C" on the bottom of the vase. I would really appreciate anything you can tell me about these two items and also what their value would be.

H.H., Los Banos, CA

A. You have two pieces of collectible 20th century American pottery. Your Roseville ewer is in the Magnolia pattern introduced in 1943. The blue background is probably a more sought-after color than the green or tan ground used. If perfect, it might be valued in the $150-$200 range. The covered jar is in Weller's Cornish pattern, introduced in 1933. It is a simple and quite elegant design but not one of the most sought-after of the Weller designs. The jar is an unusual form, however, and if perfect, I'd say it might be valued in the $100-$200 range.

Special-order plates

Q. I have a set of four of these plates. They are creamy white with tan and brown trim on the edges. They have a crown in the center with initial below, which appears to be "JBET?" They measure 9" with a 1" edge before it dips down about ¾". On the outer edge on the backside are what I think are called spur marks, three on each; no other marks on the back or front.

M.J., New Berlin, WI

A. Your dinner plates appear to be fine quality porcelain and were probably special-order pieces that may have been hand-decorated. That might explain why there is no maker's mark on the back. It would be quite difficult to determine their exact age or origin since factories in England, France and Germany were all doing comparable work in the 19th century. As a guess, I think they might date from the 1850-1880 era. Since their decoration is fairly restrained, each might be valued in the $40-$80 range.

Q. You write the most "real" answers to our questions. Thank you. My problem is this tile I have. It's 5 ¼" by 7 ¼" (the tile, not the frame). It is very well painted, dated 1950, signed "Gay Bellile" or is that a place? To get these details with only one color paint, I feel it's a nice piece of work. I do a little china painting myself so know it's painted, not just a transfer. I cannot get to the back of the tile without pulling it off the original mat and then there are old papers on the back of the frame. My question: Is it by someone well known and what's it worth?

L.W., Parowan, UT

Hand-painted tile

A. Your tile does have lovely hand-painting and it is signed and dated. I haven't been able to track down an artist by that name and without knowing where the tile was produced it's hard to know if it was decorated at the factory or by a talented free-lance artist. The name sounds French and the scene has a French feel about it. Perhaps a reader will have some additional insights. As a lovely decorator piece, I think it could be valued in the $150-$300 range at least.

Q. I enjoy your column so much! I am a novice at antiquing, but love every minute of it! The vase is 19" high. I
believe it to be hand-painted with what I think is moriage
with tiny little beading on it. The handles appear applied and
there is no mark on it. I recently bought it
at auction for $15.

The ginger jar is 10" high, no mark,
given to me 30 years ago by an elderly
friend who said it was "old." Alas, the lid
was broken. Any information and worth on
these items is greatly appreciated.

C.G., Live Oak, FL

Chinese ginger jar   *Satsuma vase*

A. Your tall vase appears to be a boldly
decorated example of Japanese Sat-
suma pottery, typical of the type exported to the West in the first quarter of the
20th century. The earlier, more traditionally designed pieces of Satsuma tend to
attract the most serious collectors, but your large piece might be valued in the
$75-$175 range if perfect.

Your porcelain ginger jar appears to be a typical example of Chinese blue
and white porcelain produced in the late 19th and early 20th century. Probably
similar examples are still being made today. Without the cover the value is greatly reduced. As a decorative accent piece, I think a value in the $50-$100 range
might be about right.

⚬⟳⟲⚬

Q. This bowl has been in my husband's family for generations. Enclosed is a picture of the front and bottom. As you can see, the gold paint is rubbing off in spots,
but it is still beautiful. The bottom reads as follows: "Limoges WG & Co. France." Could you please tell me the
price/value or history? Really enjoy your magazine.

P.E., Ephrata, WA

Jardiniere

A. Your pretty porcelain piece is a form usually referred
to as a planter or "jardinière," to use the French
term. The mark on the bottom indicates that the undecorated blank was made
by the William Guerin firm of Limoges, France. It was then hand-painted by an
amateur china painter in this country. Sometimes such painters signed their
works but you don't indicate any name on the piece. Unfortunately, the heavy
wear on the gold would reduce the collector appeal today. You didn't give a size,
but guessing it is around 6-8" high, I think it might be valued in the $30-$60
range.

⚬⟳⟲⚬

Porceleain bust

Q. I received the bust of a woman in the enclosed photo approximately 30 years ago from my grandmother. She gave us this as an engagement gift. I know she had it in her possession for many years before she gave it to us. The markings on the bottom did not show in the photo, but they include: "ESG" over a "B" with "19" over "536" to the right and "Stellnacher" over "Berlitz" to the left. We appreciate any information you can provide us, as well as the approximate value of this piece.

C.O., Duluth, GA

A. Your lovely porcelain bust of a turn-of-the-20th-century beauty appears to have the impressed name of the Stellmacher firm of Teplitz, Austria. This company is noted for the lovely detailed figures it produced around 1900 and their pieces in top condition are much in demand today. The painted trim on your young lady appears to be a bit worn but if there are no chips or cracks in her elaborate costume, her value should still be good. You didn't note the size, but assuming she stands somewhere in the 15-30" range, I think she could be valued in the $800-$1,600 range.

Camel teapot

Q. I would appreciate your comments on my camel teapot I purchased in 1935 at an old crossroads antique shop in a town in New Jersey for a dime. It is perfect, no chips, with a replaced handle. It was my first antique purchase. Camel teapot: 9" from top of nose to tail, 13 ¾" diameter at top of basket, marked "Made in Japan." I am a lifelong collector of old glass, Depression glass, old sugar bowls, Stangl cake plates, pottery of the 1940s, jewelry of the 1950s, '60s, '70s, small bisque items, etc. It makes life interesting.

C.H., Farmingdale, NY

A. The camel teapot is charming and from the marking would date from between the wars. Figural teapots are collectible today and even with the replaced woven handle it should have good market appeal. I'd say in the right market it might sell in the $75-$125 range.

Q. In a recent issue of the magazine, the Price Guide contained Rose Medallion. I am enclosing pictures of two Rose Medallion casserole dishes that belonged to my great-grandmother. These dishes are approximately 10" by 8 ½" and 2" or 3" deep.

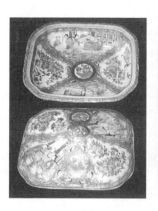

A. The Rose Medallion (or Rose Mandarin, with figures) serving dishes appear to be typical of shapes used

Rose Medallion casserole dish

through the 19th and into the early 20th century. Depending on condition and amount of wear, such pieces can sell in the $500-$1,000 range.

Q. I am a new subscriber. *Collector Magazine* is great! I hope you can give me some information on the enclosed photos. 1. Girl in pool: Figure is 4" high and pool is 6 ½" by 8". Porcelain is marked "Bing and Grondahl-Danmarq-1532 F." It has a high glaze and is in mint condition. 2. Pitcher: 6 ½" high and 7" bottom diameter, hand-painted and marked

Pottery Guild pitcher

Bing & Grondahl dish

Porcelain box

"Pottery Guild of America" (in script), mint condition. 3. Candy dish (?) with lid: 7 ½" high. Lid top is four formed roses and leaves. It is marked on the bottom "Maruhom Ware-K" in circle, "Hand ptd.-Japan." It has an ivory background and the design is in black and gold. It has a three-footed base. It has many cracks and one small chip. Mother received it as a gift in 1933. I have never seen Maruhomware listed in any of the books. Any help you can offer will be greatly appreciated.

H.S. Margate, FL

A. Your pretty Bing & Grondahl porcelain figural dish looks to me like it is a design likely introduced during the 1920s or 1930s since it has an Art Deco feel. A new book, *"Bing & Grondahl Figurines"* by Carbline and Nick Pope (Schiffer, Ltd. 2002), shows this piece as Model 1532 titled "Meditation." They don't indicate when it was made but it is relatively scarce and valued in the $100-$200 range.

The Pottery Guild marking was used by the Cronin China Co. of Minerva, OH, in business from 1935 to 1956. They made good quality earthenware products. Your pitcher has a Modernist design, which might place its production anytime from the late 1940s into the early 1950s. It is appealing but there isn't a strong market for this firm's wares as yet. As a decorative piece in fine condition, I'd say it might be valued in the $30-$60 range.

Your Japanese porcelain box is based on ornate European Rococo porcelain designs. Many firms produced good quality porcelain wares in Japan between the wars and the trade names like "Maruhom Ware" don't have much significance today. Since it is serious damaged its value would just be sentimental.

Q. I have enclosed three photos of "keepsake" items my husband's 98-year-old aunt sent. The first is a photo of a cherub figure sitting on a rose-covered toothpick holder or napkin ring? I don't know and hope you would know. There is an imprint on the bottom pressed in the porcelain, perhaps an M or W. I could not get an impression.

Victorian-style cherub figurine

Porcelain pitcher

Divided relish dish

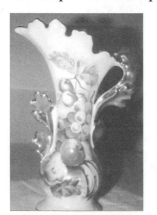

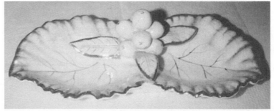

The second photo is of a pitcher brightly painted with gold on the handle and lining the lip of the pitcher. The remains of the sticker have "Cagco Ceramic Japan." There is a "V" stamped on the bottom as well.

The third photo is probably a relish dish. There is nothing on the bottom but it has remnants of a sticker. It is about 10" long and 5" wide. My husband's aunt received these items as gifts in the 1920s and 1930s. They were probably purchased in the Texas- Louisiana area. I would appreciate knowing the age and approximate value if this is possible.

C.F., Gahanna, OH

A. I'm not sure that your holder with the cherub had a specific use. It is a Victorian-style novelty piece but the mark indicates it was made in the 1920s or 1930s. In perfect condition, it might be valued in the $25-$45 range.

The decorated pitcher or ewer with the fruit is also Japanese porcelain in the Victorian style and again, new in the 1920s or 1930s. Since it over 10" high and appears to be in perfect condition, it might have a value in the $40-$60 range.

The divided relish dish with the figural fruit was also new when received in the 1930s. It may be porcelain or perhaps good quality earthenware. Some American potteries of that era were making decorative pieces of this type but without the sticker it is hard to attribute. If perfect, it too might be valued in the $40-$60 range.

Q. I hope you can help me with the pottery company that would have made this jardinière and pedestal. I've looked at all the pottery books available in my area and can't find anything close. It is 12" across the top, 10 ½" high, top portion, 20 ½" high, lower portion, 10" across the base. The number on the bottom of the jardinière is 1160. There are small hairline cracks but it's hard to see them. You seem to have contacts that maybe could help me out if you don't know.

D.W., Tobaccoville, NC

A. You have a handsome classical style jardinière and pedestal. This type of quality earthenware planter was made by numerous American potteries around the turn of the 20th century. Most were not marked well and attributing them to specific makers can be difficult. Your set is quite elegant with the dark streaky green glaze. I haven't been able to identify the maker, but if it only has the non-visible cracks, I think the value would still be good, perhaps in the $350-$700 range.

Jardinière

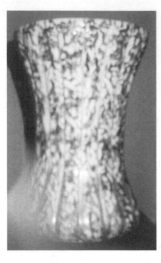

Umbrella stand

Q. This spongeware umbrella stand has a hole in the bottom with a cork in it so it can be drained out. It has been in the family for a long time. I can't find any books that list umbrella stands as to age and value.

T.M., Brook Park, OH

A. The umbrella stand looks like a great piece with the tall ribbed, flared sides and base. This type of pottery was widely produced in the early 20th century. You don't give a size but a good large spongeware piece, if in top clean and undamaged condition, could easily sell in the $600-$1,200 range.

Q. Enclosed is a picture of a plate my husband and I purchased. The plate is white trimmed in gold; around the top is a verse from Milton's "Paradise Lost": "Oh earth how like to heaven, if not prepared, more justly," The bottom of the plate is signed "© Appi00" or it could be "Appiouv," it's hard to make out. The back of the plate has gold lettering: "P.B.R. 1897." Any information will be greatly appreciated. Enjoy your magazine!

J.G., Wellford, SC

Late 19th century plate

A. Your porcelain plate appears to date from the late 19th century and was most likely made at a German factory where the gold trim was added to the border. However, I think the central theme was probably hand-painted by an amateur china painter in this country and the initials and date on the back added by this artist. The scene of the fallen angel Lucifer and the quote from Milton make for a unique scene. The figural rendition of Lucifer is adequate but not exceptional as far as painting goes. It is also not a theme that would be in great demand among collectors. Depending on the size of the piece (10"-12"), I think it might be valued in the $50-$100 range.

Q. This shell-shaped bowl was given to my mother by an old friend. It is 10" wide and has pictures of roses and 17th or 18th century figures on it. The back is marked with the crossed swords of Meissen. I would like to know

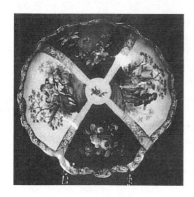

Meissen bowl

how old it is and its approximate value. I really enjoy your column and learn something new from it every month. Keep up the great work.

M.P., Pickens, SC

A. You do appear to have a nice piece of original Meissen porcelain. The difficulty is that they used the blue crossed swords from the early 18th century right through to today and pieces not made for export from the late 19th century on had that mark. An original Meissen bowl with this ornate design and dating from the late 18th century would be very rare. I suspect, without any information on the provenance, that this is more likely a copy by Meissen made in the late 19th or early 20th century. If perfect, it could still have a very good value, perhaps $800-$1,600 or maybe more in the right market.

Q. Thank you for your very wonderful articles in *Collector Magazine*. It is the very first article I read when I receive my new issue. I am enclosing pictures of a "Gypsy Head" about 12" by 7 ½" and made of some kind of plaster of Paris (?) material. I also have a photo of the backside, which is hollow with holes drilled at the top for a wire hanger. The material is very thick and the head is very heavy. It hung in my grandfather's sitting room and as a child in 1930s it was very scary for me to look at. The eyes seem to really look at you! There are no markings and so I would appreciate any information you can give me. I'm sure my grandparents had it in the early 1900s as my mother, born in 1904, remembers it also as a child. Also, is there any value, as none of my children really want it unless it is valuable.

B.M., Middlebury, IN

Wall bust

A. Your molded plaster-of-Paris wall bust is typical of such artworks widely produced in the first decades of the 20th century. Large busts and full-figure pieces were also produced and often painted in realistic colors as this piece is. Because of the fragile nature of the plaster-of-Paris, many have been chipped, cracked or had the paint badly worn. The most popular designs collected today are busts or figures of Art Nouveau maidens, Native Americans or African-Americans. Your gypsy would have a little less general market appeal but in the right market might be valued in the $75-$200 range, if perfect.

Grape with Rickrack pitcher

Plate dating before World War I

Rochester Company teapot

Teapot of Japanese origin

Q. This crockery pitcher belonged to my husband's grandmother, who was born in Norway and came here as a child. She was married in 1887. This could date from that time. The only mark on the bottom is the faint impression of a five-pointed star. It is in perfect condition. Would appreciate information about maker and value.

The plate belonged to my husband's grandmother. The center is ceramic or porcelain, the rim is German silver, I think; it is too shiny to be pewter, but it may be. It also dates from the late 1800s. The center is 7 ½" in diameter, the overall diameter is 10 ¼". I have tried to illustrate the markings on the back. It shows a bird-type figure with "B-M-F" across the bottom, followed by "N" within two dots and under that, the word "Germany." Under the country are the numbers "1345, 5 G20" (indented) and "2" (stamped).

This teapot was given to me by my mother. I'm sure it has been in the family for well over 80 years. It is 5 ½" high and 5 ½" wide. It has a metal lid, which has a dull finish but the rim is shiny. The body seems to be porcelain, hand-painted, with no cracks or chips, hinge on lid needs repair. The diamond shape on bottom has "Ohio" inside it and very faint printing that says "8 Rochester," faded and hard to read. Imprinted on the lid by the hinge is "Royal Rochester" with T-48 below. A small hole in the lid knob is for a tea ball to move through, I presume.

The teapot with braided handle is also a family piece. I have a photo of my great grandmother's parlor showing this on a tea table, which I also have. Overall height is 6 ½" and same across. The only marking on the bottom is what looks like the artist's mark, "E111" The date on the photo is 1909. I surely do enjoy the information you contribute to Collector Magazine.

Mrs. M.L., Meckling, SD

A. Your first pitcher is blue and white stoneware in a pattern called Grape with Rickrack. It would date from the early 20th century and the pitcher came in several sizes with the smaller sizes actually selling for a bit more than the largest size. Price ranges from larger to smaller are about $225-$350, if perfect.

The plate with the chrome or silver plate mount may date just before World War I and as marked, was made in Germany. It is quite large and decorative with the ceramic insert and I think might be valued in the $50-$100 range.

The teapot could date from around the turn of the century. The Rochester company made chromed metal mounts as well as appliances. For a teapot collector, I'd say the value might be in the $40-$80 range.

The final little china teapot appears to probably be of Japanese origin and could date from the early 20th century. If it was marked "Nippon," the value would be even higher but I'd say, if perfect, it might sell in the $45-$75 range.

Q. I have this Santa that seems to be made of plaster and measures 14" by 9" or 10" with no markings. It has been in the family over 50 years. Thank you for any help you may be able to give.

B.O., Fairfield, CN

A. Your charming Santa head would have great appeal among Christmas collectors and probably dates from the 1930s or 1940s. He looks to be in fine condition and might be valued in the $75-150 range.

Santa

Pitcher and bowl with Art Nouveau look

Q. Enclosed are pictures of my pitcher and bowl with the details on the back of each picture. This pitcher and bowl were bought by my aunt from a woman who was 96 years old in the early 1980s. She was told it was nearly 100 years old at that time. I would like to know how much it is worth. On bottom of the pitcher there is a marking of the letter "C" and #5836 or 5876. It is hard to tell the third number. On bottom of bowl it says, "31" and the letter "C"

M.R., Paducah, KY

A. You have a lovely pitcher and bowl was set probably dating from the 1890 to 1910 period. It is in rich flow blue and would be in great demand among those collectors. The poppy design gives it a rather Art Nouveau look which was very popular during those years. It is unusual that it doesn't have a clear manufacturer's mark and my guess is that it is a fine grade of earthenware pottery and my have been produced in Germany. English and American potters were pretty good about marking such items. If it has no chips, cracks or other damage I wouldn't be surprised if it could be valued in the $600-1,000 range.

Roseville pottery basket

Q. What can you tell me about this vase? The following information found on backs of pictures: Deep rose (all one color) "Roseville USA #710-10."

R.L., Racine, WI

A. Your Roseville pottery basket is in the Silhouette pattern that was introduced in 1952. This is in their overall deep rose glaze. This pattern featured a panel on each piece, which either featured a stylized plant design, such as this, or a profile of a nude female. The pieces with the nudes are much scarcer and more valuable than these floral examples. Since your piece is a nice size and appears to be in perfect condition, it should still be valued in the $150-200 range.

Q. Enclosed is a photograph of a plate I bought at an antique store. It is 6 ½" wide. It shows the coronation of Queen Elizabeth, June 2, 1953, and is signed on the back by Clarice Cliff. It's in perfect shape. Can you tell me its value?

K.B., Charlotte, MI

Commemorative plate

A. You have a nice royalty commemorative from the 1953 coronation of Queen Elizabeth. Such pieces are certainly going up in value these days. It is interesting that your piece has the Clarice Cliff name on the back and it's possible that the shape of this plate could have been designed by her. She did do some more "traditional" china designs which don't have anywhere near the value of the Bizarre Ware line and related wares. The portrait design of the queen is a nice quality transfer print. Your plate is good quality earthenware and not porcelain. Such a plate in perfect condition might be valued in the $50-75 range, but I don't know if the Clarice Cliff marking would add a premium to that or not.

Q. I really enjoy your column and I hope you can help me. My mother purchased this bust about 30 years ago for a quarter at a garage sale. The woman that was selling it was quite elderly and she said she had it for at least 60-70 years. It's not porcelain but seems like some kind of bisque. It's in perfect shape, which is surprising since the woman kept her pens and pencils in it. The signature (in script) on the lower right hand side is "H. Jacobs." On the bottom of the piece there is (or seems to be) an upside down seven. Right below that is a capital "C." Beside that is a circular stamp but is too small to read. It is 10" tall and 10" at the base. The color goes from purple to gray, to mauve and starts back to purple. All the gilt is there and perfect. I would like to know about it and the price for insurance reasons.

S.C., Richland Center, WI

Figural bisque dish

A. Thank you for your letter and the photos of your figural dish. This is a nice example of the Art Nouveau style so popular in the 1890-1910 period. It does appear to be bisque with nicely shaded coloring. Decorative pieces with busts of Art Nouveau maidens were widely made and many examples came from Germany and Austria. I couldn't determine from your description what the marking is but several factories did similar work back then. I don't see any chips, cracks or wear on this piece and in the right market today I think it might be valued in the $250-500 range.

Plaque

Q. This framed plaque is signed "Melizig." A hand-written note on the back of the plaque describes it as a Wedgwood plaque – England – about 1785. It is in an antique gold frame – an early Grecian figurine with cupid and darts – signed Melizig. The writing on the note looks like script from the 1800s. I hope with this information you will be able to authenticate this plaque for me.

I.M.H., Lancaster CA

A. First, I don't believe your back plaque is by Wedgwood and probably not 18th century. It looks much more like a special ceramic ware popular in the late 19th century called "pate-sur-pate" (paste on paste), which also features white classical figures on a colored ground. This technique was developed in France in the mid-19th century then brought to England and used by several English factories in the last quarter of the 19th century. The Minton factory is the one best known but any quality piece of pate-sur-pate is very desirable. I'm not familiar with the artist named on this piece, but it does appear to be in the original frame. You don't give a size for the piece but a plaque in the 8 by 10" size could sell in the low thousands if perfect.

White ironstone pitcher and bowl set

Charles and Meakin marking

Q. As a new reader of your *Antique Trader's Collector Magazine and Price Guide*, I thoroughly enjoy your "Kyle on Antiques" section. I have pieces that belonged to my mother. I kept them after her death 27 years ago, but have never had them appraised. I would appreciate your opinion. Thank you! White stoneware pitcher and bowl set and the bowl diameter is 14 ½", bowl height is 4 ¾", pitcher diameter is 8 ½", pitcher height is 11 ¼" and stamped on bottom of each is "Charles Meakin – Hanley, England." The pitcher has a small chip on top.

S.W., Providence, KY

A. Your white ironstone pitcher and bowl set was produced by the firm of Charles Meakin, which used this mark between about 1883 and 1889. He was one of a large number of Meakins making ironstone wares in England then. This pair is very simple in form and decoration and might be valued in the $150-$200 range if perfect.

Q. I greatly enjoy your column every month! I have what will probably be a very easy question for you. I collect cat statues, salt and peppers, etc. and I recently acquired this piece from my grandfather, who passed away a short time ago. He wanted me to have it because of the cats on the front. I have enclosed a sketch of the markings on the bottom. By a little research, I know it was made by George Jones & Sons, but I need your help with what you would call it – a vase? When does it date from and what is its value? Your help would be greatly appreciated!

T.M., Nebanow, OH

George Jones vase and marking

A. Your decorative vase was produced by the George Jones factory in England and the marking you sketched would date the piece to the first quarter of the 20th century. It has sort of an Oriental design with Victorian touches. The kittens are an appealing topic; however, I'm not sure how collectible the dark burnt orange glaze would be today. George Jones pieces that are in most demand today are his fine Victorian majolica wares which can bring very high prices. I think this decorative later earthenware piece would be a bit less collectible. If perfect, it might sell to the right collector in the $75-150 range or perhaps a bit more because of the design.

Q. I've enclosed a photo of a black bowl marked "Japan." It has a floral decoration that feels raised above the surface of the bowl. I'm interested to know what kind of value it might have.

V.S., Westfield, IN

A. Your ceramic serving dish in black with the pastel floral transfers looks to me like a shape popular about the 1930s. Black-glazed

Serving dish popular in the 1930s

pottery and black glass were very popular during that period. If it doesn't have any wear or damages, it might be valued in the $35-55 range depending on the size.

Pitcher and bowl set with soap dish

Q. The December 2000 *Collector Magazine & Price Guide*, page 66, outlines the Mettlach ceramics. The enclosed picture shows a bowl (15 ½" diameter by 4 ¾" deep); pitcher (11 ½" tall by 7" diameter at bottom) and a soap dish (6"oval by 4" wide) with ribbed bottom (inside). Each piece has a gold checkerboard rim around the top. The mark on each is a Mercury figure, i.e. face with winged head, "Villeroy & Boch, Mettlach, Made in Saar Basin" and the name "Bosna" at the bottom. Each piece has #9046 in black; the writing appears to be in green. Another mark (stamped on the bottom) is #33 with the letter A above. The pitcher has small air hole inside on the upper part of the handle. Since the Mettlach name and stamp are different than in the article, could this set be of earlier origin? I have no idea of date of manufacturer or value and thought perhaps you could advise. We enjoy your articles and comments on antiques; please keep up the good work.

G.C., Coffeyville, KS

A. Your pitcher and bowl set with a soap dish was part of a pottery chamber set produced by the firm of Villeroy and Boch. They also produced the "Mettlach" stoneware steins and related decorative wares, but they fall under a different area of collecting. Your set was more of a general commercial line of utilitarian wares that Villeroy and Boch also produced. From the marking and design of this set I would guess it was made in the 1920s or early 1930s. It is still collectible, but not valued in the same range as the earlier Mettlach stoneware pieces. If in perfect condition with no wear or damage, I'd guess your three-piece set might be valued in the $150-$250 range.

Victorian Moss Rose ironstone china set

Q. I am enclosing a couple of photos of some Moss Rose Ironstone China that was my Grandma's. She died in 1911, but the family owned it before that. There are about 90 pieces of it. They will set the table for 12 place settings. They were made by Alfred Meakin and Fenton Bros. England. Most are in very good condition. There are: 12 plates (10"), 12 plates (8"), 12 square sauce dishes, 12 small salts or butter plates, 12 cups and 12 saucers, one large platter (14"), one square bread or cake plate, one sauce boat, one covered butter dish, one covered vegetable dish, two lids, one sugar bowl, one cream pitcher, one footed fruit compote, one soup bowl in fair condition, two other not so good. I would appreciate having some idea of their value. Thank you for an opinion.

R.C.G., Aledo, IL

A. You appear to have a very nice, very complete set of Victorian Moss Rose pattern ironstone china likely produced in the 1880s or early 1890s. Today Moss Ross is quite collectible, and it is unusual to find large sets in top condition. Any hairlines or staining reduces the value of pieces, but as a general range I'd think your set might sell in the $1,200-$1,600 range if you found the right collector. Of course, it would also be nice if you kept it together in the family.

French porcelain wall hanging

Q. This plate has holes to hang it and below the left bottom leaf it says "Luck." On the back there is a crown, on top of that is the word "Limoges" and on the bottom of the crown is "Coronet France." It's in perfect condition. What would its value be? I thank you for your great column.

M.G., Grand Marsh, WI

A. This porcelain wall-hanging piece is French porcelain from the late 19th or early 20th century. "Coronet" was the trade name and Limoges the city where it was made. It appears to be hand-painted, with large roses and green leaves and has nice gold trim. Such plates are usually about 10-1/2" wide; if it is perfect, without any wear to the decoration, it might be valued in the $75-125 range.

Q. I am enclosing two pictures of items I have that I would appreciate some information on. The lamp is made of porcelain or ceramic, with the figurine sitting on a metal base. The figurine including the base is 17" high. I took it apart, but could find no markings. The peasant boy and girl are made of a material like bisque or something similar. They have fancy marking with "Depose" over the top; on the left side is the word "Wien" and on the right side is "Teplitz" with "made in Austria" on the bottom. The pair of figures is beautiful and very delicately made. Could you please give me age and value of these pieces? You have been very helpful in the past and I hope you can help me now. You are very informative and I look forward to your interesting column every month.

V.B., East Brunswick, NJ

Cordey figure on lamp

Figurines dating after 1921

A. The china half-figure of the elegant lady on your lamp base appears to be a product of the Cordey China Company, founded in Trenton, NJ in 1942. The famous ceramic artist Boleslaw Cybis founded the firm, which specialized in fine quality figures and plaques. Production ceased in the mid-1950s. Many of the Cordey pieces came with an impressed model number, and there is at least one catalog reprint that shows some of these numbered pieces. I didn't locate your lady in it, however, Cordey seems to be fairly scarce and doesn't show up in pricing guides too often. My guess is that your lovely piece, if in perfect condition, might be valued in the $150-300 range. The pair of figures are also fine ceramic and were produced by a factory in Teplitz, Austria. Similar pieces were produced in the late 19th and early 20th century. The "Made in Austria" marking would indicate these came out after 1921, when the United States Customs required the words "Made in" to be added to marks. You don't give a size, but assuming they are in the 12-18" range and in perfect condition, I'd think the pair might be valued in the $600-800 range.

German pottery steins

Q. What can you tell me about these? There are four small German steins 8" high and one large stein 20" high. Markings: "Germany 82/414" on the bottoms. These were given to my grandfather as a gift dated 1906. All figures on the steins are raised. All steins are in excellent condition, with no chipping or scratches.

J.J.H., North Riverside, IL

A. Your German pottery steins could date as early as 1906, but similar examples were made right through the 1930s and later. The most collectible German steins are the Mettlach examples; yours are of lesser quality than those and are not as much sought after. The tall tankard might be valued in the $100-150 range and the small mugs/steins, $50-75.

Milkmaid figure

"October" girl bisque figure

Q. "Kyle on Antiques" is my favorite part of the whole magazine. I'm so glad they have expanded the amount of space for our questions and your answers. You do a great job and I appreciate how you respond to your readers. Enclosed are three pictures of items my Mother would like for you to look at and give her some idea of their value. Mom thinks one is Little Bo Peep with her sheep. We have found lots of ceramics items listed for Staffordshire but not this item. Do you have any idea the age of this item? The birthday doll was given to her by a friend who has no idea of its value, if any. The other item, the statue of the man, we have no information about. As I get older I have come to appreciate antique items and have learned a lot from your articles. Keep up the good work.

J.R., Tucson, AZ

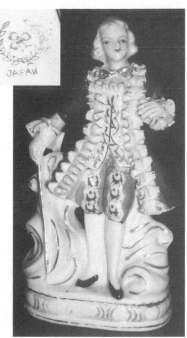

A. Thanks for your letter and pictures. The china figure group might represent Bo Peep, but I think since the animal is brown it is more likely a milkmaid and calf. The marking on the base indicates this was a "copy" of the Staffordshire china pieces popular in the 1840-80 period. The word "England" in the mark would place it in the 1900-20s time frame. This is still a charming piece and, depending on size, perhaps valued in the $40-80 range. * See Ceramics Tip #1.

The "October" girl was produced for and sold by the Lefton China Co. The bisque figure was made in Japan and sold here by Lefton. It probably dates from the late 1950s or early 1960s. Lefton has a number of figures representing the months. If perfect, this girl might be valued in the $25-30 range.

18th century gentleman figure

The 18th century gentleman marked "Japan" is porcelain and made between 1921 and World War II. Again, size is important, with smaller ones selling in the $10-20 range.

Q. I am enclosing a picture of a vase that is 31" in diameter and 24" tall. Could it be Satsuma? It originally came from an old lumberman's home in Mainstee, Michigan. It was brought back from China by his daughter. There are no markings that I can find. Any information you can give me will be greatly appreciated. Thank you very much.

Mrs. D.H., Cadillac, MI

A. Your large painted vase appears to be an early 20th century Japanese piece probably meant to imitate Satsuma pottery. From what I can see, it looks more like a porcelain piece rather than pottery, which would have a finely crackled glaze. It is an ornate form meant for export to the West. If perfect, I'd guess the value might be in the $250-450 range

Large painted vase

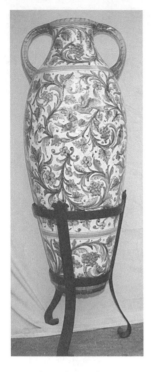

Q. Enclosed is a picture of an Italian urn. It's about 100 years old. It's very large—49" tall and 49" around the middle. It sits in a wrought iron frame. It is marked inside top of neck—"Italy."

Ref. B & C.J., Feeding Hills. MA

A. The tall earthenware Italian urn is typical of classic colorful Italian pieces. The "Italy" mark would date it from the 20th century, most likely after about 1920. It is nicely painted and an unusual decorator piece. If perfect and dating before World War II, I'd guess it might be valued in the $800-1,600 range in the right market.

Cracker jar & underplate marking

20th century Italian urn

Porcelain half-doll with whisk broom

Q. I enjoy your magazine very much and especially your column. I am hoping you can give me some information on the following two items: The first is what we called "Grandma's cracker bowl." The plate is 9 ½", the bowl is 8" and the cover of the bowl is 5 ¼". We believe she brought it with her from Norway. It is in excellent shape, with no cracks or chips. The only mark on it is on the bottom of the plate, which says "P.K. Silesia" and has sort of a bird above that.

The second is a half doll and a sort of whisk broom. The only mark on the doll is "Japan" in black letters. The overall length is about 6". I hope you can tell us something about the age of these two items and their value. Thank you very much for your help.

A.B.H., Zimmerman, MN

A. Your pretty porcelain cracker jar and underplate carry the mark of the Porcelain Factory Konigszelt in Konigszelt, Silesia. This mark was used after 1912 and until about 1928, so if you know when your grandmother immigrated, you can tell if she might have brought it with her. Much porcelain of this type was sold around the United States also, so it's more likely she acquired it here. If it is perfect with no chips, cracks or serious wear, I'd guess the set might be valued in the $100-150 range.

The porcelain half-doll with whisk broom is a sort of novelty popular in the 1920s. Some German factories made really exquisite porcelain half dolls that can sell for high prices. Your version from Japan is not as highly detailed or nicely painted. I think this piece might be valued in the $40-$60 range.

Q. I am sending you three pictures of items that I would like to know about. First, in your August 1999 magazine there were tea sets. I would like to know about my set. Can you tell me what pattern it is? How old is it? And what is it worth? The tea set service is for eight. I think that it is older than 71 years old.

Snack set popular from the 1920s to the 1950s

This plate is from a set of china I have. It is marked "Meito China Japan" in the center of a wreath. Below the wreath it says "Hand Painted."

Meito China plate

Can you tell me the pattern, how old it is, what it is worth and if this company is still in business? And do you have their address? It is trimmed in platinum. The china service is for 12 with all possible extra pieces. I want to tell you, Kyle, I can hardly wait for your column each month. You are the best that I have ever read. Thank you.

A. Your cup and plate is actually referred to as a luncheon or snack set, which were popular from the 1920s to the 1950s and made in both ceramic and glass. They often came in matching sets. Your pieces appear to be porcelain, with an Art Deco style of decoration, which would date them to the 1925-35 era. Without a mark, I can't say for certain where they were made, probably Japan. A single set like this might be valued in the $40-60 range. Meito China was one of many porcelain companies making dinnerware in Japan before and after World War II. I would guess your design might date from the 1930s. Unfortunately, there are few records on these smaller companies, and their patterns have not been cataloged. It is difficult to find matching pieces that can hold down the value to collectors, since with makers like Haviland and Noitake, there is a chance you could find missing pieces more easily. Even though it's a nice set of 12, I believe it might sell in the $500-$1,000 range.

Bisque figurines

Q. This pair of figurines shows a boy and a girl sitting on tree stumps. They are 14" high with numbers 81 and 84 on the inside. There are no other markings. They are bisque in pastel shades of blue, white and gold trim and are very delicate. An old friend of my mother's was given these as an engagement gift in the 1890s. I have had them since 1939. They are perfect. I would like a value and information about the maker. Thank you.

L.H., Hillsdale, WI

A. Your cute bisque figurines are typical of pieces made in Germany and France in the last quarter of the 19th century. Many just had imprinted numbers from the factory. Your pretty tall pair, if perfect, might be valued in the $250-300 range.

Q. I look forward to your column. I've learned a lot from it. I found this jug/pitcher on a discount shelf in an antique mall, probably because no one else could identify it. I believe it shows good style and form. Also it seems to show a good amount of age. I have checked many books, but can't find the "Rulel" mark anywhere. Perhaps you could help me with age, maker and approximate value. There are no chips or

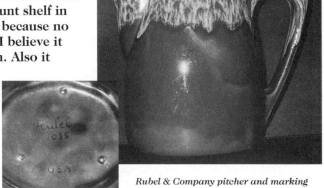

Rubel & Company pitcher and marking

cracks but some age crackle inside glaze. The dimensions are height: 7" width: 3 ½" top, 4 ¾" bottom; base length: 5 ½", 8 ½" lip to back of handle-top. Thanks for your help.

J.T.McC., Clearfield, PA

A. Your decorative brown and white pitcher appears to have been sold by the firm Rubel (not Rulel) & Company Decorative Accessories, New York, NY. According to *Lehner's Encycloepedia of U.S. Marks on Pottery, Porcelain & Clay*, this firm had pottery pieces made for it to sell and also distributed the products of various other potteries. They apparently began business in the early 1950s and operated at least into the 1980s. I don't know if they are still in operation. From the design and glaze on your piece I'd guess it was made in the period from the late 1950s through the late 1960s. Since the company is not well known, the value would be based on the individual appeal of the piece. I would guess $20-40 might be a fair range.

Q. These two wooden shoe-style planters made of ceramic or pottery (?) were found in a house my son bought in Indianapolis, Indiana. The solid blue with pink flower is marked "McCoy" on the bottom. The blue floral one is marked "hand painted Delft (Blauw)." Could you tell me anything about these—when and where they were made and value? I found listings for Delft in an antique price guide but it was white with blue flowers. As you can see, this one is light blue with dark blue design. Both these planters are in very good condition, no cracks or chips or appearance of being used. Any help would be greatly appreciated. Your articles are a welcome sight.

S.W., Howe, IN

Earthenware novelty shoe planter

A. Thank you for your two photos of the shoe planters. Each of these earthenware novelties is collectible. McCoy pottery has become increasingly popular with collectors in recent years. Your Dutch Shoe planter was first released in 1947 with a rosebud on the top of the shoe. The new type of blossom, which is on your shoe, dates it to after 1953. If perfect, the value is in the $30-35 range. Delft pottery has been collectible for a very long time, however the traditional blue and white pieces are still being widely produced in Holland. Many similar items are still being brought back by tourists, so they don't always have the name of the country of origin on them. I'm not really sure when the light blue on dark blue combination started to be used, but I would guess after World War II. This piece could be fairly new, but I'd say it might be valued in about the same range as the McCoy piece.

Czech ceramic tea set

Q. On page 70 of your October 2000 issue is a Czechoslovakian scarlet pitcher with black rim and handle with hand painted flowers on the side. We have a pitcher like it plus a creamer, sugar bowl and lid, 11 cups, 13 saucers, eight with flowers and five just scarlet with black rim, and 11 desert plates.

L.S., Hart, MI

A. You do have a great tea set in a bright Art Deco design of Czech ceramic very similar to the piece shown last October. I would call it a tea set except you don't have an actual teapot. I think the pitcher, if it has the flowers, would be valued like the piece shown before, around $125. The matching creamer and sugar set are probably in the $125-175 range, the flower-decorated cups and saucer sets about $40-60 each and the dessert plates around $25-45 each. These values would be for perfect pieces without any damage or stains so you can see as a quite complete set, it would have a good value.

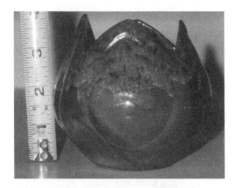

Van Briggle No. 19 Tulip vase

Pitcher dating from the 1940s to the 1950s

Q. Enclosed are three photos of things I would like to know more about. Two of these have no backstamps. The little brown one with turquoise mouth trim is marked "Anna Von Briggle; Colo. Sprgs." I've only been getting your magazine for less than a year. My husband and I really enjoy it, so we will certainly continue to subscribe. Both of us are junkers and now thinking of selling off some of it. These pieces are just a few of what we have. So if you could tell us if any of these have any value, it will be a start.

M.I., Collinwood, TN

A. Thanks for your letter and the three photos of your pottery pieces. I was able to contact Darlyn Mangus, Office Manager at the Van Briggle Pottery, and she explained to me that the "Ann Van Briggle" mark was used on a line they produced between 1956 and 1968. Your vase is the No. 19 Tulip vase, which came in several colors. I haven't found any current prices for this particular line, but since the production was limited to a specific time frame I suspect it has grown in value. I can only guess it might be valued in the $75-150 range today. The second photo of the squatty pitcher with pointed handle certainly resembles some products of the Purinton Pottery of Shippenville, PA, operating from 1941 to 1959. It's appealing and might be valued in the $30-60 range, I think. The third, taller pitcher seems to date about the same period as the Purinton piece, but I couldn't find a comparable design. It might be valued in the same range.

Pitcher resembling Purinton Pottery products

Q. I am enclosing pictures of plate that I can find nothing about after looking through all the books, and the other I am curious about. It is a lovely cream ware, pretty heavy, with leaves and quail. I did read that there was a special artist who uses these quails. The back has this mark: in a circular pattern, going from the outside to the center it says "Articles santares – Faiences part Revetements ceramiques; The Boulengea et Cle Choisy-le Roi; Terra de Fer." Marked with "A" in red. Front border outside is raised. Picture is 10 ¼" and is darker than cream.

D.B.D., Rockford, IL

A. This plate of creamy earthenware carries the mark of a French pottery

Earthenware plate with peafowl

and the words "terre de fer" literally translate to "ironstone," basically the same heavy ware produced in England and America in the 19th century. The birds, which I believe are peafowl, may have been hand-painted on the plate after it was produced but I can't tell from the photo. A hand-painted design would add much more to the value than just a transfer-printed design. If it is hand-painted and in perfect condition, I'd guess it might be valued in the $75-125 range.

Q. I bought the beer pitcher and six tankards at auction and can't find anything on them. It reads "The Leisy Brewing Co., Peoria, Ill." And on the bottom it is stamped "Haynes Balt." The butter churn is salt glazed five gallon with blue trim. There are no identifying marks. There are six blue marks on the ears and raised collar on the lid in perfect condition but I can't identify when or where.

R.W.W., Brainerd, MN

A. Thank you for your letter and photos. The beer pitcher and mugs are good quality earthenware that was produced around the turn of the 20th century by the Chesapeake Pottery operated by D. Haynes & Son Co. between 1880 and 1914. It appears to have some sort of lodge logo as well as the color desert scene. If all the pieces are perfect, with no staining, chips or cracks, the complete set might be valued in

Butter churn

Beer pitcher and mugs from Chesapeake Pottery

Butter churn

the $200-300 range or perhaps a bit more to the right collector.

When I saw the photos of your stoneware butter churn with the painted chicken, something didn't look quite right about it. Stoneware in the 19th century had the applied handles tapered down at the ends and the shape of the rim didn't look quite right. Also the bird doesn't seem in quite the right proportion for the piece. Also the "commas" on the back are not a design arrangement I've seen in old stoneware. I wanted to check my suspicions so contacted Bruce Waasdorp of Clarence, New York, a leading auctioneer and dealer in early stoneware. After seeing the pictures he agreed that his piece is a fairly modern reproduction of a 19th century churn. It could be 10 to 20 years old but basically only has value as a decorative piece.

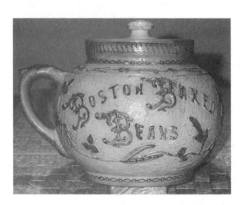 

White's Pottery bean pot front and back

Q. It is great to have an expert critique our treasures and give us an idea of their value. I have enclosed two snaps (front and back) of an old bean pot. It was given to me by a friend who recently passed away at age 92. She told me her grandmother lived with the family and always used her pot to make beans. The pot in itself is not signed and is in perfect condition, but the cover has a small chip. The blue characters and printing are of a raised design.

Mrs. A.M., Columbus, WI

A. I checked with Steve Stone, a leading authority on blue and grey pottery, to see what he knew about your bean pot. He reports that it was produced by the White's Pottery of Utica, NY, in the late 19th century. It was made in several sizes and value depends on the size as well as the condition. Any chips or cracks greatly reduce the value to collectors. The general price range he notes for this piece is $300-500.

Q. I love this magazine. I am sending a picture of our two Hull vases. We've had them for six or seven years. On one of the vases is a sticker "C & S 5.to10.00 Stores, 98c, Hull U.S.A. 108," I just would like to know the value of them. There are no cracks. They're in great shape.

Mr. & Mrs. R.S., Dayton, OH

A. Your pair of Hull Pottery vases was part of its Novelty line, produced between 1951 and 1962. The glaze on the pieces helps determine their age in that period. Your "suspended" vases, as they called the design, most likely date around 1955-60. Hull Pottery has become very popular

Hull Pottery vases

with collectors in recent years, especially its earlier pastel floral lines with a matte glaze. Your glossy glaze pieces aren't quite as sought after but if perfect I believe they might each be valued in the $50-75 range. Your original price sticker adds interest to the piece and perhaps a little collector value.

Japanese-made dinnerware

Q. Could you give me some information on the following items: Nippon-Tki Kaisha dinnerware eight place setting, with meat platter, vegetable bowl, teapot, sugar bowl, creamer? I know Nippon stands for Japan but is the rest of it the name of the area where the items were made?

A.F.S., Huron, SD

A. You are correct about the name "Nippon." It was used on Japanese-made items between 1891 and 1921. The other name may refer to a factory but doesn't greatly affect the value. From the design of your set I would say it dates to late in the Nippon era, ca. 1918-20. It probably has transfer-printed florals rather than hand painting. It is a nice set but dinner sets in Nippon are probably not as sought after as the ornate vases or other decorative pieces produced then. I think depending on the market and the condition of the pieces the set might be valued in the $500-800 range.

Spice set and marking

Q. Could you please price on this spice set I have had for 30 years? It has "Mikon Ware Made in Japan" on the bottom. I cannot find this company. I also have a cheese dish with the same markings.

A.P., Lowell, AR

A. Your spice set is probably porcelain and was produced by one of the numerous porcelain factories working in Japan between the wars. If the jars are all perfect with no chips, cracks or staining, I would guess the set might be valued in the $100-200 range. The value of the cheese dish would depend on whether it has a domed, rounded cover or is one with an angled wedge-form cover. The latter form is more desirable.

Q. I am enclosing a picture of this pitcher. I have been told that it is Sumida Gawa ware, but I can't understand why you don't have information on this in your magazine. Would you please send me some information. Where it is from? How old is it? I would like to know all about it. On the side is a marking. It is cream colored and the marking is blue. It looks like an applied piece of material. I have enjoyed your articles and have learned a lot. Thank you!

M.P., Wichita, KS

A. Your information on this tall pitcher is correct: this is a type of decorative Japanese pottery called "Sumida Gawa." It was widely produced and exported to the United States in the first decades of the 20th century and has become quite collectible. Value often depends on the types of figure applied to the surface, with more figures and more detailing raising the value. If perfect I would think your pitcher with the red background glaze might be valued in the $500-1,000 range depending on the local market.

Sumida Gawa pitcher

Q. Even though I am not a dealer and my collection is not large, I enjoy reading your column. I like using the nice and primitive antiques in decorating my home. I find the questions and answers pages interesting. I'm enclosing pictures of vases that I've had for years. Information from back of pictures: Vase 13 ½" tall. Bottom marked "17619. B.G." over "38." The rose is quite large. On bottom (in a circle): "A Little Capture – Young Bacchus." Signed in gold

Pair of vases

"TatrRa." It is 11" tall. Any history or value would be appreciated. Thanks.

D.S., Cerasco, NB

19th century European art pottery vase

A. You have some lovely pieces of ceramic art. The pair of vases has the ornate style and decoration used on French and German porcelains of the 1880 to 1900 era. It's too bad we can't read the signature but it is likely that of the decorator of the pieces. Since the titles of the scene on each is in English, that indicates they were made for export to England or the U.S. It is difficult to tell without seeing the pieces first-hand, but the lovely figural panels may be hand-painted, which would increase their value tremendously. You don't give a size, but assuming they are about 8-10" tall and hand-painted and perfect, I'd think the value for the pair might be in the $600-1,200 range. If they have transfer-printed designs the value would drop to under $500 for the pair.

The other vase with the wonderful gilt-metal mounts looks to me to be a lovely example of late 19th century European art pottery, most likely done in France. I haven't been able to track down the initials on the bottom but the French potters working in the 1870s inspired the American art pottery movement with elaborate pieces such as these. The huge flower applied on the front is fabulous and appears to be in perfect condition. I hope a reader can help us identify the exact artist since I believe this is probably a unique and wonderful piece. I can only guess, depending on size and condition, that it might be valued in the $1,000-2,000 range but further details may help establish a better guideline to value.

*"Raleigh" pattern
oval platter*

Q. This plate was purchased in the 1940s in an antique store; the platter at an antique show in the 1960s. I would appreciate knowing the origins, age and, if possible, what value they have. Information from photos: The plate is 6 ¾" in diameter. There is a standing lion in mark with "Schumann" underneath.

The platter is in perfect condition. The mark on platter says "Raleigh." The length is 19 ½" and the width 13 ¼". There is a crown with lion and "Semi. Royal – Porcelain, Co. England, Wedgwood." Other markings: "3" with "SP" in a circle and an "X" in a circle. Thank you.

N.B., Massena, NY

A. Your pretty porcelain plate with the latticework edge and the color transfer-printed scene of an 18th century couple was produced by the factory of Carl Schumann of Arzberg, Germany. This mark with the lion in the shield probably dates the piece to the 1920s or 1930s. It is a pretty piece but fairly small in size. If perfect I'd think it might be valued in the $25-45 range.

The oval platter is a piece of quality ironstone china in the "Raleigh" pattern produced by Wedgwood & Co. of England—no relationship to the famous Josiah Wedgwood firm. The gold-trimmed green pattern is typical of designs of the 1890-1920 era, however, green pieces don't tend to sell as well as blue and other colors. If perfect I'd think this piece might be valued in the $50-100 range. *See Ceramics Tip #2.

Porcelain plate from Arzberg, Germany

Q. I'm sending pictures of items I would like to know age and value. Boehm Wren 5 ½" made in England and O. F. initials; figurine – girl with mirror, 30 ½" tall to top of mirror, 22" to top of figurine head, 13 ½" across bottom and marked in circle on back "Made in Austria" and the number 307.

Mrs. D.H., Montgomery, AL

Boehm wren

Peasant girl figure

A. Your wren by the Boehm company was produced at the Malvern, England, factory, probably in the 1970s or 1980s. They are collectible but the market is fairly narrow. If perfect I'd guess it might be valued in the $200-600 range.

The figure of the peasant girl and mirror appears to be molded plaster-of-Paris with a painted finish and the marking would indicate it was made in Austria in the 1920s or 1930s. It is a nice size and looks to be in fine condition. I think in the right market it would be valued in the $250-500 range.

Q. I have a collection of steins and I would like to know more about these three. #1—I believe is called a serving stein. It is 17 ½" tall. On the bottom it reads "Royal Bonn" and below that "Delft." There are two numbers, #3902 in blue and #1304 incised. I don't know the identification of the "character" portrayed here. #2—An Indian head—0.5L—there is only one mark on it, and appears to be a #46. The outside of the stein is matte finish, but the inside is glazed, including the head-gear. It is about 6" high. #3—Marks on this stein include "CAC" in a brown wreath (I think this stands for Ceramic Art Company)— underneath it reads "Lenox." The top is copper with a silver cut-out frame around it. I would like to know the value and age of these three steins. I have owned them approximately 40 years.

F.L.S., Tavares, FL

Royal Bonn China stein

American Indian Chief character stein

Ceramic Art Company stein

$A.$ Thanks for your letter and the nice selection of steins. Your first example was a product of the Royal Bonn China Manufactory of Germany. They were noted for making high-quality chinawares in the last quarter of the 19ᵗʰ century. The "Delft" probably refers to the blue and white stylized decoration. The form of this tall stein is rather traditional but its size and fine portrait decoration certainly make it very desirable. I suspect the portrait is copied from an early Dutch or German painting. If perfect I'd guess this piece might be valued in the $500-1,000 range at least.

Your American Indian Chief character stein is a very desirable piece, probably produced by the firm of E. Bohne of Sohne, Germany. This half-liter size could sell today in the $600-1,000 range I believe.

You are correct about the "CAC" markings on the third stein. The undecorated blank was produced by the Ceramic Art Company, which then became Lenox. Again, the nice hand-painted portrait of the Native American chief makes this an especially desirable piece, both for collectors of American porcelain and stein collectibles. I wouldn't be surprised if it might fetch in the $800-1,500 range in the right market.

$Q.$ Enclosed is a picture of a couple of approximately 7" tall figures I bought years ago from an old couple. I thank you in advance for your assistance.
R.W., Elizabeth, NJ

$A.$ Your pair of isque figures probably date from around 1900. If perfect the pair might be valued in the $125-250 range.

Bisque figures

English Staffordshire platter
front and back

Q. The pattern on this platter is not listed in anything I've seen. It is 17x13 ¾". It says "Bride of Lammamore" and "Selby's Illustrations" on the reverse side. A number 16 is indented on the back. The front and rim are in good shape and the back has a little flaking of glaze only. It is probably stoneware rather than porcelain. We enjoy your column and the fact that you don't put down the folks who ask for your expertise.

P.S., New Port Richey, FL

A. Your lovely large oval platter is early English Staffordshire earthenware featuring a desirable transfer-printed scene. Titled "Scott's Illustrations—the Bride of Lammermoor," the scene is based on a popular work by writer Sir Walter Scott. The Davenport firm produced this piece with the deep pink transfer around the mid-1840s. Such large platters in top condition today can sell in the $250-500 range and sometimes more.

Q. I enjoy your column and hope that you will be able to help me find out about the pitcher that I have enclosed pictures of. The pitcher is a music box and has no chips or cracks. It is marked on the bottom "Fieldings Made in England Rd. No 755789-1930." The signature on the side reads "John Peel" and I believe the words on the front may be the words to the tune it plays. Thank you for any information you can give me.

C.L.W., Cuba, MO

Ceramic pitcher with English hunting scenes

Ceramic pitcher with English hunting scenes

A. Your colorful molded ceramic pitcher, with the English hunting scenes, poem and fox-shaped handle, was produced by the firm of S. Fielding & Co. The registration number on this piece indicates it was registered in 1930 so it is a revival of an early 19th century piece. It is still attractive and has lots of appeal. If perfect I'd guess it might be valued in the $150-250 range, especially since it still has a working music box.

Bisque porcelain centerpiece

Q. Your column is such a welcome addition to the magazine. Enclosed is a photo of a very ornate pedestal with attached bowl on top, which I hope you can help identify and value. It stands 16" high, and the bottom is marked "#6768, N [circled by a larger "C"]." There is also a paper label marked "hand-painted—wile China," (the first few letters preceding "wile" are missing). Many thanks in advance for any help you can provide.

Mrs. R.M.K., Cheektowaga, NY

A. Your elaborate bisque porcelain centerpiece is a copy of the rococo-designed pieces made in Germany and France starting in the late 18th century. This style was revived in the late Victorian era and even is found on newer wares. From the description of the marking, including the "NC" mark, I believe this is one of the more modern pieces. It was likely produced in Japan sometime in the 1960-80 period. It appears to be nice quality but wouldn't command the prices of the Victorian era pieces. If perfect, with no chips, cracks or wear, I'd think it might be valued in the $200-400 range even though it's not "antique."

Q. I have a vase that is described by the following information: on the bottom it has incised, "6118, H&Co. Selb Bavarian;" and has written, "A Bloemker 12-13-21." It is 10" tall, 3 ¼" across, and 5' ¾" handle to handle. It is in mint condition. The vase has a pale bluish white background a lady with a celadon green robe and hat in front; a lady with a blue robe and hat on the back with purple hanging flowers and gold handles. Please let me know what you think it is—who made it and what it is worth today. Could the mark be Haviland?

T.P., Columbia City, IN

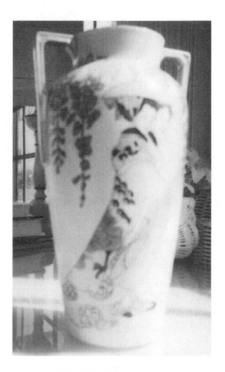

Heinrich & Company vase

A. Your vase is a lovely example of American hand-painted porcelain. Although the "H. & Co." mark could be confused with a Haviland mark, this mark with the crown and "Selb - Bavaria" indicates that the undecorated vase was produced by Heinrich & Company of Germany, which operated from 1896 right up to the 1980s at least. China painting was a very popular pastime for ladies in the late 19th and early 20th century. Your piece is signed by the artist and dated "Dec. 13, 1921," a fairly late date for an American decorated piece. The design of the graceful Geishas and wisteria vines is very pretty and appears to be very well painted. I talked to Dorothy Kamm, an expert on American hand-painted porcelain and author of *Antique Trader's Comprehensive Guide to American Hand-painted Porcelain*, about your piece. She feels that due to its size and fine decoration it could be valued in the $250-450 range. Dorothy also has a book out on hand-painted porcelain jewelry, which is also a growing field of collecting.

Little Red Riding Hood cookie jar

Q. I have enclosed a photo of a Little Red Riding Hood cookie jar I have, made by Hull Pottery. Can you tell me what its value might be? Thank you.

N.J.B., Greenvale, NY

A. You are correct that the Little Red Riding Hood design in pottery was originated by Hull, however, as author Brenda Roberts points out in her book, *Roberts' Ultimate Encyclopedia of Hull Pottery*, a vast majority of the figural pieces in this line were actually made by Regal China between 1943 and 1957. Collectors still refer to such wares as "Hull," however. Your Red Riding Hood with the closed basket design cookie jar appears to be in excellent condition with great paint and decal trim. This piece has been known to sell in the $400-500 range, however, you should be aware that a number of Little Red Riding Hood pieces have been reproduced in recent years. Buyers should be wary and purchase from reliable sources.

❧❧❧

Q. Enclosed is a photo of a shallow 11" bowl. The bowl is unmarked, but it's quite lovely and the photo really doesn't do it justice. Again, any information as to identity, age and value would be appreciated.

Mrs. R.M.K., Cheektowaga, NY

A. Your porcelain bowl is a real treasure. Although unmarked, it is easily recognizable as a piece of R.S. Prussia, produced in the late 19th and early 20th century. This molded design is referred to as the "Lily" mold, referring to the border blossoms. The piece is especially desirable because of the color-printed center portrait of Madame Recamier, a design based on an early 19th century painting. Also, the iridized panels feature what collectors call a "bronze iridescent Tiffany" finish, which makes it even more sought after. The piece appears to be in excellent condition; if there is no wear to the design and no chips, cracks or flakes to the bowl, it might sell to an R.S. Prussia lover in the $1,200-$1,400 range. *See Ceramics Tip # 4.

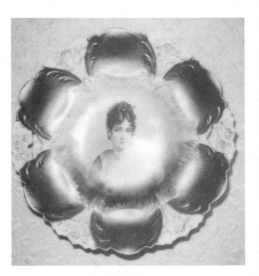

R.S. Prussia bowl

Q. My father told me this bowl is now fourth generation. He received it from his mother, who was born in 1882. She received it from her mother, who came from Norway. (The family name was Raad). The name on it, "Rancaise Porcelain," is in a ribbon. There is also a little mark in gold. I would like to know as much as possible about the company, age and value.

L.W., Snohomish, WA

A. Your china plate is an early piece, but was actually made in this country. I believe the mark is partly worn off and should read "La Francaise Porcelain." This was one trademark used by the French China Company of Sebring, OH, which

La Francaise Porcelain plate

operated under that name from 1900 to 1916. They used a French-sounding name to add to the market appeal of their wares. The transfer-printed horse design is appealing. Depending on the size and overall condition of the plate, it might be valued in the $30-$60 range.

Lady head planter

Q. We learn so much from your section on antiques and we thank you. We bought this at an estate yard sale, and would appreciate information on who the figure resembles and its value. It is in excellent condition, with no chips, cracks or crazing. The netting is slightly faded. A number, A5047, is on the bottom in green. It has a "pearl" necklace and is approximately 7" tall.

M.T., Arboles, CO

A. You made a nice buy at the yard sale! This is a nice example of the very popular lady head planters that were widely popular in the 1950s and '60s, often used by florists at that time. Most of these were made in Japan and sold here by such companies as Napco.

References usually list them by the code number on the base. Your lady has all the most desirable features—eyelashes, a hand by her face and a large hat, this one especially unique because it appears to have its original net trim and green leaves. I would guess in that market your piece might be valued in the $250-$450 range.

Molded chalkware bust

Q. I have enclosed a photo of a statue we have had in our family for many years. I inherited it from my aunt after she passed away. Many people have looked at it, but no one seems to know anything about it. I had an antique appraiser look at it, and she did not know what it was or who had made it. On the bottom of the base is a chalky substance. I was told the statue is chalkware. Some people think it might be a likeness of Clara Barton. On the base is a mark, a large circle with a letter "C" with a letter "B" inside of it. I would appreciate knowing if the statue represents anyone in particular and the value of it. It has a gray finish.

G.B.McG., Dayton, OH

A. Your pretty bust is made of a fine molded chalkware, and is a style of bust widely produced in this country in the late 19th and early 20th centuries. It was a less expensive way to copy more expensive porcelain pieces produced abroad by firms such as Royal Dux. Many of these chalkware examples are large and finely detailed, and popular designs included Native Americans, African-Americans and pretty Victorian ladies, especially those in the Art Nouveau style. Your bust is of a young woman in Dutch costume (nothing like Clara Barton, I'm sure). All sorts of decorative items with "Dutch" designs were popular early in the 20th century. Many of these busts had colorful hand painting, and they would bring more than your example with the subdued gray tones. Your piece appears to be in top shape, however, with no chips or flaking, which often happens to these pieces. Depending on the size, I would guess this attractive piece might be valued in the $400-$800 range, perhaps a bit more to just the right buyer.

Clocks & Furniture

Q. My clock and candelabra are solid brass. The clock is 24" tall and the candelabra 25-1/2" tall. The center of each candelabrum lifts off and can be used as a candle snuffer and a candle inserted in its place. There is an insignia that I cannot identify. I cannot find out anything about them.

Solid brass clock   *Solid brass candelabra*

A. These appear to be very fine quality. Many such brass and gilt-brass three-piece sets were produced in the last half of the 19th century. A great many are probably French. Without knowing the mark, it is difficult to say for certain. If all the pieces are perfect and the clock works, such a set could be valued in the $2,500 to $5,000 range, depending on the local market.

Reproductions of such pieces have been on the market and are available today. The details of the casting on your pieces lead me to believe they are 19th century examples based on French Rococo 18th century designs.

Q. Please help me with two items. The first is a Windsor chair left to me by my grandparents and also a child's rocker (the rocker was recaned in the '50s). Any idea of the makers and a price would be appreciated.

K.C., NJ

Lady's Grecian-style rocker   *Windsor bow-back armchair*

A. You have two collectible pieces of furniture. The Windsor "bow-back" armchair is a reproduction piece probably dating about the 1920s when there was a great interest in Early American furniture and many styles of Windsors were copied. The piece is probably walnut-stained hardwood and the value might be in the $125-$200 range unless it is marked by a notable maker. The rocker, although of a small size, doesn't appear to really be a piece of children's furniture. I would call it a lady's Grecian-style rocker, sometimes called a "sewing" rocker. It appears to be walnut with a caned seat and back. Such rockers were popular for a long period of time in the mid to late 19th century and from the shape of the crest on your piece, I'd date it around 1870-80. It appears to be in excellent condition and might be valued in the $150-$250 range depending on the market in your area. *See Clocks & Furniture Tip #1.

Q. **I am enclosing pictures of my walnut Victorian desk. I have not been able to find one similar and would like to know if it is circa 1880 and of Rococo style.**

R.L., WI

A. I would date this piece, made of walnut and walnut burl veneer, ca. 1875-85, however, the style would generally be referred to as Renaissance Revival. The Rococo sub-style generally has more rounded, scrolling designs and was most popular in the 1845-70 era. Because of the unique design and fine condition of this piece, I would think it might have a retail value in the $1,500-$3,000 range, depending on the local market.

Renaissance Revival desk

Q. **I have enclosed a picture of a mirror we purchased several years ago. It has a beveled glass mirror, a tin-like back, two kissing angels at top in center, and full-bodied angels, one on each side; it seems to be a cast metal. The numbers enclosed and printed are on the back: "#2002 – NB81W." Could you help me identify this piece? Could you estimate the value also? It is very pretty.**

R.H., Dewitt, MI

Turn of the century mirror

A. I can tell that you have a nice cast metal bronze-finished oval table mirror. The general openwork design, romantic motif and beveled mirror would probably date its time of production right around the turn of the century. The impressed letters and numbers are difficult to attribute today but because of its decorative appeal, I'd guess it might be valued in the $150-$250 range.

Q. We really enjoy "Kyle on Antiques." You have been a big help to us in the past. Would like information on this chest of drawers. We have had it in our family for years. Original finish and we think beautiful.

R.B., Paxton, IL

A. Your photo shows a nice example of an early chest of drawers made of mahogany veneer and tiger stripe maple. The style is transitional between the late Federal and early Classical style. The deep upper drawers and shaped short legs are typical of the Classical style and the rope twist columns might have appeared on pieces from the

Chest of drawers with transitional style

1815-35 era. This is a handsome piece and appears to be in fine, original condition. Size and condition, as well as design and wood, affect the value, and the regional market will also vary. In the Midwest, I'd say this chest might be valued in the $800-$1,200 range or more to the right buyer.

Q. What can you tell me about my Coca-Cola wall clock?

A.B., Cumming, GA

A. After checking through *Allan Petretti's Coca-Cola Price Guide*, the major reference in this field, I think your clock is probably a 1970s reproduction based on early wall regulators. The new clock shown in the book has the same molding in the frame but came with a higher cornice at the top and a scroll-cut backboard at the bottom. These would have been removed from yours or never added. The new clock also had a battery-operated works. The fancier example shown in the Petretti book was valued at around $350, but yours would probably bring quite a bit less.

1970s Coca-Cola clock reproduction

Q. Enclosed is a picture of a sideboard, which has been in our family many years. This piece stands 5'5" tall, is 24" deep, and 6' long. The oak is elaborately carved with winged lions flanking the beveled mirror, and is in excellent condition. The rest of the piece is adorned with hand-carved lions and figures, which appear to be laughing faces. Any information regarding its age, origin, or value would be greatly appreciated, as the piece has always been a mystery to us.

K.N., Easton, PA

Baroque Revival oak sideboard

A. Your elaborate oak sideboard is in a style I refer to as "Baroque Revival" and probably dates from the last quarter of the 19th century. Such large and ornately carved pieces were take-offs of the Baroque style of the 17th century and many such pieces were made in the late 19th century in northern Europe as well as this country. Such a sideboard might have originally been part of a set with a matching dining table, chairs and perhaps other pieces. Today a Victorian example of this ornateness and quality can sell for several thousand dollars in the right market.

Q. I inherited this washstand. Someone told me it could be from Civil War time; has brass knobs on door and drawer. It is 12-1/4" deep, 17" wide, 28-3/4" high. I was told it is a spoon design on the stand.

M.M., Felt, OK

A. Your oak washstand is a late Victorian piece in the Eastlake substyle and probably dates from the 1890s. The simple stylized carving on the door must be what someone referred to as a "spoon carving." This nice piece could be valued in the $250-500 range. *See Clocks & Furniture Tip #4.

1890s oak washstand

Q. Enclosed are two photos of a Mission style oak desk type secretary. Could you please identify what the piece is? We are guessing the age as turn of the century. We would appreciate any other information you could furnish and a possible price range of value. We really appreciate your column in the magazine.

S.V., Waukesha, WI

A. Your small oak piece would generally be referred to as a secretary-bookcase, in other words, a combination desk and book storage cabinet. I agree that it dates around the turn of the century. Although the lines are simple, I think the scroll-carved crest puts it more in the Golden Oak style than the Mission Oak style, which is very flat and plain. This piece appears to be in excellent condition with probably the original drawer pulls too. Smaller pieces like this are much in demand for today's smaller homes so it should have a good collector

Secretary-bookcase

value. I'd guess it might sell in the $800-$1,200 range, depending on the local market.

Q. Enclosed find three pictures of what is called a "plantation desk." There is no kind of identification on it anywhere. It is made of mostly fruit wood and mahogany. It was bought from a farm or ranch in Kentucky in the early 1950s. It belonged to a soldier's grandfather who died and the soldier offered to sell it. He did not know anything about it except it had always been in the family. I would like a little history as no one knows anything about it. And price if you know anything about this type of furniture.

F.T., Alexandria, LA

*American Classical
Revival secretary*

A. Your handsome secretary appears to be a nice example of American Classical Revival furniture made of mahogany and mahogany veneer. I would guess it would date from about 1835-45 and was most likely produced at a factory in New England and shipped south. Some people call secretaries of this type with a wide fall-front a "plantation desk," but they could have been used in any better home of that era. Your piece appears to be in excellent original condition. Classical or "Empire" furniture of the first half of the 19th century hasn't always been highly regarded in antiques circles but prices are starting to rise for better pieces such as yours. Depending on the local market, I'd say this piece might be valued in the $800-$1,600 range or higher to the right collector.

Federal Revival dining room suite

Q. Enclosed are pictures of a dining room set my husband inherited after the death of his grandmother. This set includes one table, six chairs and a china cabinet. The wood, as you can see, is dark. I do not like this set and am interested in selling it, however, I have no clue as to its value. It does need to be refinished and we know that his grandmother had it approximately 30-40 years. If you could give me an estimated value, I would greatly appreciate it.

K.A., Rowlett, TX

A. Your Federal- or Hepplewhite-Revival dining room suite is a style widely popular from the 1920s through the 1950s. I would guess your pieces might date between 1935 and 1955. They are probably mahogany or mahogany veneer. The style is still popular with those interested in an Early American look and even needing a little refinishing I would think you might be able to offer it in the $600-$1,200 range to the right collector or decorator. A dealer could only offer about half the retail price, and the amount of work in refinishing also will determine how it will sell, as well as demand in your area. I noticed damage to a foot on the china cabinet, which would lower the possible resale value, too.

French mantel clock

Q. I read your column every month and extremely enjoy it! Enclosed is a photo of a French mantel clock which has been in my family for many years. I hope you can help me determine its age and value as well as its origin if I am incorrect. The clock is approximately 20" high and is very ornate. Thank you in advance for your help and keep this great column going.

B.I., Oceanside, NY

A. Your French mantel clock appears to be a top quality example of French workmanship and probably dates from the 1875-1900 era. The main case is probably bronze or gilt-bronze and I can see banded trim of fine cloisonné enamel in blue and white as well as the shaped base made of greenish onyx or marble. The glass front and sides and the fine condition of all the ornamental details also confirm that this was a fine quality piece when made. If it is in working condition without any damages to the case which don't show in this photo, I wouldn't be surprised if this clock might sell in the $1,500-$2,500 range in the right market.

Q. Enclosed you will find two pictures of a bed that I can find nothing about. There are no identification marks at all. It is a beautiful carved bed that will take your breath away with the design. Would appreciate anything you can tell me; if the design has a meaning, would might have made it, when and value.

F.T., Alexandria, LA

Renaissance Revival sub-style bed

A. Your Victorian bed appears to be a fine example of quality workmanship. The style is a version of the Renaissance Revival substyle, which was especially popular in the 1865-85 era. Your piece has fine carving, especially with the winged grotesque mask on the crest, as well as lovely burl panels in walnut and perhaps rosewood. Most likely this was a part of a bedroom suite produced at a larger furniture manufacturer perhaps in New York City or some other Eastern city. Sets always bring the highest prices, but your handsome bed might still be valued in the $1,500-$2,500 range alone.

Q. **I am sending you two pictures. The two smoke tables have been varnished; the hutch has been in our family for years and it is the original finish, also have four dining chairs to match hutch. What can you tell me about them?**

S.S., Osceola, MO

Early 20th century hutch

A. Your little smoking stands are typical of the types popular in the 1920s and 1930s. Originally they usually had a very dark varnish finish. They are popular as accent pieces today and yours might be valued

Smoking stands

in the $60-$100 range each. The hutch was probably part of a full dining room suite that originally could have included a matching dining table and sideboard. It is walnut veneer and is an early 20th century copy of a 17th century "court" (French for "short") cupboard. These were popular in the Netherlands, England and some were even made in New England. Your piece appears to be in fine shape and might be valued in the $400-$800 range. The chairs would also have value, perhaps in the $400-$600 range if in top condition.

Q. **Enclosed are pictures of a chair and matching rocker (Windsor?). Bought them in February 1952 from an elderly gentleman who said he had purchased them for his wife at the turn of the century. Labels on the underside of the chairs are difficult to read as they appear to have been shellacked in place and have turned brown. The labels read: "American Chair Company, Sheboygan, Wisconsin, The Merikord Line." I would appreciate any information you can give me as to the company, if the chairs are Windsors and, possibly, the value. I enjoy your portion of *Collector Magazine* very much an only wish it were lengthier.**

Bow-back Windsor-style armchair

A. Your bow-back Windsor-style armchair and rocker are nice examples of "Centennial" type reproductions of Colonial furniture. Beginning shortly after the 1876 Centennial celebration American furniture makers began to reproduce and adapt early American styles of furniture to meet public demand. By the turn of the century this production was very large and competed with the so-called "Golden Oak" style of furniture and the newer simpler Mission Style furniture. Colonial Revival furniture has never completely gone out of style and was especially popular during the 1920s and 1930s. Having your chairs labeled adds some to their collectibility but many of the newer Windsors are still to be found. Nice examples will often sell in the $100-$200 range. The very accurate reproductions made by Wallace Nutting, a pioneering collector and writer on Colonial furniture, are bringing even higher prices.

Writing-arm armchair

Q. I recently acquired three chairs like the one in this picture. They are larger than a tablet-armchair that one might find in a school room and the arm and marble utility tray is flat. The bottom, back and elbow pad is upholstered with black leather-like material and they were manufactured by Teasier Brothers, Northampton, Mass. It is my understanding they were originally used in the local NYC or B&O depot as "snack" chairs as the marble surface on the tray is washable. There are no other markings that indicate they were railroad property. I look forward to reading "Kyle on Antiques" each month and would appreciate learning about my chairs.

R.H., Scarbro, WV

A. Your interesting writing-arm armchair is basically in the Mission style popular around 1905-1925. I'm not familiar with the maker, but marked pieces generally are more sought after than unmarked ones. I wonder if the tablet on the arm is really marble, as that would have been quite expensive for such a utilitarian piece. Could it be a heavyweight opaque white glass or perhaps even enameled metal? Those would have been more common materials for such heavy-duty pieces. It may well have served as a snack table in a railroad depot but without a railroad marking on it there's no way to tell for certain and it wouldn't add any great value unless it was so marked. This piece looks like it's in good clean condition so I'd take care not to refinish it or reupholster if you plan to resell it. As is, I'd say it might be valued in the $175-$225 range.

Q. The information I have on this mantel clock is very limited. It was purchased in Italy. It was one of two clocks designed for King Louis XIV and was to be displayed at the Palace of Versailles. The clock makers were Henricus, Jones and Londini. Unfortunately the history of the clock was done in Italian and is missing. Do you notice the cherubs in each corner?

This fire screen was purchased in China between 1932 and 1935. I was told the porcelain screen is or was pre-Ming Dynasty. I know that the stand is at least 200 years old. What can you tell me?

L.W., Big Bear City, CA

English bracket clock

A. Your attractive clock is a style referred to as an English "bracket clock." These were first made in the late 17th century and have been produced up through today. The name on the works is the Latinized name of Henry Jones of London, England, the first clockmaker to produce this type of clock. It had nothing to do with France or Louis XIV. Even though the general style of the case and the name on the works would lead you to believe differently, it is more likely a late 19th or early 20th century reproduction. The style of the brass handle on top is not quite right and, though handcrafted, it just doesn't quite look right to me. I would suggest you contact some major auction houses to see what they can tell you. Even if it's not 17th century it's an attractive, well-made clock.

Chinese fire screen

The screen is Chinese and the hand-painted panel is porcelain but again, I seriously doubt it is nearly as old as you believe. The Chinese have been copying their early furniture and artworks for hundreds of years and many "antique" style pieces were exported to the West during the late 19th and early 20th century. You should have an expert in Oriental art look this over first-hand, but my guess is that it's about 75 to 100 years old. With some apparent veneer damage on the frame, I'd say it might be valued in the $1,500-$2,500 range.

Q. Would appreciate any information you might have on this chair. I received it about 35 years ago from my father-in-law. The seat and back were originally covered in leather, which became so hard and brittle that it cracked and was falling apart. The tip of the back is 54" from the floor, seat is

Throne armchair

15" from the floor and 31" wide at the widest part. The arms are well worn, showing a lot of use. Would like to know, if possible, the type of chair and possible value. I like your articles and really look forward to them.

J.L., Titusville, FL

A. Your unique "throne" armchair is certainly an impressive piece. I believe the overall design is based on French and German 17th century Baroque pieces, but I would guess your example would date from the 1880-1910 era. The Victorians loved to copy and adapt the designs of earlier centuries. This piece could have been made in this country by a larger furniture firm with trained craftsmen, or perhaps was produced in Europe. A chair of this size doesn't fit in every home but would work well in a larger Victorian home. Sometime size does limit the marketability of a piece, but I think in the right market it might be valued in the $1,500-$3,000 range.

Q. My mother left me this oak china cupboard, 42" wide, 61-1/2" tall. I was told my great-grandfather's second wife brought this to his house when they married about 1900. This had dozens of coats of paint; I had the paint taken off. I know so little about these items. Are they of any value? I cannot find them in any book.

P.C., Charlotte, NC

A. The oak china cupboard is typical of pieces dating around 1900. It is a nice design but the curved-glass cabinets are generally most valuable on the market today. Your piece might be valued in the $450-$850 range.

Oak china cupboard

Q. I inherited this beautiful old table from my aunt. She bought used furniture in the 1930s and now it has turned collectible. The top measures 39" by 23" at the longest points and looks to be inlaid wood veneer of various kinds, some leaves and flowers stained with a little color. The table looks like it could be mahogany, ornately carved with cherubs and leaves. I've looked closely and each cherub is carved differently from the other; could it have been hand-carved or just made to look that way? It's a small table and stands 30" high with a glass curved to fit the outline of the table top. It is in very nice

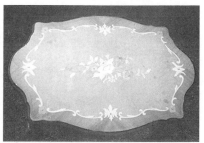

condition with no chips or dents in the wood. I can find no markings of any kind so I don't know who the maker was. Do you have any idea as to its age and value?

G.G., Silver City, NV

A. Your table appears to be a nice example of revival-style furniture popular in the first quarter of the 20th century. The top may well have inlay work and the sides are nicely pierced and carved. It is basically a take-off on an 18th century European table and may have been imported from there as a new piece around 1900-1925. Because furniture of that era is growing in value and this is a very ornate example, I'd say it might bring in the $300-$650 range in the right market or more to the right collector.

Revival-style table

Q. I purchased this wonderful old chair several years ago. It has a splayed seat and all the original finish. What can you tell me about the value and age of the chair?

J.W., Stephenville, TX

A. Your Windsor-style bow-back side chair appears to me to be a reproduction piece, likely produced in the 1920s or so. The thinness of the seat and the evenness of the spindles seem to indicate this. As a nice revival piece I'd say it might sell in the $40-$80 range.

Windsor-style bow-back side chair

Q. I am a subscriber to your *Collector Magazine* and would like information on the "Morris Chair" as shown in enclosed pictures. I have been advised that the wood is American chestnut. Any information you can provide will be greatly appreciated, value, age, etc. Note: There is an attached "swing out" footrest not shown in picture.

T.T., Gowanda, NY

Wingback rocker

A. Your rocker may be chestnut or a combination of chestnut and oak. The wingback style is a bit unusual as is having the adjustable back on a rocker. It probably dates from about 1900-1915 and could have been made in any number of furniture factories of that day. As an interesting collector's piece, I'd say it might be valued in the $300-$400 range. *See Clocks & Furniture Tip #2

Colonial Revival

Q. We bought a table, buffet and five chairs about 13 years ago. It's burl wood, in mint condition. A metal tag in the wood inside the drawer says "The Lammert Furniture Co., 911-119 Washington Ave., St. Louis." There's a date on the underside of the table, May 23, 1923. Everybody who sees it wants to buy it. What do you think it's worth?

J.S., Imperial, MO

A. Your dining room suite is nicely documented and is a fine example of Colonial Revival furniture sets of the 1920s. It has a nice carving and fine burl trim. I think, in the right market, the set might be valued in the $2,500-$3,500 range.

Q. I am enclosing two pictures of furniture that belonged to my family. I would like to know what they are worth. The secretary belonged to my grandmother who lived in Dubuque, Iowa, most of her life. I believe it to be quite old. It has a lot of detail. The mirrors are beveled and the glass on the door is curved and original to the piece. The love seat was acquired at a yard sale many years ago by my father. I would appreciate anything you can tell me about these items.

P.R., Jefferson City, MO

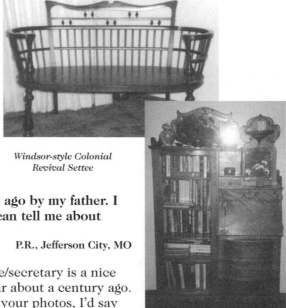

Windsor-style Colonial Revival Settee

A. Your combination bookcase/secretary is a nice example of the type popular about a century ago. Most were made in oak but from your photos, I'd say yours might be birch with a burl design and stained reddish to resemble mahogany. It has lots of nice

Bookcase/secretary

detailing with the mirrors and shelves. It looks to be in perfect shape and might be valued in the $800-$1,200 range.

The settee is a Windsor-style Colonial Revival piece, perhaps dating from the 1915-30 period. Most likely it is a walnut veneer. It's not a direct copy of an early Windsor piece, just a later "interpretation" of the style. Depending on size and condition, it might be valued in the $250-$450 range.

Q. Would appreciate information on the worth and identification of this table. I feel it is Empire, all hand-carved and in excellent condition. Willie (Nelson) signed these several items at the Colorado State Fair: Copy of original sale, sombrero, bandanna printed "Red headed stranger" and "Willie Nelson Inc." Also have pen that was used to sign.

W.C., Fowler, CO

Oak library table

A. Your oak library table is typical of the types produced in the late 1890s and early 1900s. It has nicely carved scroll detail and large metal claw feet holding wood (?) balls. It appears to be in excellent condition and might be valued in the $400-$800 range. Your pieces signed by Willie Nelson are certainly collectible to his fans, but since he is still active, their individual value is hard to judge. It would be a matter of a fan's special interest.

Q. We bought this piece from a dealer locally. He said he purchased it an at estate auction in Alabama. We have no idea what it's worth but would be interested in any information you could give us. He said it was an 1830s court cupboard. It looks hand-carved and possibly one of a kind.

A.S., Colona, IL

Court cupboard

A. Your decorative hand-carved piece is indeed referred to as a "court cupboard," the word "court" referring to the French word for "short." This design was originally popular in the 16th and 17th centuries and was used all over Europe and England as well as Colonial America. I don't believe your piece is quite as early as the 1830s. There was a great revival in this style of Renaissance-style furniture in Germany in the last quarter of the 19th century and many pieces have made their way to the U.S. It is still a fine piece of workmanship and might sell in the right market in the $1,500-$2,500 range.

Drop-leaf side table

Q. I love your considerate and thorough answers. I have enclosed two photos of a small (drop-leaf) table my great-aunt gave to me. My son said the drawers look like they're carved from one piece of wood and it could be valuable. Can you tell me about it and its value? Also, on top of the table is my nude lady vase (8" high) that I've also wondered about. It is old, but has no markings on it at all.

S.R., St. Louis, MO

A. Your drop-leaf side table is a style of country furniture that was popular from about 1850-1880. I see this form with two drawers and block- and knob-turned legs quite often around the upper Midwest. It was made in a variety of native woods including black walnut and cherry. Your piece is a bit fancier in that it has a crotch grain mahogany veneer on the drawer fronts. I think that would place it closer to the 1850s era. As a nice, handy table it might be valued in the $350-$450 range. I can't see your nude figurine too well but it appears to be in the Art Deco style of the late 1920s and 1930s. It may be porcelain and perhaps made in Germany. The shaded blue glaze is appealing. If perfect, I think it might be valued in the $100-$200 range.

Walnut and walnut veneer dining room suite

Q. Enclosed are pictures of a dining room set I inherited. There's a total of 10 pieces. Any information on the style, age and value will be appreciated. Looking forward to your column.

J.B., Cumming, GA

A. Your walnut and walnut veneer dining room suite is typical of the "Colonial Revival" sets popular during the 1920s. Overall I would describe the style as "Federal Revival," but the chair backs have a touch of Chippendale design. This mixing of design elements was typical in that era. Your suite appears to be in excellent, clean condition and such large sets are quite marketable. Although not as ornately carved as some sets, it should have good market appeal. Even though some of the furniture knobs seem to be missing or replaced, I would think in the right market this set might be valued in the $1,200-$1,500 range.

Q. All I can tell you is that this chair has been in the family for 60-70 years. Where it came from, I don't know. Any information regarding origin, maker, age, etc., and estimated value would be appreciated.

J.M., DeWitt, IA

A. Your rocker is a classic example of Empire Revival furniture sets popular in the 1890s. It was probably part of a parlor suite. It features heavy lines with a dark mahogany finish and bold carving. Some of these pieces are

Empire Revival rocker

fairly simple in design but your rocker has nice quality classical head carvings at the ends of the arms and paw feet. Although the seat needs a little work, it appears to be in overall good condition. I would try to have someone carefully clean but not refinish this piece since the dark finish is original. In the right market, I would say this chair might sell in the $400-$600 range.

Pressed-back platform rocker

Q. First of all, I enjoy your column very much in *Collector Magazine*. It is very informative and helpful! I am hoping you can help me determine the value of an old platform rocker that belonged to my wife's great-grandparents. The only marking on the rocker is as follows: "Mfg. by Buckstaff_ ED, Oshkosh, WI, VK_Y." This chair was being made in the 1880s through 1890s, I believe. The dimensions are 3'5" high from tip of back to floor, 17" from front tip of seat to floor, 19-1/2" wide at widest point of frame. Base of frame is 14" wide at back and 15" wide at front. This chair is an excellent condition, however, I have been unable to find it in any reference book. I would like to find out the estimated value. Your help will be very much appreciated!

B.B., Excelsior Springs, MO

A. Your nice pressed-back platform rocker could well date to the 1890s and is typical of the mass-produced manufactured furniture made at many furniture factories around the Midwest during that era. It is nice that your example is marked but I don't know that that adds a great deal to the market value. The pressed (stamped) detailing on the back is a major factor in valuing such chairs and most collectors like designs featuring faces, scenes, bold flowers or fruit. Your delicate scroll design is pretty but not especially unusual. The scrolled seat and platform base are nice details. In the right market, I think your rocker could be valued in the $250-$325 range.

Immigrant trunk

Q. Enclosed are photos of a trunk, 17" high, 20-1/2" wide, 38" long. Can you tell me a little about my trunk and price? The cabinet is 31" high, 18-1/2" wide, 5-1/2" deep. Can you tell me how old this cabinet is and price? We have received your magazine since 1975 and enjoy everyone.

W.B., Hastings, MN

Shaving mug cabinet

A. You have a couple of very nice antique pieces and you sent some good photos, which are appreciated. The shaving mug cabinet would be a much sought-after piece by collectors in the barberiana field. Your example has a very decorative front done in the pyrography (burnt wood) technique so popular in the early years of the 20th century. It looks like a color print was then glued onto the center of the door. Because of its appeal as a choice piece of pyrography as well as a shaving mug cabinet, I wouldn't be surprised to see it sell in the mid- to upper $100s in the right market.

Your immigrant trunk is another wonderful folk art piece and was produced in Scandinavia, most likely in Norway or Sweden. Certain designs were used in various regions of these countries so further research would be needed to provide more history. The paint appears to be in great shape, especially on the interior, which also still has its original till at one end. In the right market, I would say this piece could sell in the $1,500-$2,500 range.

Victorian chest of drawers

Q. I own this black walnut chest, marble top has two cracks (not through), 39" by 17-1/2" by 32" high, drawers have hand-cut dovetails, drawer pulls hand-carved as they are not exactly alike. I stripped four coats of paint and put on Pilgrim oil finish; left all dents and scratches. Age? Value?

A.V., Mosinee, WI

A. This walnut Victorian chest of drawers dates from about 1860-1875 and is in the Renaissance Revival style. The white marble top adds a lot to the collector value. A nice three-drawer chest like this might be valued in the $500-$750 range.

Q. Enclosed are photos that I hope you can help me with. The china cabinet dates from about 1920 or 1922, but I can't seem to find this style in any books as to value.

T.M., Brook Park, OH

A. Your oak china cabinet with the curved glass sides is typical of the style popular in the 1910-25 era. It has simple lines and is fairly delicate in appearance. These cabinets are always in demand and a nice clean piece such as yours could be valued in the $500-$900 range.

Oak china cabinet

Q. Enclosed are several pictures of a cabinet I bought about eight years ago. I'm so curious about it. I have been told it is rosewood (Brazilian?). It is very dark red in color and very well made. It's put together with square nails and the glass (original) is held in place by wooden pegs. It measures approximately 6'3" tall, 26" wide and 13" deep. It also has a lot of carving. I would like any information and a value, as I am thinking of selling it.

K.I., Waimaualo, HI

A. Your photos make it a little difficult for me to get a good idea of exactly what you have. The wood could be mahogany but would need to be examined more closely. The carving is based on early rococo designs but the piece itself doesn't seem to fit into any specific stylistic form. As a guess I think it might have been made in Europe in the early 20th century. As a decorative display cabinet with interesting detailing I'd say it might be valued in the $750-1,500 range, depending on the local market.

Dark-colored cabinet

Late 19th or early
20th century chair

Late 19th century parlor table

Could you help me identify this chair and small table? I think they may be European. Also, any value you think they may have.

K.G., San Antonio, TX

A. You appear to have some very nice decorative pieces of furniture and I would agree they are most likely European, perhaps German or maybe Dutch. The armchair and matching side chair are based on ornate 18th century Rococo designs but I suspect they date from the late 19th or early 20th century. It appears they may have hand-inlaid scenic designs in the seat and back which would add much to their value. If they are all hand-carved and inlaid, I would say the pair might sell in the $2,500-$4,000 range in the right market. The parlor table appears to be a late 19th century French piece in the Louis XV style. Again, the top may be hand-inlaid, which would add a lot to the value. If all hand-done, it might be valued in the $1,500-$2,500 range.

Q. We purchased this Gothic looking piece from an estate auction in central Minnesota. The story goes that it was purchased in the 1920s as an antique by the family. They believed it was from Belgium from the late 1500s. The piece measures 50" wide at the back, about 39" high and 17" deep. It is obviously hand-carved and the hardware appears to be hand-wrought. It gives the impression of having another cabinet that may have sat on top. Could you give your impressions and estimated value to help validate the "story?"

D.D., Young America, MN

Gothic style cabinet

A. Although your Gothic style cabinet may be an "antique" today I seriously doubt that it dates back much before the mid-19th century. There was a great Revivalist movement in Europe in the second half of that century and many copies or "adaptations" of very early pieces were handmade. Your piece may be the bottom of a two-piece tall cabinet and, of course, the complete piece would have a much higher value today. Just as a nicely carved Revival piece, I think it might still sell in the $1,500-$2,500 range.

Q. This settee has the celery pattern on the back. What does this mean? Do you know its age and value? Thank you for any information.

J.L., Salem, OR

A. The settee is late Victorian, ca. 1890s, and combines elements of Colonial Revival and Art Nouveau. This mixture of designs was very popular then. It appears that it may be mahogany or mahogany veneer, which would have made it more expensive then. The "celery" or leaf cluster on the crest may be

Late Victorian settee

actually inlaid and if so is another sign of quality manufacture. It appears to be in top condition and might be valued in the $450-650 range in the right market.

Q. I have an item I can't find any information on. I bought several books and can't seem to find any information. This chair is from my great grandfather's home. The chair has its original finish but new upholstery. It is 46" high in back and is 25" arm to arm.

A. Your upholstered armchair is in what I'd call the "Jacobean Revival" style, a type of furniture widely popular in the 1920s and early 1930s and based roughly on 17th century designs. Such pieces are beginning to grow in value on the antiques market. Your attractive chair might be valued in the $175-250 range.

Upholstered armchair

Q. I have enclosed a photo of a wall clock which I purchased a few years ago and would appreciate any information you might be able to provide. I have not been able to find a manufacturer name on the clock. However, the envelope containing the key had "Junghaus Regulator c 1913" written on it. I am also curious as to the significance of the eagle on the top of the clock.

D. C. S., Monticello, NY

A. Your German-made regulator wall clock is typical of the large number of such clocks produced in Germany and Austria in the late 19th and early 20th century and exported to the United States. Of course, some American clockmakers also made similar models but you still see a great many from Europe. I

German-made regulator wall clock

doubt the eagle finial has any significance other than decoration. I doubt it represents a "republican" eagle, more likely an "imperial" eagle. The case is most likely walnut or a hardwood with a dark finish. From the clock face it doesn't appear that the clock chimes and that type of clock is a bit more in demand. If it is in good working order, I would guess it might be valued in the $450-900 range.

Biedermeier corner cupboard

German cupboard

Blanket chest

Q. The whole magazine and your column in particular are the most helpful sources I have found for information about current antique values. I am sending too many photos of items for you to evaluate, but I'm especially interested in the first two. The first photo is of a German cupboard (1799) with mostly original paint and original wood, hinges, latch and key. It is 6" high with 1-1/2' wide side panels and 8" wide side panels with front doors plus wood trims that are 3'10" wide. The second photo is of a German chest (1834) with original paint. It is 4' long by 2-1/2' high by 26" deep with an inside shelf. The third photo is of a German Biedermeier corner cupboard, which is 5'8" high including 6" legs. I appreciate your help and look forward to comments in your interesting column.

D.C. B., Virginia Beach, VA

A. You have some really wonderful German country furniture with super painted decoration which looks quite original. Such pieces are in great demand in this country. Your large cupboard or wardrobe appears to be spectacular and if all original and dated might sell in the $3,000-5,000 range in the right market. The blanket chest is a more common form but again has fine painting and detailing. I think a value in the $800-1,600 range wouldn't be far off. The Biedermeier corner cupboard may be a period piece, ca. 1830, or a later copy. It appears to be finely constructed and even if not a period piece would have a good value.

Q. I have a bookcase/china cabinet I need to sell and would like some idea of the value. It is 8' long and 7' high and has three sliding glass doors, four adjustable shelves and three large bottom drawers. It was cut off at the left side top molding to fit into a corner with a slanting ceiling, but it could be replaced with the same kind of molding. There is also a piece missing from the right top side that could be replaced with half-round molding. The top section is attached to the bottom drawer section with screws and can be lifted off, so the doors and shelves come out. I don't know what kind of wood it is, but it's light colored and very heavy. It has

Late 19th century cabinet

some small chips and normal signs of wear. It was originally in a building dating to the 1880s (late) and I believe it may have been put in at that time. Thank you for your column; it is such a help. I need to clean out as I am 82 and must part with most of my collections.

N.B., Montpelier, VT

A. You do appear to have a nice three-part store cabinet that would date from the late 19th century. An 1880s date should be correct. It is hard to say for certain what wood it is, but it might be birch or perhaps cherry since it has a deep orangish tone. Such large pieces are sometimes a little hard to sell because a buyer has to have the space to use it, but the right collector or decorator certainly should find it of interest. If the damages are only minor, they shouldn't detract from the overall value. If you found just the right buyer, I'd guess this piece might sell in the $2,500-$3,500 range at least.

Highchair/rocker combination piece

Q. My wife recently bought this chair at an auction and I am hoping that you can tell me something about it. This is a child's rocker/ high chair combo. It is in good condition and was very well cared for. It is raised and lowered by means of the screw on the bottom. The seat is 24" (from the floor) when up and is quite stable considering the mechanics involved. There are no marks on the chair anywhere.

J.B., Camdenton, MO

A. Your dual-purpose child's rocker appears to be made of oak and most likely dates from around 1900. There were some fancier rocker-stroller-highchair models made as far back as the 1880s, but your piece is simpler in design, so probably dates later. Such children's furniture is quite collectible, and I'd guess your piece might be valued in the $150-225 range.

Q. I enjoy your column so much and have taken the magazine for years, always turning to your pages first. Enclosed are pictures of an old rocking chair my grandparent had in the 1800s. I don't know what the seat is made of, but it is not wood. Could you tell me when these types of rockers came out? My dad was born in 1890 and remembers it in their home. Does it have a value? How much?

M.G., Grand Marsh, WI

A. Your rocker dates from the late 19th century and was likely produced in the 1890s. Because of the stamped design on the crestrail of the back, these sorts of chairs are referred to as "pressed back." The seat is a stamped fiberboard material that was popular at that time. It is in overall very nice condition and might sell in the $250-300 range in the right market.

Late 19th century rocker

Q. Enclosed please find a picture of a small rocking chair I have. Could you please give me any information and value? Thanks. We all enjoy your magazine.

M.K., Liberty Hill, SC

A. Your little rocker appears to be composed of a simple wicker design and probably dates around the 1890s. The seat looks like it may have been replaced; the original might have been a pressed board insert or perhaps woven cane. Such children's pieces are always sought after, and your rocker appears to be in overall good condition. I think it might be valued in the $125-225 range depending on the local market and the amount of work needed to fix it up a bit.

Rocking chair

Q. Enclosed are photos of a Heywood Bros. wicker rocker I purchased at an estate sale in excellent condition. I tried to find out about this rocker by purchasing a Heywood Wakefield catalog, but found nothing on the age, year, and if this is a special pattern. I showed pictures to a few local antique dealers who all loved the chair but knew nothing about it. I hope you can help, value, etc. Thanks.

D.N., Crescent City, CA

Wicker rocker

A. Your charming wicker rocker was made by a leading manufacturer of such furniture. Heywood Bros. was in business before it became Heywood Wakefield, so I would guess your rocker might date from the 1885-1910 era. It appears to be in excellent original condition, and having the original label would add to its collector appeal. It is fairly restrained in design, and such pieces generally sell in the $350-450 range, but I think your piece would bring a premium because of the condition and label.

Q. I love your column on appraisals of different items. I have enclosed photos of a chair I recently purchased at an auction house. I was told it is an old photographer's chair. Any information would be appreciated. It looks like it is all hand-carved.

A.G.S., Colona, IL

A. You have a nicely carved novelty chair probably dating from the late 19th century. It is possible that a photographer used it as a prop in the studio, but wicker furniture was more commonly used there. Ornate pieces like this were more often used as accent pieces in Victorian hallways or offices, and many were carved and imported from Europe, especially Germany, during those years. It is basically a takeoff on 17th century European designs. As a finely carved novelty chair, I would guess it might be valued in the $450-800 range depending on the local market. The round indentation in the seat might suggest it either had a cushion insert or perhaps could also have served as a plant stand.

Late 19th century novelty chair

Walnut Victorian armchair

Q. I need help! I have an old chair that belonged to husband's family—his dad was born in 1860—and I find it necessary to sell it. I guess what I'm really asking is for an idea of its worth. The chair is lovely, with original wooden castors, carvings on back, arms and front of seat that are, what I've been told, Eastlake design.

Mrs. L. D. McC., Kansas City, MO

A. You are correct, your walnut Victorian armchair is in the substyle we call "Eastlake," named after the English Victorian tastemaker Charles Eastlake. It was a factory made piece, ca. 1880, and probably was part of a matching parlor suite with sofa and rocker. By itself I would place the value in the $250-350 range.

Hammered brass mirror frame

Arts & Crafts style tabouret

Hammered brass mirror frame

Q. What can you tell me about this mirror? It measures 10" and has a beautiful beveled glass. The back is heavy tin with an iron hanger. Please tell me what you can and what price it might bring on today's market. I presume it's Arts & Crafts period but I've never seen another like it.

Is this octagon-shaped table the same era? It is walnut, 15-1/2" across, 18-1/2" tall. What price?

L. P., Col. City, IN

A. Your interesting hammered brass mirror frame does look like the style of work that would have been done during the Arts & Crafts era, ca. 1905-20. Many workshops produced hand-hammered works in copper and brass, but those that are marked by a well-known firm will bring the highest prices. An unmarked example such as yours, provided it hasn't been over-polished (collectors want the original patina), might be valued in the $150-350 range.

The small table or "tabouret," as they are called, is also in the Arts & Crafts style although most furniture of that era was produced in oak. Walnut was not generally used by the major manufacturers such as the Stickleys or the Roycrofts. Again, signed examples bring the premium prices and original finishes are very important. Many smaller factories and even amateur craftsmen made pieces in this style at the time, and your piece may be of that origin. It does have nice keyed tenons through the legs, which shows quality construction. As a nice unmarked piece I would guess it might be valued in the $150-250 range.

Q. My mother called this a war chest, and told me that there were only about five ever made, and that one is in Thomas Jefferson's home, Monticello. Can you tell me if this is right, and what the value might be? It is in perfect condition.

A.A., Orlando, FL

A. Your pretty chest of drawers is an early piece but I haven't heard this design ever called a "war chest." It is a nice country-style piece likely hand-crafted around 1820-30 but I doubt Thomas Jefferson ever owned a similar piece and although a rather unique design, I doubt you could say for certain only a few were made. The woods appear to be cherry and maybe wavy birch. The style is transitional between the Federal style and the Classical. The shaped crest on top and the drawers with beveled edges or a rounded front are designs from the Classical style, but the delicate turned legs are carry-overs from the earlier Federal era. Country

Chest of drawers

craftsman often mixed various design elements in their pieces. Maybe your family has some idea of where it might have originated, but Pennsylvania or Ohio are possibilities. It looks to be in great condition and might be valued in the $1,000-1,600 range.

Q. Enclosed are pictures of my antique chair. I was told it is of Italian origin. Circa? I have had it for more than 40 years.

A.S., Ormond Beach, FL

A. Your nice armchair is a revival piece based on the 18th century French Louis XV style. It is nicely carved and finished. Although it is possible it was produced in Italy, it is more likely that it was produced somewhere else in Europe or even the United States. It is possibly 75 to 125 years old, and since it is a well-done piece in good condition, it might be valued in the $350-650 range today. In some markets it might even bring a bit more.

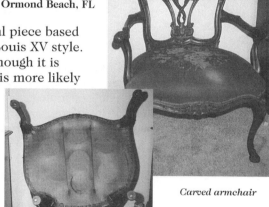

Carved armchair

Carved armchair seat

Q. Enclosed is a picture of an early sleeper/couch. It's in fairly good condition. I believe it's leather. It has an inner-spring and is quite heavy. It stands on wooden casters. The couch is 59-1/2" wide x 31-1/2" deep, 33-1/2" high (back) and 26-1/4" high (front). As I've had trouble locating any information, I would really appreciate your help. Is it Mission? Also I would like to know its age and value. Thank you.

C.R., Oconomowoc, WI

Mission Oak style sofa-sleeper

A. Your sofa-sleeper certainly appears to be in the general Mission Oak style although the best Mission Oak pieces usually have slats under the arms and in the back. Leading makers also featured details like corbels (brackets) under the arms and through-tenon construction. Of course any maker's label adds to the general value. Still, this is a nice piece and looks to be in fine condition with nice old upholstery. I think in the right market it might be valued in the $600-1,200 range. Of course, the right collector might pay more. *See Clocks & Furniture Tip #3.

Q. Could you please tell me something about the clock in this picture? What is the history and value? It's been with us for over 80 years, has no identification on it and no markings. It is 13" tall. Thank you very much.

D.R., La Crescent, MN

A. Your pretty clock is in the French Rococo style and was most likely made in Europe in the late 19th or early 20th century. It is nicely cast but I suspect it is a base metal with a gilded finish. If you can check the works by opening the back see if you can find any marks or wording. The clock and base could both be French but sometimes American-made clockworks were put in imported cases. Since it appears to be in great condition with no damages or serious wear it would have a nice value. Size is also a factor in value and I guess this piece is about 12" to 16" tall. If working and in great shape I think it might be valued in the $300-600 range or perhaps a bit more to the right collector.

French Rococo style clock

Q. I have enclosed photos of a revolving table. It has four open sections and is oak. The carving on the top and the sides is quite attractive. It measures 22" in height and is also 22" wide. I would really appreciate any information you could provide on this piece.

P.H., Manorville, NY

Oak bookcase/side table

Oak bookcase/side tabletop

A. Your attractive oak table is a combination bookcase/side table. The carving is attractive and appears to have been finished by hand. It shows fine workmanship and I would guess it might date from the 1910-1940 period. Well-made pieces with unique designs like this are always in demand. Your piece is unique enough to attract a good deal of collector interest. Depending on the local market I feel it might be valued in the $350-650 range.

Q. This coffee table is reportedly from France. The wood is mahogany and the marble is white. It measures 60" long, 30" wide and 20" high. I think that when this was made they did not have coffee tables, so this was most likely a cut-down hall table.

F.G.T., Alexandria, LA

A. Your marble top table does appear to be a mid-Victorian parlor table that was cut down to make a coffee table. This was done quite often in the 1940s and 1950s. These "re-worked" tables can still sell quite well although their antique value may be lowered. In the right market your table might sell in the $400-800 range.

Marble top parlor table

Arts & Crafts style oak armchair

Q. Enclosed please find pictures of a chair that belonged to my grandfather. It was passed on to my father and thereafter to me. Do you have any idea of its origin or value? It has been refurbished over the years.

H.E., Grovetown, GA

A. Your hefty oak armchair is basically a simple Arts & Crafts design although the curved ends of the arms and shaped feet were not used on the very plain "Mission Oak" style also popular in the early years of the 20th century. In refinished and reupholstered condition I suspect it might be valued today in the $250-325 range.

Q. My wife and I inherited this clock. It is marked "Ansonia" and measures 18-1/2" x 16-1/2". We would appreciate information.

B.B., Bellmore, NY

A. Your Ansonia mantel clock is a fine example of the decorative mantel pieces this firm was producing in the 1880s and 1890s. Old catalogs show that each model was given a name, however, I wasn't able to identify the figure on your piece in the catalog reprint I looked through. The classical figure with armor

Ansonia mantel clock

perhaps represents Julius Caesar. The piece is made of patinated metal and has a wonderful original finish. In good running order, without any damage to the metal designs, I believe this piece might be valued in the $1,000-1,500 range.

Q. I purchased this coffee table at an estate sale a few years ago and hope you can give me some information and value for it. It stands 14" high and the top is 55" long and 28" across. I was told the bottom of the table and the inner area on the top is abalone. Really enjoy your column and am looking forward to any information you can give me.

C.N., Tolland, CT

Coffee table

A. Your most unusual coffee table is certainly a unique piece. It is rather a fantasy design, perhaps loosely based on ornate Venetian gilt furniture of the 18th and 19th century. It is possible that the oval base and inner rim are decorated with a thin veneer of abalone shell. My best guess is that it was produced in the 1955-75 era. Although not antique, it has lots of pizzazz and might have a decorator value in the $400-600 range or perhaps more to just the right buyer.

Late Victorian library table

Q. **This table was given to our son-in-law by his grand-mother years ago. We have always wondered about the age, era and value. I think it is cherry wood. I feel it's very unusual and valuable.**
B.J.S., Wykoff, MN

A. Your late Victorian library table is an unusual and decorative piece. It features nice carving, bobbin-turning and bold spiral-turnings with ball-and-claw feet. The wood could be cherry or perhaps walnut or mahogany. It is also possible that it is a less expensive hardwood given a dark reddish mahogany finish. That was often done in the period of 1890-1910. Such unusual tables are always in demand in the collecting market. You don't give a size, but I'm guessing it's about 24" x 40" or so. In the right market I'd think it could be valued in the $400-600 range, but the right buyer might pay more.

Extra large wall regulator

Q. Enclosed are a few photos of a clock I recently purchased. It is about 7' tall, is a Waterbury and it seems to keep perfect time. I would like to know the value of it.

J.L, El Dorado, AK

A. I'm afraid your photos of this large clock were too dark to reproduce, but I'm having a drawing from a catalog of a similar Regulator reproduced here. This example was produced by the Ansonia Clock Company in the mid-1880s but since the Waterbury Clock Company was producing very similar clocks it can be used as a comparison. These extra large wall regulators were used throughout the country in the last quarter of the 19th century and into the 20th. Generally they would have been used in public buildings such as courthouses or perhaps train depots. They often came into walnut or oak cases and the style and ornateness of the base as well as the condition of the movement are factors in determining their value today. From what I could see in your photos you appear to own several antique clocks so perhaps you have followed the clock market. You don't really give any specific details on your piece but it appears to have a walnut case with nice detailing. If it has a time-and-strike movement and is in top running condition I've seen similar pieces listed in the $4,000-6,000 range with some outstanding versions perhaps bringing a bit more.

Q. I found this rocker in a landfill some years ago. It seems to be all original and in good, sturdy shape. The old circular green paper attached to the bottom says: "John A. Dunn Company Chairs and Ratian Products NO. 149-6" (the paper is torn so there might have been more numbers.) Any information you might have will be appreciated.

A.K.C., Mountain Home, Idaho

A. Your rocking armchair is in the Federal Revival style and was probably produced by this firm in the 1920s when such revival styles were widely popular. It looks like it could stand a good refinishing and some new upholstery. Refinished in top condition I would guess it might be valued in the $100-150 range.

Federal Revival style rocking armchair

Reader Update

It was a real pleasure for me to receive the following informative letter from my long time associate, Connie Morningstar. Connie is now retired but was the original "answer expert" for *The Antique Trader Weekly*, with her column "Ask Connie" starting in 1972. She has written extensively over the years and has a special interest in decorative arts and American furniture. It was great to have her expert input on the following subjects:

"Dear Kyle, Regarding the John A. Dunn rocker also in your Dec. 2001 column (page 38), I found that Dunn was born in Westminister, Mass., in 1831. He moved to Garnder, Mass., in 1855 where he was employed by the Heywood Chair Manufacturing Company. A number of associations followed until 1902 when then sole owner Dunn incorporated the business as the John A. Dunn Company. Manufacturing remained in Gardner but large warehouses were located in Chicago, Boston and St. Paul, Minn. I have no record of the firm after 1903. I do have to keep my hand in, don't I? Best, Connie"

Q. I have been a subscriber to *Antique Trader's Collector Magazine* for many years. Your column was a great addition when they changed the format. I hope I have enclosed enough description of these items to obtain information as to the age and value of them. Sideboard: 39-1/2" highest point (with back), 66" long, 37-1/2" wide, legs 17-1/4", two drawers (in the middle), one 8-3/4", one 8-1/4" door on each end, original pulls (no other holes). It is dovetailed throughout. Top drawer has a silverware sliding tray.

Federal Revival style sideboard

Secondary wood appears to be pine. The top drawer has a center lock. It looks to be veneer. Desk: roll top 34" in height, 24" wide, 15" deep. It is in excellent condition. I think it is oak. I appreciate your help. Thank you.

Mrs. P.W., Ozark, AR

Roll-top desk

A. Your sideboard is in the Federal Revival style and probably dates from the 1920s. It is nicely made with lovely mahogany veneer. It may have been part of a dining room suite at that time. As a well-made copy of an early 19th century piece I feel it might be valued today in the $250-500 range. The little roll-top desk and chair also probably date from the 1915-35 era. The very simple lines and tall legs indicate it's not as early as many of the larger roll-tops. It appears to be in various hardwoods rather than solid oak. I believe the set could be valued in the $350-650 range.

Q. We have been unable to find any information on several items. An estimate of value on these items would be frosting on the cake. The first item is a footed clock, made in The People's Republic of China. It is made of brass with enamel overlay. There are front and back doors of beveled glass. The second item is a cuckoo clock. The word "Germany" is printed on the brass works inside of the clock and on the wood on the back of the clock. There are two little doors, top front, one for the

Modern clock

cuckoo bird and the other for a little man sitting. The first appears on the hour and the latter on the quarter and half hour. The third is an anniversary clock, stamped "made in Germany" and made of brass.

E.L., Bonifay, FL

A. Thanks for your letter and photos. Your first clock with the "People's Republic of China" mark is, of course, quite modern. The cloisonné work does look like fine quality, and the overall design is meant to emulate French designs of the late 19th century. Since major trade with China only began here during the 1970s, I believe this piece is less than 20 years old—a nice decorative piece but not an antique. German cuckoo clocks are classics that have been carved and exported in great numbers since the 19th century. Your carved design is fairly simple and the word "Germany" would indicate early 20th century production. In top working order

German cuckoo clock

I'd guess it might be valued in the $200-$400 range. The glass-covered anniversary clock appears to be a fine quality piece likely made in Germany between the wars. It's another classic design and values depend on the type of works and detailing. Perhaps a fair range in top working order would be $250-$500.

Anniversary clock

Reader Update

This letter provides more information on the People's Republic of China enameled clock. In part it reads: "China made clocks copying European makers for the English and American trade from the 1880s through the late 1940s as well as clocks (mostly bracket and wall types) for their own use.

"The clock manufacturing trade was situated mostly in Jianjiang, Province of Sichuan and after 1950-55 moved to Beijing. The clock belonging to E.L., Bonifay, Fla. is a Japy Freres copy and I doubt if the enamel work (champleve) is overlay work but more inlaid as champleve is another form of cloisonné.

"Usually these clocks have an applied tag on them of enameled brass stating where made that's easily removed and the entire exterior metal works (are) usually gilt brass instead of bronze dore. Later on, due to political unrest and other problems, the clock makers of China were moved to Beijing and the work became quite coarse and shoddy until, due to a demand from U.S. and European importers, they became more sophisticated in their production again, after 1960…"

Rabbi Feivel Shiman-Gedalia
The Painted Lady, Inc., Chicago

Rabbi Shima-Gedalia, a Life Member of the American Watchmakers Institute Assoc., Estate Jewellers Assoc. of America and the National Assoc. of Watch & Clock Collectors, and retired horologist, also notes the E.L's bracket-style clock, without seeing it close-up and from the photo presented, could be valued in the $400-$1,200 range. That depends on when and where it was made, as well as how it was made. Some People's Republic of China bracket clocks have sold for as much as $2,800 with some for as low as $150.

Q. The enclosed Victorian chair has been in my family since before my time (I am 83). Frankly, I don't ever remember seeing it without its cover. I am in the process of selling ever so many antiques that I fell heir to, but I have misgivings about this chair as I don't recall having ever seen a Victorian

Mid-19th century rocking chair

rocking chair. Is this for real, and what would you think its value would be?

G.L.C., Grand Rapids, MI

A. You do indeed have a nice rocking chair dating from the mid-19th century. The rocking chair first appeared in the late 18th century and by the mid-19th century was widely produced. The upholstered examples such as your were more of the "upscale" models. A high-back upholstered version is today called a "Lincoln" rocker because Abraham Lincoln was sitting in one at Ford's Theatre the night he was assassinated. Your "barrel-back" style would also date from the 1850-70 era. It appears to have nice velvet upholstery in top condition and a nice finish on the walnut frame. In the right market I would say your piece might be valued in the $400-$600 range.

Q. This chair belonged to my wife's great-grandparents, who lived in Maine. It has older re-upholstery that covers what I believe is the original upholstery. The frame is oak and has the original finish in very good condition. It has a brass rod to adjust the angle of the back. I would appreciate it if you could comment on the age, origin and value of these items.

B.M., Plainfield, IL

Morris armchair

A. Your oak armchair is an American factory-made piece, ca. 1900. It is a form of the classic "Morris" chair, an early type of recliner first introduced in England by the famous designer William Morris. You often find Morris chairs in the simpler "Mission Oak" style today, but his fancier designs also have good market appeal. I think it could be valued in the $400-$800 range today at least.

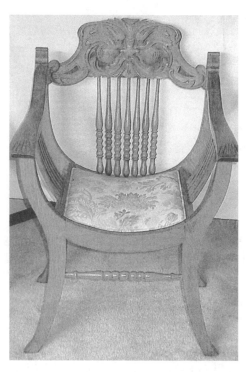

Novelty oak chair

Q. I look for your section in the *Collector Magazine* each month when it arrives in the mail. I have wanted to write for some time. I bought the pictured chair at an antique mall several years ago. I've looked for it in books from time to time but haven't found it. I was told at the time I bought it that it was called a "West Wind Chair," and may have been the captain's chair for a dining room set. The name seems reasonable from the design on the back. I love the chair, but I would really like to know more about it. The wood, I think, is oak. The seat is not original. I can find no manufacturer's markings on the chair anywhere. I'm more interested in origin or history than price, but anything you can tell me would be great. Thanks in advance for anything you can tell me about it.

E.M.W., Moses Lake, WA

A. Your attractive chair is an example of the novelty chairs so popular in the late 19th and early 20th century. They generally were used as accent pieces in hallways, parlors or libraries. It is oak, and the overall style is referred to as "Roman," being a take-off on an early Roman design. The carving in the crest is referred to by various names like "old man of the North," "West" or "North" wind, etc. It's basically a grotesque face design based on 17th-century baroque motifs. Since the frame and legs are fairly simple ones, the value wouldn't be quite as high as more highly carved examples. Still, I would say a value range of $300-$650 would be fair.

Q. Enclosed is a picture of a chair that has been identified as a "bustle chair." I purchased it some years ago at an auction. The wood has the original finish, but it has been reupholstered. I have tried to find information

about the chair but have not been successful. I would appreciate it if you could provide any information as to the era, the use,
and probable value. I enjoy your column in
the magazine.

G.P., Mt. Vernon, IN

A. You have an interesting little late
Victorian settee. I suppose someone
could call it a "bustle" chair, but I don't see
that it would have made it easier for a
woman wearing a bustle to sit down comfort-
ably. Most likely it was just a novelty piece.
The design is in the Victorian Eastlake style,
popular from about 1880 to 1895. The wood
is likely black walnut with some walnut burl

Late Victorian settee

panels. The upholstery is a nice complement and having new upholstery
shouldn't hurt the value. I would guess this piece would be valued in the $500-
700 range, depending on the local market for Victorian furniture.

Tilt-top table

Q. I bought this piece in 1940. It
is a tilt top table—27" square
and 27" high with black and gold
paint. I am looking forward to seeing the information. Thank you,
again!

J.K., Johnson City, NY

A. Your tilt-top table appears to be
a revival-style design meant to
imitate Victorian laquerware tables.
It probably dates to the 1920s. I
suspect the color designs are transfer-printed rather than hand-painted.
If that is the case, I'd guess it might
be valued in the $150-300 range. If it
should happen to be hand-painted
the value would be quite a bit more.

Q. I own this grandfather clock. It is mahogany and marked "Jung Hans
Westminster Chime Clock, Hastings, #2879." There is an old, yellowed
card inside the clock—a square with an 8-pointed star with the word "Jung"
inside and the letter "J" under the word "Jung". What call you tell me about

its age, origin and estimated value? Any help you can give me will be appreciated.

J.B., Chicago, IL

A. Although this clock was made in Germany, it was made for the English or American market. The simple style of case would help date it from the 1910-40 era. It probably has a top quality works with nice chimes. In top working order I suspect it could be valued in the $1,800-$2,800 range.

Grandfather clock

Q. This oak table is 20" tall, 30" across and has hand-carved legs, and metal (cast iron?) recently painted gold claw with bluish tint with bubble glass ball feet. The apron just above the legs is one piece formed around. The piece contains old screws. I purchased this piece around 40 years ago from a friend. It had belonged to her parents or grandparents. It is obviously quite old. If possible, I would like to know its age and value. I enjoy your column.

A.J.S., Peoria, AZ

A. Your round oak table with the turned legs ending in cast-metal claw feet with glass balls is a fine example of factory-made pieces from the 1890-1915

Round oak table

era. Such attractive and practical pieces remain very popular in today's antiques market. In top condition I believe this table could sell in the $250-400 range.

Q. I would like your opinion on the chair pictured. I purchased this chair in Kaoshung, Taiwan, in the late 1950s. At that time I thought it was made of teak. It is hand-carved. Is there any value to it and where might I find a buyer?
P.F.C., Orlando, FL

A. Your ornately carved armchair may well have been made in Taiwan about the time you purchased it. It has a certain decorative appeal, but what I have learned about the market for older Chinese furniture is that the most advanced collectors prefer the very simple traditional style pieces which would have been what were used in an upper class Chinese home. The ornately carved pieces such as yours in general were made for export to the West, starting in the later 19th century and some examples are probably still being turned out. They can feature some nice hand work but the market is with

Ornately carved armchair

people who like showy, decorative pieces. Presuming this piece does date from the 1950s, I'd say it might sell in the right market in the $200-$400 range but could go for more to just the right buyer.

Q. I enjoy your column on antiques. I am enclosing a picture of an old icebox that was in our cellar when we bought our farmhouse back in 1965. My husband knew the previous owner since he was a child and he said they had this as long as he can remember. He is 77 years old now. It is very elaborate with the carving on it, mirror, etc. In the top is a lid to lift off to put ice in (see knob on lid). Doors open to store food in. I am enclosing a picture of doors open. The faucet is where water comes out from melted ice. Could you give us information about how old this would be, what it is worth and anything else you can tell us about it.
E.D.M., Southhampton, NJ

Late Victorian ice box

Late Victorian ice box interior

A. You were lucky enough to find and preserve one of the fanciest and most unique late Victorian ice boxes I have ever seen! Most of the ones on the market today are much simpler oak models produced during the first quarter of the 20th century. Your example is truly a high quality piece of Victorian furniture, decorative enough to have been kept in a fine dining room of the era. The wood is probably black walnut and the overall style would today be referred to as Victorian Eastlake. It is a very rare survival, especially with the decorative superstructure with the turnings, carving, shelves and mirror. It even appears to retain the original hardware and lining. Since this is such a one-of-a-kind piece it is a bit difficult to set a specific value. The demand for this should be very high. Just a ballpark range I think that might be realistic is $1,500-$3,000. This is a case where the final sale price is really the best gauge of value.

Q. I have searched everywhere to find someone to tell me about the item in the pictures I'm sending you. I saw your column and felt like at last, I have the answer. I look forward each week to see the goodies you help people with. The secretary I bought in Atlanta. I don't know if it's made of poplar or what. The carving on it looks similar to Eastlake—it has the original glass in the door and all the original hardware.

H.J.T., Casper, WY

A. You are correct that the style of your unique secretary-bookcase is Victorian Eastlake. I don't believe I've run across a similar example with the three-section tall, narrow case. It was probably factory-made in the 1880-1900 era and may be a hardwood such as you mention. Although black walnut was the most popular wood for pieces such as this, sometimes less expensive woods were used and stained to resemble walnut. Because of its nice, smaller size, it would probably sell even faster than the larger versions, which don't always fit well in modern homes. In the right market I think this piece might sell in the $1,800-2,800 range.

Victorian Eastlake secretary-bookcase

Q. Enclosed is a photo of an end table that has been in the family for many years. It measures 24" by 13" across the top and is 22" high. The carved figure appears to be a gladiator or knight carrying a sword and a shield bearing an image of a face. It is in excellent condition.

R.J.K., Cheektowaga, NY

A. Your table appears to be a half-round console-style table and may be made of walnut. Although the overall look of the piece is Victorian, this style of half-round table was most popular in the 1920-40 era. It may date back to the late 19th century but it would be necessary to check the construction of the piece to know for

Half-round console-style table

certain. It is quite unusual with the carved gladiator so it would have a strong market appeal. I would guess it might be valued in the $300-600 range due to the carved design.

Floor model humidor copper interior

Q. I am an 82-year-old avid reader of your column who, needless to say, respects your knowledge and opinions. Because of my advanced age and the process of attrition, I have come into my possession many lovely old things; since I wish to divide these things as fairly as possible among the children in my will, I must have some idea of value. I have chosen a few articles—which seems to be a bit greedy—but I'm sure you will decide

Floor model humidor

which items to use. The first two belonged to my husband's grandfather who emigrated from Ireland in 1850. One is a solid mahogany standing humidor— 32" high, 21" wide and 13" deep. The legs are hand carved Roman gladiators. It is completely copper-lined and has a copper mesh square "frame" on the left door into which a damp cork square fits. My inexperienced eye finds no manufacturer's mark except 2" stamped black numbers 0600 and the obvious marks of a missing paper sticker.

V.L., Tuscon, AZ

A. Your attractive humidor is a fancy example of the type of floor model humidors widely produced around the 1920s. This is an especially fine and unusual version with the copper lining, nicely veneered case and the finely carved legs. I recently answered another question on a table of this era with similar Roman gladiator forming the front leg. Without a mark it would be difficult to determine which factory produced either of these pieces but they certainly were top of the line at that time. Today, because of the fine details and top condition I wouldn't be surprised if this cabinet could sell in the $600-1,000 range to the right collector.

Colonial Revival chair

Q. Your column is most interesting. We live in the country in Texas. A neighbor was going to put two chairs in the trash. He ended up putting them in my garage. Could you help identify the chair, period and worth? The seat says "150" on the bottom. The front of the chair has a slight curve. The height is 33", depth is 20" and width is 17". It appears to be oak.

S.P., Kerrville, TX

A. Your dining chair appears to be an example of a simple Colonial Revival piece probably produced in the 1920s. The front turned legs reflect the designs used then, which copied 17th and 18th century furniture. The chairs may need some restoration but in top condition the pair might be valued in the $75-125 range.

Q. Enclosed find a picture of an old secretary desk. It has three drawers on the bottom, under the desk. The wood is believed to be mahogany. With this meager information, would you please try to tell me how old it is and its approximate value as an antique. Thank you.

K.R., Tracy, MN

A. Your photo is a bit dark and cropped off, but from what I can see I believe this secretary is a Federal Revival style piece likely produced around the 1920s. The wood is probably mahogany veneer. Such Colonial revival styles were widely produced during that era and are becoming collectible today. The value depends on the quality of the construction, wood and detailing. Your piece appears to be fairly simple without very much carved detail. If the finish is in good condition, I'd guess it might be valued in the $400-$800 range. More ornate examples can sell for much more.

Federal Revival style secretary

Brass and cast-metal plant stand

Q. I love learning more about antiques and your column is one of my favorite resources. My question concerns a stand, possibly a plant stand. I have enclosed pictures. It is 29" high and is made of pot metal and brass. The center ball appears to be marble and I have replaced the top with a piece of marble. Can you tell what you think it is and its age and value? Thank you.

L.M., Havre, MN

A. Your brass and cast-metal plant stand is typical of the types that were popular in the late 19th and early 20th centuries. The ball is probably onyx and the top shelf would probably have been onyx also. Marble is a good second choice. As is, I would think this piece could be valued in the $150-$250 range.

Q. Enclosed find pictures of an old rocker that we have. It could be one of the first "recliners" that I have seen. The back reclines at different levels. The wood is oak. I realize this is not much, as far as information is concerned, but could you tell us about how old it is and if it has any antique value? Thank you.

K.R., Tracy, MN

Early 20th century rocker-recliner

A. Your interesting rocker-recliner follows the general style of Mission Oak furniture of the early 20th century. A few recliner designs were introduced in the later 19th century but they don't seem to have gone into mass-production until decades later. The tall back with the flared wings is not typical of Mission furniture. Does it appear to have always been upholstered? Most Mission armchairs had wooden backs with vertical slats. If the back and seat were always upholstered I suspect originally they would have had a much plainer upholstery like leather or mohair. It is an interesting early 20th century piece and could probably be valued in the $350-450 range because of its unique design.

Q. Enclosed is a photo of one of two chairs I own. I think they are covered in tapestry.

B.K., Piscataway, NJ

A. These armchairs appear to be a version of Classical Revival furniture and probably date from the 1930s or 1940s. They appear to have some nice carved detail and might be valued in the $150-$200 range for the two.

Classical Revival armchairs

Q. Enclosed are photos of objects for which I'd like to know the approximate date of manufacture and value. The first is a table/desk that has a paper tag on the back which reads "Master made Furniture No. 341." It stands 30-7/8" high, is 36" wide and 20-1/8" deep. It has two drawers and three cubbyholes. It was purchased by my grandmother at an estate sale in the 1930s. The second is an old rocker that has been in my family for at least four generations. It was reupholstered some time in the 1940s or 1950s. It stands 35" high, the width at arm rests is 20-1/2". There are no visible markings.

W.H., Synsset, NY

Spinet desk

A. Your little "spinet desk" was a popular piece during the 1920s and 1930s. The design is based loosely on early 19th century spinet pianos; their "early American" look appealed to buyers of that era. Some old Victorian spinet pianos had the works taken out and were converted to desks, but this piece was just made as a small desk. Such pieces were usually made with walnut or mahogany veneers. Your piece appears to need refinishing so that would keep the value down a bit. If it was carefully restored and refinished it might be valued today in the $150-300 range.

Your rocker is a Victorian piece, factory-produced about the 1880s or 1890s. This type of turned "spindle-style" furniture was very popular then and many rockers were made in this style and had upholstery panels used in the backs and seats. Your piece looks like it has nice finish and if it is good and sturdy I think it could sell today in the $175-250 range.

Victorian rocker

Q. Enclosed are photographs of a writing desk that my grandmother owned and gave to me. There are no nails and it has wooden pegs, except for the brass hinges and handles. This is over 100 years old. Could you give me some value on this piece of furniture?

H.G.W., Marion, IN

Mahogany veneer writing desk

A. Your mahogany veneer writing desk looks like a type that would have been stylish in the very late 19th or early 20th century. It is a take-off on Classical Revival furniture that was popular at that time. The finish appears to be excellent but I notice several of the brass pulls are missing. With some searching you may be able to find some that match the originals. As is, I'd guess this piece would be valued in the $350-450 range.

Country Collectibles & Folk Art

$Q.$ I have a weathervane that I hope you can identify and date. I purchased it recently in a secondhand store. It is made of two copper sheets soldered together. The head is made of zinc. It is 31" long and 9" tall at the head. I suspect it is very early 19th century due to the crude soldering. There is nothing on the piece to identify it, no engraving or stamping. The rider has become unseated and from handling, the arms have become unsoldered from the body. I am reluctant to have these re-soldered if it would detract from the value. Kovel's 1998 price guide lists a Horse, Sulky with Driver, 32" long at $6,500, so naturally I am interested in its authenticity.

I.C., Rochester, WA

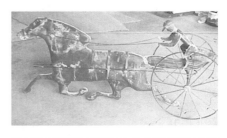

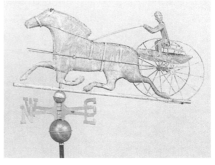

Horse and sulky weathervanes

$A.$ I'm sorry to be the bearer of bad tidings, but I'm afraid your horse and sulky weathervane (shown top) is a modern reproduction. I have had a photo of the same piece copied here from a 1992 reproduction wholesale catalog. Several antique-style shapes have been produced in the Orient in recent years and their crudeness is one of the danger signs to watch for. Early weathervanes, especially of this style, were carefully finished and soldered. Unfortunately, copper is easy to "age" using chemicals or simply leaving it outside to weather for a few months. The original wholesale price was $80 for this piece but most collectors would avoid them; their main appeal is just as a decorative accent. I hope you didn't get stung too badly, but weathervanes are one of those areas of "folk art" which require a lot of study in order to find quality early examples.

Metal spectacles

$Q.$ Please find enclosed pictures of a pair of spectacles. Could they be a trade sign for an old eye doctor? The frame is some sort of cast metal and the lenses are mirrors. There is a chain attached to one side and a bracket for mounting on the opposite end of the chain, probably for wall mounting. The only marking is the word "Wilton" stamped in the metal. The mirrors are held in by cardboard with four metal clips. The measurements are: width, overall, 21", height, 8-3/4", lens, oval, 6-3/4" by 5-1/4" inside, and 8-3/4" by 7-1/8" outside. Any information regarding date, use, maker and value would be appreciated.

J.H., Milburn, OK

A. Your metal spectacles most likely were a figural trade sign for an eye doctor. They are probably cast iron and the Wilton firm was active early in the 20th century making cast iron items, most notably figural bottle openers. From the style of these glasses and the fact that the mirrors are held in place by cardboard rather than wood I would say this pair probably dates from the 1910-30 era. Early painted wood trade signs from the 19th century are very much in demand but I don't recall coming across many that were made of solid cast metal like this pair. Your pair is interesting and nicely done, so I'd guess they might be valued in the $300 to $600 range, but might sell for more to the right collector.

Q. I am enclosing two pictures of a grinding wheel. The seat is 29" from the ground, the top of the wheel 39-1/2", the wheel 20-1/2" across the center and 1-3/4" thick. There is a large "R-W" on the top of the seat, raised letters. I would appreciate any information you could give me, including the value. A sample copy of *Collector* was sent to me, and after reading your column, I decided to subscribe. I'm learning a lot and look forward to each issue.

P.G., Yancey, TX

Whetstone

A. Your grinding wheel or "whet-stone" was a piece of machinery necessary on early farms and in black-smiths' shops in order to sharpen and hone tools and knives. Your example appears to have a bent steel frame which would lead me to think it is probably from the early 20th century. I don't know if the initials in the seat stand for the maker of the whole machine or just the iron portions. Items like this fall into the category of "primitives," and collectors of such pieces like them for their decorative appeal or perhaps as part of a restoration project. There probably are people interested in your whetstone, but I don't think the demand would be high or the value great.

Q. Can you give me any information about this old butter churn? It is marked "Bellows Falls Vermont-Vermont Farm Machine Company."

L.M., Vidisi, TX

A. Your interesting crank-action butter churn on frame is certainly a very large size and must have been meant for major use on a dairy farm, perhaps. I found designs for similar pieces in a reproduction of the 1897 Sears catalog and they were originally sold in several sizes. It is an interesting primitive, however, the size makes it a little hard to display and would probably keep the collector interest down a bit. In the right market, it might be valued in the $100-$200 range.

Crank-action butter churn

Bench wringer

Q. I am enclosing two photos of a folding bench ringer stand in good condition. It has been in the family at least 80 years. It is in excellent condition and the hinges are in good shape. Please advise as to value.

E.B., Blaine, WA

A. You have an interesting primitive item relating to home life around the turn of the 20th century. I don't know how this bench wringer operated but it was obviously meant to ease the labors of the housewife on washday. Many such unique pieces were designed and produced from about 1880 to 1910. Once again, however, the value depends more on how a modern collector could display or use this piece rather than on its actual age or uniqueness. Someone interested in washday artifacts might find it intriguing, but value depends on what a person would offer. Somewhere in the $75-$150 range probably wouldn't be out of line.

Q. The windmill weight was on a windmill on our ranch that was victim of a tornado in the early 1930s. I found the windmill weight in a shed some 40 years ago and have it mounted on the wall in our family room. Could you give me an estimate on the value?

E.D., Gillette, WY

A. Early cast-iron figural windmill weights are very collectible today. I didn't find a listing for your specific "short-tailed" horse, but some other horse-form weights can sell in the $2,500-$3,500 range in the right market.

Cast-iron figural windmill weight

Enameled wood-burning stove

Q. Recently I read some back issues of *Collector Magazine* and ran across the issue on stoves. Immediately the stove in my grandmother's house came to mind. She says it came with the house when she bought it approximately 60 years ago and she still lights a fire in it to warm her kitchen. It is a Lady Hibbard made by Hibbard, Spencer, Bartlett and Company, Chicago, Ill. The serial number is 36 18 56. What is the approximate age and value? My grandmother and I would appreciate any information.

R.H., Arena, WI

A. Your grandmother's enameled wood-burning stove appears to be a fairly late model, as far as such stoves go. The simple design with a creamy white finish looks to me like it should date the stove to about the 1920s. By that time, wood-burning stoves were fast disappearing from the market as electricity and gas became more available. In rural areas such stoves remained popular for a longer period, into the 1930s at least. There is an interest in old wood-burning cook stoves or ranges, but the older, black cast-iron models with nickeled trim are most in demand today. However, someone restoring a 1920s period kitchen might find this piece of interest. I'd say the value might be in the $300-$600 range, but it perhaps could bring more in the right market.

Q. I have this early stove, marked "Regal Oak," made by The Brinkman Stove Co. of Cleveland, Ohio. It's numbered 213. I can't find any information on the stove, even though I live in the Cleveland area. I really enjoy *Collector Magazine* and your column.

T.M., Brook Park, OH

A. Your "Regal Oak" round stove also probably dates from the 1900-30 era. It is a simple form without the fancy detailing that attracts serious collectors. If it is clean, not rusted and ready to use, it might be valued the $300-$600 range.

"Regal Oak" round stove

Q. I have enjoyed your articles that are published in
Collector Magazine regarding identification and
values of items submitted by the readership. I have
purchased this scrimshaw piece and would appreciate it
very much if you could give me any assistance whatsoever
in identification and value. I have used a "black" light,
and it maintains its ivory color. The total length is
16-1/4"; it is 3-1/2" at the widest part, and tapers to 2". It
bears the following inscription: "Whaler Tapaz off Mari-
giesas [not sure of the spelling] Is Jan 1880." It also has
initials "J. A." and "J_Ne_s (James?) F. Allen." The top
photo shows the back of the piece. The middle photo
shows a close up of the whaling ship. The bottom photo
shows the entire front of the piece. The work is very
intricate and finely done. Again, any information you
could provide for me would be greatly appreciated.

B.R., Port Charlotte, FL

Scrimshaw piece

A. Scrimshaw (pieces carved from whales' teeth and
ivory) is a big field of collecting but in recent years has been swamped by
modern fakes. From your photo I can't be completely certain but I suspect this
piece was cast from resin to resemble a whale bone and then incised. A great
many similar pieces are on the market and you should only buy scrimshaw from
dealers who will guarantee its authenticity. The flattened end of this piece might
show fine parallel saw marks and likely does not show the fine graining in real
ivory. You might try the "hot needle" test on a small, inconspicuous spot. Heat a
needle red hot and try to push it into the material. If it is resin, the needle will
penetrate it, at least a little. It won't penetrate real ivory.

*Part of a home
vegetable slicer*

Q. I have enclosed a photo of, I believe, some kind of a
household item. I have been trying to get a fix on it
for two years and would be grateful for help.

C.T., Covina, CA

A. Thanks for your letter and the photo of your "mystery
item." I'll be happy to run it here and see if any
readers have a clue as to its original use. It looks like the
metal band might swing down, and the curved part reminds
me of old potato mashers. Any other ideas?

Reader Update

Re: *Collector Magazine & Price Guide*, May 2001, page 21--The "mystery item" is part of The Home Vegetable Slicer patented Feb. 22, 1898. I have a well-used complete unit with its paper label which describes its Instructions, Points of Merit and the maker: Catawissa Specialty Mf'g Co., Limited on Catawissa, Pa. My grandmother used it in 1900 for making Saratoga Chips, now known as potato chips. My mother frequently used it as a cabbage cutter for making coleslaw. The part shown in the article is the "pusher block" which pushed the vegetables over a set of serrated blades which were fastened in the bottom of an open rectangular wooden trough. The trough is approximately 2-3/4" wide by 1-1/2" high (inside dimensions) and 20-1/2" long. Six blades produce the slices while the slanted end of the pusher forces the vegetables forward and downward. The metal wire device pulls the vegetables back on the return stroke! And it really works!
Mike Graham

Thanks for the info, Mike--Kyle

Home vegetable slicer or kraut cutter

Several more readers wrote in to explain that the mystery item shown in the May 2001 issue was used as part of an old-time vegetable or kraut cutter. It was used to push down the food being cut and keep it in the tray of the cutter while protecting the fingers and hand of the user. One reader even sent a shot of her cutter complete with this device. My thanks to Mary H., M. Morgan and J. Carroll for their informative update.

Q. I appreciate and enjoy your column. It seems I have a lot of company. In a recent issue of the *Collector*, your column shows very many more inquiries. I would also like to be a part of it. I am enclosing two pictures of two canes for your inspection, comments and valuation. The curved cane is of a wood unknown to me. I am speculating that it was at one time a living plant that was stripped of its leaves or branches and left to age to its present prickly appearance. The second cane is of light and dark woods, with an ivory inlay and several ivory ring separators. It disassembles into four pieces. Most prominent, of course, is the clenched fist handle, which suggested an African relationship, but over the years the clenched fist symbol has also been adopted by other cultures and movements. Any pertinent information on these objects would be greatly appreciated.

Early cane and walking stick

Late 19th or early 20th century cane and walking stick

P.K., Hillsdale, NJ

A. You do have a couple of interesting canes. You are correct about the one being made from a natural branch that was stripped of branches and bark. I'm not sure what sort of tree or shrub would have such closely set thorns or tiny branchlets, but it makes a decorative piece, perhaps valued in the $75-100 range. The other cane or walking stick is much more desirable with the mixture of woods, inlay and the fist handle. It probably dates from the late19th or early 20th century so would not relate to more modern movements. A fist was a popular design on many early sticks of that era. You don't describe any of the other inscribed or inlaid designs and that is important in determining a value. Carved animals or names and inscriptions add greatly to the value of a piece like this, which would range from the low to upper hundreds with really rare examples bringing even more.

❧

Small corn stick pan

Q. Enclosed is a picture of a small corn stick pan. I'm wondering if it is a reproduction and what its value is. The overall length is 8-1/2" and width is 4". There are indentations for seven cornsticks. I appreciate your help. We enjoy your column very much.

J.C., Hampton, IA

A. I'm afraid from just a photo I really can't confirm if you have an original No. 262 Griswold Crispy Corn or Wheat Stick Pan or not. The original came out in the early 1930s, but reproductions are now on the market. An experienced dealer or collector in kitchen cast-iron wares would have to examine the piece to help you determine the age. Unless it is a family piece or one that you know the history of, you may have a hard time authenticating it. An original example in top condition might be valued in the $80-100 range.

Walnut box with marbles

Q. Some time ago—25 years—some friends and I were treasure hunting with coin detectors out West around an old mining camp (town?) not on any map. In one of the cabins we found some items, including this box with the marbles. I kept the box and all marbles I could locate. They are rough, not machine made. The only thing I did with the box was clean it up and use lemon oil on it. Any idea what it was used for and its value? Thanks.

F.H. Grand Forks, ND

A. I believe your interesting walnut box with marbles was probably used by some early fraternal organization or private club. Such boxes with various colored marbles could be used for voting purposes during meetings, each member selecting a color to represent his vote. You may have heard of someone being "black-balled." That happened when "no" votes, using the black balls, outnumbered the "yes" votes in white. This voting method could be used to accept a new member to the group or expel a member for some reason.

Q. I am sending you these photos of an Oriental vase. I believe this to be authentic and made out of ivory. I heated a needle until it was red-hot and the needle would not penetrate the vase. It stands 12-1/4" high, 7-3/8"

top, and a 5" base. Its weight is 9.89 lbs. This vase has been in the possession of the owners for many years and they have hired me to act as their agent to possibly sell this item. I have been in the antique business for many years and have never encountered such a pristine Oriental vase such as this. I am not as knowledgeable on the Oriental objects as I should be, so I am asking you if you think this is indeed ivory on an ebony base and the approximate value of the vase. Please notice on the bottom is some writing and you can read it with a good magnifier. Please keep up the good article and please let me know what you think this item is and its value.

C.M., Delco, NC

Oriental style vase

A. Thank you for your letter and the photos of the Oriental style vase. I appreciate your efforts to research this piece and trying the "hot needle" test. Although that test can be helpful, on some modern resins it may not be foolproof. In the view you took looking down into the piece I can see that the walls are very thick and somewhat rounded at the rim which is not typical of fine ivory carvings. Also, I cannot detect any overall fine veining which true ivory would have. The piece also seems to be very heavy compared to an antique ivory piece. Is that base attached to the vase? That would also be a sign that it is a more modern piece. You could have the piece examined first-hand by someone who specializes in Orientalia, but my feeling is that it is not true ivory and probably not too much over 25 or 35 years old.

Q. Enclosed you will find a photo of a basket. From my research I found that the basket is a Nantucket, swing handle, wood base, 3 deep rings, 8-1/2" x 13".

J.H., Los Angeles, CA

A. Your woven wicker basket with the high arched handle probably has some age but it does not really resemble the fine quality, tightly woven baskets

Woven wicker basket

woven over the years on Nantucket Island. They are in a class by themselves. Your piece is a nice country accent piece and might be valued in the $40-80 range.

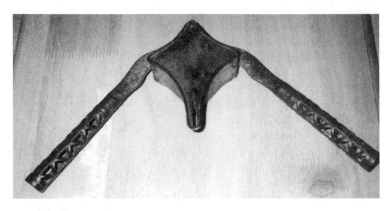

Orange reamer

Q. We are enclosing pictures of an antique article that we have been unable to identify. We have inquired of several antique dealers and farmers and numerous people who have no idea what this is used for. We purchased this at a farm auction about five years ago, and I suspect we paid too much for it at $40 but there were several bidders and no one knew what it was and everyone wanted it. I have included on the back of the pictures the measurements. This item is made of heavy metal, much like stove lifter handles, and weighs about 1 pound. It has riveted hinges on the movable parts. Box size is 2-1/4" x 2-1/4". Handle length from connection at top of box is 9-1/2". Open work handle is 4" long. The left open work handle has what appears to be a spring of some sort the full length of that open work handle and extends up handle, across the open end just inside the end. We would appreciate any information you could give us. We subscribe and enjoy your column and all of the other information. If you can identify this item do you have any idea of its value?

M. & J.S., Genesee, ID

A. I've done lots of research on this "whatsit," including old Sears catalog reprints and references on old tools and kitchen items. So far I've found nothing like it either. The pierced long iron handles would seem to indicate it was meant to be used around heat but what exactly the folding compartment was for I don't have a clue. Let's see if one of our sharp-eyed readers can identify what this curious antique was used for.

Reader Update

In answer to a "What's It?" question, I ran some time ago (November 2001 issue), I have received the following replies: J.R. of Rochester, NY suggests perhaps the mystery piece had something to do with shaping horseshoes.

However, L.S. of Visalia, CA wrote: "Your 'What is it' is an orange reamer. One very similar is shown on page 202 of Mary Walker's book, *Reamers – 200 Years.*"

Looks like the mystery is solved. Many thanks for this input.

Q. Enclosed are photos of a cast-iron letter box. My father was a rural mail carrier for years, but I don't know where he acquired this. It has two areas with raised lettering, one saying "US Mail," and one on the side that says "letter box." The top and front both have an American eagle emblem. The glass on the side is broken, so the paper underneath is water damaged and illegible. It measures 15" high, 7" wide and 12" deep. As you can imagine, it is very heavy. It looks to me as if the top hinged letter slot has been repaired. It doesn't show in the picture, but on the side it has a large hinge and bolts. One woman suggested that it might have hung in a hotel lobby. I'm interested to know the history of this mailbox and approximate value. I've searched the Internet and cast-iron collectible books, but have not come up with any information. I'm hoping you can solve the mystery.

Cast-iron letter box

M.C., Medicine Lodge, KS

A. You do have an interesting relic from our postal history. This cast-iron box does look like it was an official government issue, and I would think it dates from the first quarter of the 20th century. It may have been mounted inside a building, with the small window indicating mail pick-up times. Does it have mounting holes along one side or on the base? If so, it might also have been mounted outside on a building. Any repairs would, of course, lower the value somewhat, but overall this is an appealing piece with nice traces of the original paint. I haven't run across similar items offered recently either, but it has great "decorator" appeal and I'd think it might well sell in the $200-$400 range in the right market.

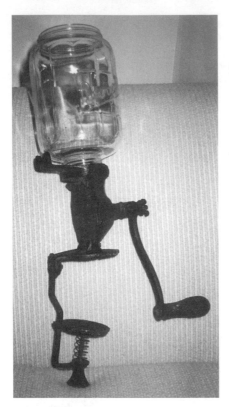

Wall-mounted coffee grinder

Q. Enclosed are photos of my "mystery item," possibly a coffee grinder. The glass jar says "Crystal no. 4" and the iron part behind the wheel crank says "ARCADE Freeport, ILL. No. 40 reg. U.S. pat. off. made in USA."

T.S., Southampton, NY

A. Your mystery item is indeed a wall-mounted coffee grinder. The Arcade company introduced a number of versions of these "Crystal" models in the early 20th century. Yours should have a metal lid on the top jar and a smaller receiving jar at the bottom. You might someday be able to replace these with matching old ones but it would be difficult. Prices seem to vary widely on these Crystal model grinders. We've listed an Arcade No. 3 in complete, original condition for $350, but a Model 25 with replaced bottom jar for only $150. I suspect your incomplete model would be at or below the lower price.

Q. I own this World War I shell casing, 11" high, of hammered brass, made by a disabled veteran. It says "PVT G.F. Ross 318 CoE," with a carving of a castle. On the reverse side is a lovely poppy. The underside is stamped in a circle "75 DE C. C.1539L. 17.D" and a small "F" appears on the outer rim.

V.L., Tuscon, AZ

A. Your hand-crafted brass shell casing is a prime example of what collectors now call "trench art," since it was done mainly by American soldiers in France, many of whom worked on pieces while recovering from combat injuries. For many years it was a neglected art form but today there is a growing appreciation for these very personal mementos of our Doughboys. Prices are rising on nice examples and some can sell in the low hundreds.

Brass shell casing

Q. **What can you tell me about this basket? Is it Nantucket?**
R.S., Euclid, OH

A. Your tightly woven covered basket does not look to me like a true "Nantucket" basket since these usually had deep sides and a high arched bentwood handle. My guess is that this is more likely a Chinese-made basket produced in the early 20th century. Such covered baskets, sometimes trimmed with Chinese coins and glass rings, were widely exported in the first decades of the last century. Nice ones can sell in the $40-80 range.

Covered basket

Tea caddy and birds

Q. **I would greatly appreciate your expertise on these items. The sewing box is over 100 years old and so are the birds.**
S.G., East Moline, IL

A. Your box is a lovely piece with its walnut burl exterior featuring a star inlaid on the lid. Although it is used for a sewing box, I think perhaps it was originally meant to be a tea caddy, hence the separate covered compartments inside and the lock on the front. The mirror inside the lid looks like it was added later. The size and form of this box indicate that it was made in England in the late 18th or early 19th century. Quality tea caddies of this type can now sell in the $300-600 range. It would be interesting to know more history on the carved birds. Whoever carved them left us some nice examples of folk art and they appear to be in great shape with the original paint. Values for folk art pieces vary widely and usually depend on the appeal a piece has to a specific collector. Certainly $50-100 each for your birds wouldn't be out of line.

Q. **I am enclosing pictures of two carved figures. They are 14" and 13" high. One figure is of Charlie Chaplin. It is all handmade with a wind-up mechanical back.**

Carved wooden figures

On the bottom of the large one is "Germany 407A" and signed "Hans Fritz Stultz." I have been told they are automatons yet a clock dealer calls them "whistlers." I'd like some information, plus values on each figure plus the date if possible. They are carved beautifully. A small bellows is in the back.

R.J.S., Brevard, NC

A. It's too bad your photos are so blurry. These charming carved wooden figures are very appealing. I am not familiar with the maker who signed them but I would date them from the 1920s, during the height of Charlie Chaplin's popularity. Since they have mechanical bellows in the backs I would agree that they were probably "whistlers," meant to make that sound when wound. An "automaton" is a doll or figure with moving limbs or head which moves in conjunction with a music box when wound. These have no moving parts. In top shape I'd value the Chaplin figure in the $150-300 range, the double figure of two men a bit less.

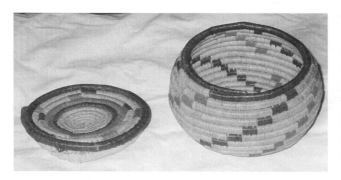

Coiled basketry container

Q. I would certainly appreciate your help on this little basket. It was purchased in about 1936 in Phoenix, Ariz., by my mother (unfortunately, when she was alive, I had no interest in it), but it was supposedly an Indian artifact. It is in excellent condition and is 5" in diameter and 3" high. The material, both core and wrappings, appear to be vegetable fiber, even though the wrappings are glossy. So, is it genuine Indian (hopefully)? Can you give some specific identification and what is your estimate of market value?

P.D., Foxfire Village, NC

A. Your coiled basketry container is typical of souvenir pieces marketed in the Southwest during the 1930s and 1940s. Native Americans in the region certainly were offering woven pieces for sale to tourists during that period, however, the bright red and purple bands on this piece lead me to believe it was more likely made in Mexico and sold in Arizona. Such Mexican-made items are starting to become collectible and if perfect I would value this in the $30-60 range.

Q. I'm enclosing a picture of something that has stymied me and I don't know what it is. It has the name "Badger" and was manufactured by an Appleton Mfg. Co. in Wisconsin. It has a circle under "Wis." It was patented in

1883. It seems that it was operated by means of a belt or chain, with two pulleys (one's missing). Please let me know what I have bought. Is it a mill or crusher?

A.G., Questa, NM

Cast-iron piece

A. This cast-iron piece is obviously part of some farm apparatus. My suspicion is that it was part of a pulley system, perhaps for loading hay into a hayloft. What can our readers suggest as the original use for this "what's it?"

Reader Update

D.P. of Ludington, Mich., writes regarding the wheeled cast-iron piece sent in by A.G. of Questa, N.M., that appeared in the August 2002 issue. He notes that there was a car ferry named "Badger" which ran across Lake Michigan between Michigan and Wisconsin. At one time he believes it was part of the C&O Line but today it is still operating but is privately owned. It seems likely that this was a piece of machinery originally used on this early ferry.

B. R.C. of Tennessee wrote in with more information on the Appleton Manufacturing Co., which produced the iron item shown in the (August 2002) column.

This firm was founded in Batavia, Ill., around 1880 and made iron grinders, hay equipment and other farm and home tools. The "Badger" (shown) appeared in 1883 as a hay hoist that ran on tracks or rails inside and outside the hayloft of many barns in the western United States. The example shown dates between 1884 and 1907 or 1917 depending upon which source of information you refer to. The one shown is missing several pieces, such as the block and tackle and hayforks. In good, complete condition this might sell in the $85 to $150 range; as is, perhaps $25-45.

As R.C. further notes, farm items are becoming "hot" and sought after but need to be in top condition to be of serious interest to collectors.

Old carved canes

Q. I own these two items that are canes or walking sticks, I'm not sure I know the difference. The bird head cane measures 42-1/2". The carving on the bird is beautiful and exacting. Its eyes are brown - possibly glass but I'm not sure. The other cane is carved from the top to the bottom with places and ports the sailor has been. There's also scrollwork between the ports. It's a life story of a sailor or merchant marine. How does one value such a unique piece? It starts in 1923 in Glasgow, World's Fair London, Guttenburg, Sweden - all in all there are about 40 places carved. It tells a story. It is 35" long. The only other date is 1926.

L.T., Lewiston, ID

A. Old carved canes and walking sticks are very collectible today. In general a cane will have a curved or angled handle, such as your pieces, while a walking stick will have a simple knob at the top. The detail of the carving is important in determining the value of such pieces. Your bird-handled cane is probably the more valuable of the two. It has some nice details but not as elaborate as the choicest examples. I think it might be valued in the $250-500 range. The other cane is interesting with the carved names and dates but most collectors prefer canes carved with figures or animals at the handle or down the sides. I think $100-200 would be a fair range for that one.

Q. Could you tell the value or some information on this juicer? "Holmes Juicer Extractor, Holmes Mfg. Co., Los Angeles" is printed in large letters.

P.T., Paradise, CA

A. I wasn't able to turn up any reference specifically on old juice reamers, but I checked some other references that include them. In general I can tell you that the all-glass models in color tend to be the most sought after. Linda Campbell Franklin, in her classic *300 Years of Kitchen Collectibles*, does a list of a variety of these "mechanical" juicers made in the first 40 years of the 20th century. Holmes Mfg. Co. was a major producer of kitchen utensils, I believe. Your

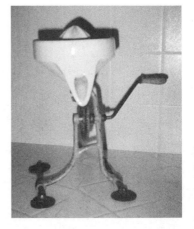

Old juice reamer

machine, which appears to have a porcelain reamer on an iron base, might interest some reamer/juicer collector; however, values seem to still be fairly modest for this sort of design. I'm guessing it might be valued in the $50-75 range, but the right enthusiast might offer more.

Q. I have tried several antique dealers and a friend of mine tried the Internet to find out what this is. It has a felt cup in the bottom - the ball is hollow. There is a slide at the bottom of the ball to let a small marble out. It opens at the top and spans 360 degrees. It is made of cherry as far as I can tell. I believe its a gambling device but can't find anyone who knows. Can you help?

M.M., Dubuque, IA

Likely gambling device

A. You are correct about this handsome piece having its origins in gambling. I'm about 99 percent certain that it was used to mix the balls used in the game of Keno. I haven't been able to find any current photos of similar pieces or get the lowdown on how Keno was played, but it did use the balls. There is a good deal of interest today in older gambling items and even newer casino chips; however I haven't seen a nice piece like this offered recently. It was obviously beautifully made and appears to be in super condition. I think a value in the $300-600 range might be about right.

Ivory carving of the Japanese god Hotei

Q. After reading your column I was urged to write to you about a Japanese piece we have had for several years. We have shown it to several people who couldn't come up with a value for it. I hope you have better luck.

C.H., Eustis, FL

A. Your interesting figure appears to be an ivory carving of the Japanese god Hotei with children. The carving is good quality but not outstanding and it is signed in the little box on the base. The rounded form of this piece made me think it might be a netsuke, the special toggle that serves as a counterweight to a little box called an inro. However, I don't see any hole through this piece, which would be needed for the support cord. Without a hole it is not considered a netsuke.

Netsuke and other carvings have been done in Japan for hundreds of years and are still being produced and widely reproduced. I'm afraid I'm not able to give you a specific date or origin for this piece. Some more modern carved pieces can sell for under $100 while early, rare pieces, especially netsuke, can sell in the upper hundreds and thousands.

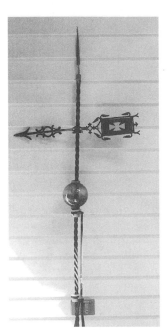

Q. I own this weathervane from the top of an old farmhouse. It is an arrow design with a red glass insert etched with a Maltese cross. It has a clear glass ball, which is still intact. I also have the pair of lightning rods that were mounted with it on either side of the roof. Imprinted on the metal rim of the glass ball is "Cole Bros. Pat. Dec. 12 1893." Imprinted at the base of the point at the top of the weathervane is "Miller Quality." It measures 70-1/2" high and the span across the directional arrow is 22-1/2".

G.F. Edgemoor, SC

A. Your lightning rod complete with glass ball and the nice cast-iron directional with a ruby-stained glass panel in the tail is a great country collectible. I believe in the right market it could sell in the $500-1,000 range.

Lightning rod with glass ball

Q. I have a small tin that has a flint and a fuse that fits in the small round wooden bottle and they fit into the tin can. My husband says it was his grandfather's.

I.B., Traverse City, MI

A. Your flint striking kit probably dates from the mid-19th century since wooden matches became fairly common by the late 19th century. It is an interesting "primitive" and might be valued in the $25-50 range.

Flint striking kit

Q. I have this object that is called a "coal cooker" made by the Toledo Cooker Co., Toledo, Ohio, U.S.A. I bought it at a yard sale for $20. I was told it was at least 92 years old.

D.L., Dover, NC

A. Your coal cooker was a self-contained oven that was made to be portable so was perhaps used on camping trips or other outdoor activities. It is an interesting "primitive" but I don't know that it would have a great collector appeal. If it didn't have the slightly domed top someone might find it useful as an accent table in a den. It does have possibilities as a storage unit (wine or liquor perhaps), but I would guess it wouldn't sell for much over $50.

Coal cooker

Q. We purchased this cane some time ago. It is engraved walnut with a horn base and horn on the handle - beautifully done and in perfect shape. It is for sale but I haven't a clue of what the value is. Many that have seen it say it is a real antique. I would appreciate your knowledge as to its value.

L.B., Shepherd, MI

A. Older, hand-carved canes can certainly be very collectible. Values tend to depend on the style and how ornate the carving is, with canes with well-carved figures and animals and painted trim being considered folk-art. From what I can see your piece has fairly simple geometric carving without figures or animals and apparently no inscriptions. There are some specialist dealers in early canes and you might check sources such as that but the best price would be from an avid collector. Without any special unique details I can only guess it might retail in the $75-100+ range.

Hand-carved cane

Q. I am enclosing a photo of an old basket I bought at a garage sale. It is 8-1/2" high and 12" wide with a circumference at its widest part on the outside of 38". It

Mexican-made basketry basket

has woven designs of colored cane that is faded on the outside but still bright on the inside. There are two identical large flower spray designs in opposite sides in red and green. On the other side are identical skirted figures about 5" high in red, dark blue, and brown. Near the top opening are light woven-in letters about 3" high in dark blue. They are "RECUEROO." The lid still has good color as it was detached and inside the basket. It and the handle had been attached with thread. The handle is loose. I could repair it and also re-dye the designs, but that may not be a good idea. Any information you can give me about this and its value will be greatly appreciated.

A.E., Brewster, MN

A. Your basketry basket appears to be a Mexican-made piece, probably produced for the tourist trade in the 1920s or 1930s. The colors and designs, not to mention the inscription, seem to confirm this. There is some collector interest in these although Native American pieces of the same era tend to have greater appeal to collectors. It would be acceptable to carefully re-stitch the handles but definitely do not touch the designs or you will only lower the value. This is mainly of decorator interest today and I think might retail in the $35-55 range or perhaps a tad more depending on the local market.

Q. I have a three-burner enamel gas stove with a blue marble-ized top. It is 36" high with the top down, 15" deep and 27" wide. There is no manufacturer's name. Can you tell me its age and value?

C.M., Rocky Hill, CT

A. Small early gas stoves from the 1920s era are quite sought-after today, especially ones with a nice blue and white marbleized top such as yours. People redoing period homes or who like the vintage look can have them restored and refitted for use

Three-burner enamel gas stove

today. The nice small size probably adds to its appeal for someone with a smaller kitchen. I don't see any signs of serious rust, chips or corrosion. I think in the right renovation market this piece might retail in the $800 to $1,600 range.

Country store bin

Q. Enclosed is a picture of a coffee storage box that came from my grandfather's store. I have two requests. The first concerns finding out the monetary value and the second concerns finding any information about Hersey Coffee Company. A description of the box follows: 31-1/2" x 16-1/2", tongue and groove, pine, with a split on the side with an old repair at the top. Also there is a split on the top board. I think it is from the early 1900s, but I am not sure.

M.L.F., Columbia, SC

A. You have a very nice country store collectible that is especially neat because it came down in your family. I hope you intend to keep it in the family since its sentimental value would exceed any monetary value. Similar country store bins might retail in the $200-400 range, depending on the brand noted on them. I'm glad to see you have left this piece in its original condition with the worn finish and lettering. That aged look is so important to collectors. I think it will be hard to track down information on the Hersey Coffee Company unless you know what city it operated in. During the late 19th and early 20th century there were dozens of firms that would buy and sell products such as coffee beans wholesale, so trying to find the history of a specific one can be difficult.

Q. I purchased this carving of a woman's head about 25 years ago at a yard sale. I hope you can give me a clue as to age, origin and value.

L.W., Snohomish, WA

A. The hand-carved wood sculpture you have is quite attractive,

Hand-carved wood sculpture

but without any background on who carved it and when it is very difficult to evaluate. A trained artist may have done it but a piece like that normally would have been signed. If a talented amateur carved it, then it only would have value as a decorative accent piece.

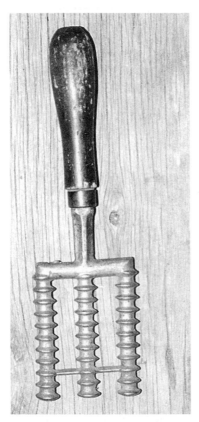

Late 19th or early 20th century kitchen piece

Q. Enclosed is a photo of something we can't identify. There are no marks. It is 10" x 3", made of heavy "silver" metal with wood handle. No one seems to know what it is. Do you? We paid $5 for it at a yard sale about eight years ago.

D. & M.H., Ignacio. CO

A. Well here we go again! It looks like another "what's it?" This appears to be some sort of kitchen implement since it seems to have galvanized or aluminum tines and a wooden handle. I guess it dates from the late 19th or early 20th century. But what is it? I've checked through all the references I could think of including Linda Campbell Franklin's encyclopedic *300 Years of Kitchen Collectibles* (Krause Publications, 5th Edition) and a reprint of the 1897 Sears, Roebuck catalog. Nothing like this shows up. Another reference showed a single primitive rod with ridges something like this piece and it was described as a "cookie dough mixer." I suppose this implement could have been used to stir up thick cookie dough. It would not stick as much to the grooved, galvanized tines. Anyone have other ideas?

Q. Enclosed is a photo of a hoe that measures 6-1/2" x 7-3/4" and weighs two pounds. On the left side there is a crown. In the middle there are two circles. On the right side is the name "John Pruks" (I am not sure of the "uk"). Would you please give me some information and a value on this cotton hoe?

M.J., Alpena, MI

Primitive iron cotton hoe head

A. Your primitive iron cotton hoe head is an interesting relic. There isn't much information available on garden tools such as this, but I suspect it was produced by hand in the first half of the 19th century. The crown mark seems to me to indicate the piece may have been manufactured in England and exported to the South. I'm afraid I don't have any leads on English toolmakers of that era. However, the value would depend on the interest in such early farming implements used in early cotton fields. I believe the value would be higher in areas of the South where cotton is and was a major crop. Just as a guess I'd say it might be valued in the $50-100 range but as a marked example a specialized collector might offer more.

Q. This recent purchase from a yard sale is a wooden statue 7-1/2" tall. It is marked "Anri, Italy." There was a book with it. *Novena Devotions to the Infant Jesus of Prague [drawing of statue] Enthroned Statue, National Shrine, Prague, Oklahoma.* The booklet sold for 25 cents. I assume from the writing in the book this was from 1948-49. What can you tell me about Anri and the value of something like this?

L.W., Snohomish, WA

A. Anri is an Italian company that is best known for the carved wood figurines that were widely produced during the 1970s onward. Some of these were "limited editions," but I couldn't find specific information on this Infant of Prague statue. It was probably a special order piece meant to be sold at the shrine in Oklahoma. I can't verify the age but it may date from the late 1940s or early 1950s. There is a market for Anri figures and some collectors do seek out religious figures such as this. However, in general, that market is fairly narrow. I can only guess that your piece might be valued in the $75-150 range but the right person might offer more.

Carved wood figurine

Q. I have enclosed a picture of a wooden box. I wonder who would have made it—seaman or military man. It took a lot of time as it is made of tiny little pieces of inlaid wood and quite thin. Some pieces are missing and the hinges are missing. The two flags have 17 stars, so is that the Civil War era? It is about 16" x 12" wide and 7" tall. There is also an inlaid heart with an arrow through it on back, stars on all sides and eight stars on top with the two flags. It looks like two or three different colors of wood. The bottom is scalloped with four small legs. It is tattered and torn but it still is a nice piece of

Inlaid chest

American history. I paid $150 for it and thought it well worth it. I would really like a story to go along with it.

A. You have a wonderful piece of American folk art. This wonderfully inlaid chest may well date from the Civil War era because of the American flags and shield on the top. The American flag during the war had from 33 to 35 stars but if you added up the total stars on both flags you come up with 34, which would fit. Since this piece doesn't have any nautical designs, I doubt that it was made by a sailor. A Union soldier may have made it but with the workmanship involved he would have needed a lot of free time. The heart inlaid on the side might indicate this was made for someone's wife or sweetheart. It could use some professional restoration, but be sure and take it to someone with experience and expertise in this area. I would check with any museums in your area for guidance and some of the major New York City auction houses also have restoration departments. One-of-a-kind pieces like this are hard to value, especially in "as is" condition, but given the workmanship and design I would think somewhere in the low-$1,000s wouldn't be out of line.

Kerosene burner

Q. What can you tell me about this kerosene burner? It is 11" tall, 9" in diameter with the burner 4-1/2" and 6" in diameter. The oil can is 20 ounces. Was this miner's or camper's stove? I have no history—it belongs to a friend. I would like its age and value.

C.F., Parishville, NY

A. Your burner was probably used as a portable camping stove during the early years of the 20th century. Unfortunately it is in pretty rough condition so the value would be fairly modest, perhaps $15-25.

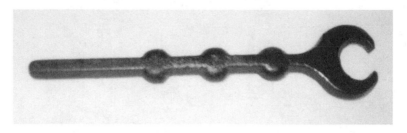

Railroad spike puller

Q. My friend has been carrying this "thing" (a tool?) to antique shops for some time. No one has been able to identify it. It is 12" long. The width at the top is 2-1/2". The width of the three bumps is 1-1/4". It is 7/8" thick and weighs 2-1/4 pounds. The handle has a little green paint on it and bears the stamp "GD." What the heck is it?

P.S., Slater, MO

A. I checked through a number of references on old tools but wasn't able to identify the exact use of your wrench. Not as much is written on old wrenches as on other types of old tools. Early woodworking tools, especially planes, are most sought after by collectors and wrenches just don't command the same interest. I'll open this up to our readers and see if someone out there can fill us in on this unique piece. By the way, lovers of old tools should watch for the new *Antique Trader Tool Price Guide* that I edited and which was released earlier this year.

Reader Update

I have had several readers come forward with the identification of the unusual iron tool shown on page 16 of my November 2003 column. It turns out that this is a railroad spike puller that could be used to reach the spikes in tight spots. The three "bumps" down the handle allow it to be used for different sized rails.

My thanks to all those who shared their expertise.

Baskets

Q. It is my understanding that some baskets can have value and I am curious about these two baskets that I have. The smaller basket is 8" in diameter and 3-1/2" tall. The handled basket is 8" across the bottom and 11" tall. It is held together with twine and has twigs attached to the front. I'd appreciate knowing if they have any value.

V.S., Westfield, IN

A. You provide no background on these baskets and it would be a help to have some idea of their age. All I can say is that the one with the high, arched handle could date from the early 20ᵗʰ century. The other one is a simple low, round design that could have been made anytime in the past century. In the right market I feel the handled one might be valued in the $50-125 range while the smaller one, maybe $30-50.

Q. I wonder if this wooden box might be a Shaker one. I'm quite sure it came from Maine or New Hampshire.

C.C., Tacoma, WA

A. Your wooden bentwood box is not Shaker-made. Their storage boxes were made using "finger lappets," i.e., pointed, tapering bands that were tacked in place. Your box has a flat-tacked seam. It might date from the early 20ᵗʰ century or a little before but without the fitted cover the value would be modest, perhaps $25-45.

Wooden bentwood box

Late Victorian iron fence

Q. This iron fence is around 100 years old. It is 262 feet and has two walk-in gates and a driveway gate. It was put in to keep the neighbors' geese out of the yard. Our son removed it and installed it on his own property.

R.B., Paxton, IL

A. You have a wonderful large late Victorian iron fence and it appears to be in great condition. There is a great demand for such fencing among people restoring Victorian homes. Quite often the separate segments of fencing are sold by the piece. Because of the amount of fencing you have, as well as the gates and gateposts I certainly think you should insure this fence in the $2,500 to $3,500 range at least.

Glass Items

Pitcher and tumbler set

Q. The enclosed photo shows a drinking glass and pitcher, family possessions for many years. It was a wedding gift in October 1891. I could find no marks of any kind. The pitcher (8-1/2" tall) is in good condition but the glass has been chipped. The matte finish is of splotchy pink shades and white with black spots in a few places. The handle appears to have been attached as a separate piece rather than a part of the pitcher mold. Any idea of value? As you can see from the ribbed sides, the top is quite fluted.

A.M., IA

A. Here's an example of glass produced by the famous glassman Harry Northwood. This pattern, today called "Ribbed Pillar," was introduced by Mr. Northwood at his factory in Martin's Ferry, Ohio, in 1889, so the dating of 1891 would be just right. This type of decoration with the pink and white splotches is commonly referred to as "spatter" glass and your pieces have a satin finish obtained by briefly exposing them to acid fumes during manufacture. Early Northwood pieces are always in demand and Dr. James Measell shows a similar pitcher in his first book on Harry Northwood covering the maker's early years of glass production. The pitcher today in perfect condition might be valued in the $250 to $300 range. The tumbler, because of the chips, might sell for under $50, but they are great mementos to keep together.

Q. I am enclosing a picture of one of two vases I have. I have been told these are Bristol vases. I can find no mention in any book with Bristol and the markings on bases. Can you identify these vases and their value?

B.S., MA

A. Your decorative glass vase is a type that is sometimes lumped together

Decorative glass vase

with other pieces under the general misnomer "Bristol" from the former belief that many of these pieces were made and decorated in Bristol, England. Most actually came from Bohemia, some from France and even some from England, although not Bristol. The "PK" monogram on the bottom of this piece has been discussed in glass circles for some time. I'm still not certain if it has been attributed to a specific glassmaker or a decorating firm, but such examples are considered to be Bohemian in origin. From the form I would date it to the 1885-1905 era. The shaded dark brown ground and large stylized florals are not quite as desirable as more delicately done designs, so depending on the size, I'd guess the pair might be valued in the $150-$250 range.

Q. After reading the July '98 *Collector Magazine* and seeing the millefiori paperweights, I realized the paperweight I got from my aunt may be worth more than I thought. Enclosed is a picture of it. Could you tell me what its name may be and what it's worth?

C.R., Windsor, CT

Millefiori paperweight

A. I am not an expert on antique paperweights, but I do know this type of millefiori weight has been widely produced and reproduced since the mid-19th century. The simple design of rings of canes is not unusual and I can see around one side interior bubbles in the glass, which would not have been allowed in the fine early French paperweights. The Chinese have made this style of weight for many years and my best guess is that this might be Chinese and made between the two world wars. Values for this type of weight are quite modest, probably under $100.

Hobnail bowl

Q. Enclosed are photos of my deep amber hobnail bowl. It measures 8" across the top and 5" across the bottom. Any info you have on age and value is appreciated.

V.S., Westfield, IN

A. Although your amber Hobnail pattern glass bowl is similar to pieces produced in the late 19th century, I believe your example was made by the Imperial Glass Co., probably in the late 1950s or early 1960s. It was shown in their catalogs of that era. Some of their products carried the pressed "IG" trademark. As a pretty bowl, it might have a collector value in the $15-35 range.

Figural powder jar

Q. Enclosed find a photo of a pair of candlesticks and what I assume is a powder container. The three are not of the same set. The candlesticks are unmarked. The container, however, has on the bottom: "Paris, Ramses, New York." I've not been able to find any information in any book about this piece. I would appreciate any help.

S.S., Olympia, WA

A. According to Margaret and Kenn Whitmyer in their book *Bedroom & Bathroom Glassware of the Depression Years* (Collector Books), your figural powder jar was advertised in the 1930-31 Montgomery Ward fall and winter catalog and was meant to hold Ramses perfumed bath powder. It sold then for 93 cents and came in frosted pink or frosted green. Today collectors refer to the figure as "Pandora" and in perfect condition the box can sell in the $75-$95 range - nice appreciation. Your spiral-twist pressed glass candlesticks are also from the early 1930s, when several makers produced similar designs. I'd say your pair might be valued at $60-$90.

Q. This pair of green glass bottles was given to family members in 1870. If you can add possible dates and value of any of these items I would be most appreciative. I'm 93.

H.S., Lebanon, NH

A. These tall decanters in a light frosted green may be of French origin and dating would be around 1850-1870. If perfect with little wear, I think $125-$200 each is a fair range.

Frosted green decanters

Q. **Please tell me the value/price and make of this basket. Also please describe/name and tell me the price/value of these vases.**

M.D., Peoria, AZ

A. You have a lovely late Victorian bride's basket, so-called because they were often given as wedding presents. Your cased and shaded golden yellow bowl features hand-painted flowers and a decal of cupids. Complete with the nice silver-plate

Late Victorian bride's basket

frame it might be valued in the $350-$450 range. Your pair of vases are a milky white mold-blown glass sometimes referred to as "Bristol," although such wares were not made in the late 19th century in Bristol, England. Almost all such pieces were produced in factories in Bohemia and they are still quite common on the market. Your pair, depending on size and condition, might be valued in the $80-$150 range.

Bristol vases

Q. **My wife loves this satin overlaid glass. However, we find it hard to come by. Pictured is her collection, less a vase broken by our fly-chasing cat. Can you tell us who made it, when it was made, the approximate value and what it is called?**

C. & A.J., Lindenhurst, IL

A. Your cased satin glass pieces feature applied fruit, leaves and curled legs. From the general design and colors, I think these are most likely Venetian

Satin glass pieces

imitations of Victorian originals. The Venetian pieces were nice quality but not as lightweight and well finished as the originals. Often the pontil marks on the bottoms are not polished. Even if these are later Venetian wares they still have some collector value, probably ranging in the $50-$75 range for the smaller pieces and $150-$200 for the larger example. *See Glass Tip #1.

Carnival glass punch set

Q. I have enclosed a copy of page 16 of *Collector Magazine*, January 2000 issue, also a photo of a Carnival glass punch bowl set which I own. This set my mother had for at least 30 years and I acquired the set five years ago. It is green glass with that metallic gold look. It has the large bowl, stand and eight cups, approximately 11" by 10". Initial on bottom of stand shows "+." I would very much like to know if it could be of any worth, the age and who would be interested in the set. The set is in perfect condition.

R.M., Estes Park, CO

A. Your carnival glass punch set is in the Acorn Burrs pattern produced by the Northwood Glass Company in the early 20th century. Green is a popular color and if your bowl, base and eight matching cups are all perfect and don't have any wear, I think the set might be valued in the $1,600-$1,800 range. *See Glass Tip #2.

Q. The photo is of what I think is a glass ashtray. It is 91/2" by 8" and is marked "Higgins" in the lower left corner. I would like to know the age and value.

V.S., Westfield, IN

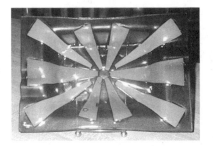

Large glass ashtray

A. Your interesting large ashtray is a nice example of the glass artistry of Michael and Frances Higgins, a husband and wife team. They specialized in making glass by the "slumping" technique, in which pieces composed of fused segments of glass were reheated and allowed to slump down over a prepared mold form. They began their work in the late 1940s and by the 1950s had become associated with the Dearborn Glass Company of Bedford Park, Ill. Their designs were a major part of that firm's output until the mid-1960s when they went independent. They continued working and although Mr. Higgins passed away a couple of years ago, and Mrs. higgins a few months ago, production continues. A book on their glass, *Higgins - Adventures in Glass* by Donald-Brysan Johnson and Leslie Pina, was published by Schiffer Publishing Ltd. in 1997. Early pieces from the 1950s and 1960s can now sell for hundreds of dollars.

Q. Enclosed are pictures of a bottle I have. I call it a "pinch bottle;" it's clear glass, with triangular pinched in sides and covered in sterling silver embossed with roses. On the bottom it says "Sterling-Sterling-Sterling." I can find no other markings. The stopper in the photo is not the original stopper. What was the original stopper like? What was the bottle used for and what would the value be? The bottle, not including the stopper, is between 7" and 8" tall.

V.E., Valley Springs, CA

A. Your sterling silver-encased bottle probably dates from the first quarter of the 20th century and most likely was meant to hold cologne or toilet water on a lady's dressing table. I believe some of the markings on the base may relate to the maker, but they can't be read clearly. There is a lot of interest in decorative bottles of this type today but not having the original stopper would lower the value. Very likely the original stopper was a silver-encased knob. Even "as is" I suspect this might sell in the $100-$200 range or more.

Sterling silver-encased bottle

Tantalus set

Q. This Tantalus case is oak with brass hardware. It is 18" high, 13-1/2" wide and 9" deep. It has this top drawer holding shot glasses and the bottom drawer has a hidden button in the rear that opens it. The lock is on the middle of the top wing. It has three cut glass decanters that cannot be removed without opening the swing door.

F.T., Alexandria, LA

A. Your Tantalus set is undoubtedly English and such sets were popular throughout the 19th century. I think your set might date from the first half of the century and the bottles should be fine cut glass. If the bottles are perfect, the set would be very sought after today. A complete Tantalus such as this might be valued in the $400-$600 range.

Q. Would you please help me with my paperweight? I know it is old because my great aunt gave it to me. But with no markings, how can you value it? I've read in your magazine that paperweights can be very valuable.

S.R., St. Louis, MO

Millefiori paperweight

A. Paperweights first became widely popular around the middle of the 19th century when several French factories began producing beautiful examples in a variety of designs. These are the ones that advanced collectors cherish. Among the designs used in paperweights are the colored millefiori (thousand flower) canes such as you see in your weight. Because of the colors of the canes in your piece, the quite simple design and the controlled large bubble, I would say your weight was probably produced in China. They have imitated European-style weights at least since the 1920s and 1930s and are still making them. They are generally not marked and even older examples have a modest value, perhaps in the $40-$60 range.

Q. Enclosed are photos of a glass piece we have. It stands 11-1/2" tall, and is smooth on the top and bottom. Please help us identify and place a value and age on this piece as we have not had much luck with the reference books.

J.W., Endicott, NY

Late 19th century vase

A. Your tall, very elaborate vase would appear to be a fine example of the artistry of English glassmakers in the last 20 years of the 19th century. Its tall elegant form with the white opalescent stripes in the yellowish green ground looks similar to designs produced by the famous Stevens & Williams firm. The pink applied and curled leaves around the shoulder and leaf-form feet are also typical of the appliqued work this factory was noted for. Since this is a large piece and quite elegant, the value will be good provided there is no damage, especially to the applied section. If perfect, I would say it might be valued in the $300-$400 range in the right market.

German beer bottle

Q. This is a beer bottle purchased in Germany at an antique store in the late 1960s. I have never found another; perhaps you can give me some information on it. It is 11" tall. The handle may be pewter. The marking on the neck band says, "Glasindustrie Dresden D.R.G.M.E. No. 102886." The flip top appears to be Dresden china. I would appreciate any information and the price on this bottle.

H.M., Ft. Collins, CO

A. Your German beer bottle looks to me like it would date from the first quarter of the 20th century. My German isn't great but I think the marking on the stopper indicates the porcelain stopper was patented and made at a factory in Dresden for use by the glass producer. This type of wire closure was most popular in the late 19th and early 20th century and the metal bands and dolphin handle are typical Germanic touches. As a decorative piece, I'd say it might be valued in the $50-$100 range or perhaps a bit more.

Q. Enclosed are photos. I would appreciate your comments. I enjoy your column immensely. The vase I purchased at an estate sale 28 years ago. It is perfect, with no chips or cracks, and clear glass. I've seen a couple since but usually broken. Here are some details about the items. The vase is possibly blown glass, with rough pontil mark on bottom, scallop on top edge, 13-1/2" tall, 13" around widest part, 11" around neck, 4-1/2" wide at bottom, 6" wide at top.

C.H. Farmingdale, NY

A. The clear glass vase has a Victorian look to it and may have been blown in a mold around 1900, possibly imported from Bohemia. Clear pieces generally don't have strong market appeal so I'd say it might be valued in the $30-$60 range.

Clear glass vase

Q. These bottles are old and believed to have come from France, but there are no markings of who made them or when they were made.

J.J., Gillette, WY

A. Your blue glass bottles with stoppers are figures of the Virgin Mary and were meant to hold holy water. They could have come from France but similar examples also were made in Mexico. Generally they were sold at pilgrimage sites such as Lourdes in France. They could date from the late 19th or early 20th century. Although pretty, they aren't too much in demand in the bottle market. I'd say they might be valued in the $50-$75 range each if perfect.

Late 19th or early 20th century bottles

Ornately decorated glass vase

Q. This vase was one of my mother's wedding gifts in 1914. It is milk glass with a raised flower decoration outlined with gold, 7-1/2" tall with a top opening 1-3/4" in diameter. No one has been able to identify it. There is a pale blue "x" on the bottom. It's in perfect condition.

D.C.B., Virginia Beach, VA

A. Your ornately decorated glass vase may have been a gift in 1914 but it has the look of earlier enameled wares produced in Europe in the 1880-1900 era. Factories in Bohemia produced some of the most decorative wares of that era. Most such pieces are not signed by the maker. Some similar wares also came out of England and France, but Bohemia took the lead. If the enameling is in perfect condition without any wear or chips a decorative piece like this might be valued in the $150-250 range.

Flame-shaped globe

Red Crown globe

Q. I really enjoy your column. I am hoping you can help with these two gas pump tops. My father worked for Standard Oil for over 40 years and got these when they were updating the gas pumps. Both are made of glass. The "flame" top is 20" tall and 35" around at the middle. The other one is 18" tall and 50" around the middle. I would greatly appreciate any information you can give us and would also like to have names of people that would be interested in purchasing them.

M.R.B., Miles City, MT

A. Thank you for your letter and the photos of your old gas pump globes. There is a lot of interest in these today as well as other early gas station items. Your Red Crown model comes up for sale fairly often and can bring in the $300-500 range, depending on the condition of the paint and if there is any other damage. I haven't turned up a recent listing for the flame-shaped globe so it may be scarcer and possibly of more value, but it also appears to have some paint flaking which would affect the value to a collector. In regard to selling the pieces, there are some auction houses which specialize in auto related items and you could also run ads in trade publications such as *Collector Magazine & Price Guide*.

Q. My daughter gave me a subscription to your magazine as a birthday gift and I have enjoyed it very much. Enclosed are pictures of a vase I would like help in identifying. This was in a box of junk that I bought at an auction for 50 cents. It has no markings on it and is in excellent condition. When held up to the light it has a lot of fire in it. I go to a lot of antique shops and have a lot of books on glassware, but I have never seen anything like this. I have been told (but not by an expert) that it is Fenton. Could you tell me what it is and its value. Thank you so much for your help.

E.F., Salina, OK

Duncan & Miller Glass Company vase

A. Your little blue opalescent vase is the Three Feathers or Horn of Plenty pattern vase produced by the Duncan & Miller Glass Company around the 1930s and 1940s. This piece came in both a short and tall form. The short version is valued around $85 and the taller version, which I think you have, is valued around $185.

Q. I believe this vase is Wheeling Peach Blow. It is 9" high, blown glass, with stick neck. Am I on the right track? Pontil is on the bottom. The base is 2-1/2" and the top is 1-3/8". What is this worth? The other piece is 70" high with a fluted neck. The top of the neck is 7" and the footed bottom is 3-1/2". There is a darker color from top to bottom of flute.

W.C., Fowler, CO

A. Your tapering slender vase with the Amberina-like coloring is not Wheeling Peach Blow. That scarce Victorian art glass is always lined with a creamy white

Tapering slender vase with Amberina-like coloring

Jar/vase with Amberina-like coloring

inner layer. The form and coloring of your piece lead me to believe it was probably a product of the 1960s or early 1970s. The most likely producer was the Blenko Glass Co. of West Virginia, but there were several firms in the area using similar colors and forms at that time. Blenko produced blown pieces with modern firms, copies of early American blown and some Victorian shapes. I believe your jar/vase could also be a Blenko product. Such pieces are becoming collectibles, especially those with Amberina coloring, but they are not true "Amberina" in the Victorian sense.

Mouth blown ornaments

Q. Just received my *Antiques and Collectibles 2001* book and went to the section on Christmas ornaments. There were only a few. The enclosed photo is of ornaments purchased in early 1960s. They are 5" to 6" tall, made in Germany and Italy, mouth blown. I have not seen any of this type in books. It would be greatly appreciated if you could tell the value of these.

L.R., Warwick, RI

A. For further information on Christmas collectibles you can check our *Country Americana Price Guide, 2nd Edition (2000)*. We listed and illustrated these later blown figural ornaments, which can be quite valuable. We showed a crescent moon example similar to the one in your photo listed at around $100. Other figural ones, depending on how ornate they are, their size and the design, seem to range from $50 to $80. Of course, they must be in perfect condition, and values quoted are what a serious collector might be willing to pay.

Q. I am enclosing pictures of a clown decanter. I would like to know its value and if it should be insured. This item was purchased at an estate sale. It had been in storage over 30 years and is in mint condition.

H.L.J., Gorden, NE

A. Your clown decanter is typical of examples in blown glass made in Venice in the 1950s and 1960s. The non-decanter figurals are a bit more in demand, but there is a good market for these novelties. Take note, however, that reproductions are coming on the market from Mexico. If yours is an older original and perfect, it might be valued in the $125-250 range.

Blown glass clown decanter

Pitcher and tumbler with "Bird and Strawberry" pattern

Q. All the dishes in these pictures are very old. They have no markings, dates or anything. My mother would have been 95 and these dishes belonged to her mother before my mother was born—so I've been told. The designs on the dishes with feet are grapes and birds. The candy dish is very heavy. The glass and mug on each side of it have grapes. The set of bowls and glasses and pitcher are all the same set. There are six little bowls, one round and one oval shaped, and six glasses. The baskets were on a marble topped dresser (wish I had it). I want to know all about these dishes and how much they are worth. I will sell them if I feel I'm offered enough.

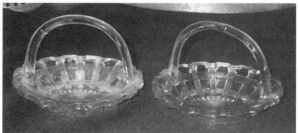

Baskets with "Open Plaid" pattern

Dishes with simple grape design

J.J., Vernon, AL

Clear frosted glass bowls

Footed oval bowls with "Bird and Strawberry" pattern

A. American pattern glass is one of my favorite fields of study, and you have some collectible early pieces. The footed oval and round bowls are in a popular pattern known as "Bird and Strawberry," introduced in the period around 1910. Your water pitcher and tumbler also appear to be in that pattern although the photo is fuzzy. This pattern also comes with the birds decorated in blue and the berries in red, but it is much more expensive in that version. Even in clear the pieces are sought after; the larger bowls might be valued in the $60-80 range, the small sauce dish $15-25, the pitcher $150+ and the tumbler, $40-80. The shallow round dishes with applied handles look like a pattern called "Open Plaid," which was introduced in the late 1880s. I haven't seen this form before, and basket as well as pattern glass collectors would enjoy them. Value might be $50-75 each. The clear frosted glass bowls and covered butter dish are a plain pattern I don't recognize but also probably date from the 1890s era. The large bowl might sell in the $25-35 range, the small bowls $8-10 each and the butter dish, $40-50. The last group shows simple grape design pieces probably mass-produced around 1900-1910. Each might be valued in the $10-15 range. The square dish with cover is sometimes called a "honey dish" because blocks of honey were served in it. I'm afraid I don't recognize the pattern, but it again would date around 1900 and might sell in the $50-100 range. Keep in mind the values are for perfect pieces.

Q. Enclosed are pictures of some items I would appreciate some information about. I was given the milk glass bowl and candleholders about 40 years ago. On the bottom of the inside of the bowl are the words "PresCut." The bowl is 7-1/4" in diameter and 3-1/4" high. The two metal bells are brass. The large one is 6-3/4" high and 4-1/2" in diameter. The smaller one is 4" high and

McKee bowl and candleholders

2-1/2" in diameter. The number 1811 is impressed on the outside of the large bell. I tried to show the number on the bell in the picture but it didn't come out well. Could the number 1811 indicate the year it was made? I bought these at a yard sale about 20 years ago. The glass bell I bought about 25 years ago at an antique shop. The gold design is, I believe, etching and not painted on. I was told it is German glass. It is 7-1/2" high and 3-1/2" in diameter. Could you tell me the value of these items? I thoroughly enjoy the magazine, especially your column. It is the first thing I look at and read when the magazine arrives.

Two metal bells

I.M., Wellsburg, WV

A. The "Prescut" name was a trademark used by the McKee Glass Company for a line of patterns introduced in the early years of the 20th century. Most of these patterns were imitation cut glass designs and I believe your bowl and candlesticks may be in the Fentec pattern. Pieces in this line were produced in milk glass, and this console set probably dates from the 1920s or 1930s. McKee glass is quite collectible but their early milk glass animal dishes and Depression-era kitchen glassware are most in demand today. I would guess your set might be valued in the $100-150 range. Your two metal bells appear to be fairly modern copies of early bells. The metal appears to have been artificially aged to make it appear antique. This has been done with many newer metal bells produced in the past 50-60 years. I'd guess the smaller one might be valued in the $15-25 range and the larger one perhaps $20-40. The ruby glass bell may well be from Germany but it is from the second half of the 20th century and I feel was most likely exported during the 1950s or 1960s. As a pretty ruby glass with gilt-trimmed etching it might have a value in the $30-60 range or perhaps a bit more to the right collector.

Q. I enjoy your column very much. Can you give me any information on this Venetian vase? I purchased it some time ago, and I do not have any background on it. I could not find any marks. There is some damage to the applied fruit. Any information and value would be greatly appreciated. Thanks.

L.G., Sidney, OH

Blown glass vase with applied glass fruit

A. Your blown glass vase with the applied glass fruit and leaves was a decorative type of Victorian glass produced mainly in England by firms such as Stevens and Williams but also made by factories in Bohemia. The amber color of your piece with the applied blue rim and the gilt metal stand that holds the vase are more typical of pieces made in Bohemia in the 1880s and 1890s. In checking through a reference on Bohemian glass, I found some examples similar to yours that were made by the Harrach company. Any damage to the applied parts of the decoration will lower the appeal to collectors. Depending on the size and condition, value could range from $75 to $100. Larger and perfect pieces might sell in the $250-$450 range.

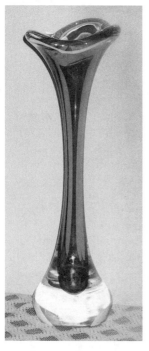

Q. This cranberry glass vase is 17-1/4" tall, with a base 4-2/5" across. Where it shows white at the base, it is clear. On the base is an old sticker which says "Flygsfors-Crystal-Sweden" and "Coguille Flygsfors-59." It is heavy and beautiful and has a ground base.

D.L., Houston, TX

A. Your tall blown glass cranberry and clear vase, fortunately, does have a nice marking. The Flygsfors factory in Sweden produced a range of decorative glasswares exported to the United States during the 1950s. It is not as sought-after as works by Orrefors or Kosta Boda of Sweden, but the "modern" design would appeal to collectors. I'd guess it might be valued in the $100-200 range, but I haven't seen much pricing information on these wares yet.

Flygsfors vase

Q. I hope you can help us identify this vase. My mother got it from her mother who got it from her mother! The part of the country was Thomasville, Ga. My mother was born in 1923. I thought it might be early Fenton and sent photos but they say it isn't. The vase stands 5-1/2" high, with an opening of 3"; flute across is 3-3/4" wide. The vase is unmarked and has a clear overlay of glass over the second layer. Any help you can give will be appreciated.

B.L.A., Athens, AL

A. I can understand why you thought this vase might be early Fenton since during the 1940s

Cased spatter glass vase

and 1950s they did reproduce a great deal of Victorian style glass. However, this cased spatter glass vase is a period piece likely made in the 1880s or 1890s. It is fairly small but quite appealing in the pink, maroon and white swirled spatter cased over in a swirled rib design in clear. If perfect I think it might be valued today in the $75-150 range.

Q. I have found a picture very similar to this small vase in the *Antique Traders Price Guide, 1984 First Edition* on page 592 under Monot & Stumpf. What is your educated guess? Can you confirm from the pictures that this is possibly Monot Stumpf? If not what is it, who, when and where was it made and what is its worth? The other picture is of an art glass vase. It is very beautiful and different from any I have seen before because of the brass ring around the neck. What kind of glass is it, who might have made it and when, and what is its value? Thank you for your time. I look forward to seeing you in the magazine. I have found your magazine more helpful than a lot of books I have read, there's so much variety.

P.O., Red Mound, OR

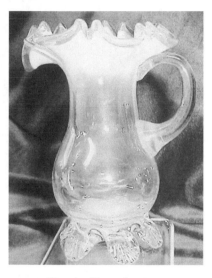

Victorian blown glass vase

A. The small blown glass pitcher is a decorative Victorian piece with opalescent treatment. I haven't come across too much Monot Stumpf on the market, but what I have seen generally has deeper colors and not the applied color rim of this piece. My guess is that this is from a Bohemian glasshouse, made in the late 19th century for export. Value depends on the size, color and condition. Any cracks or chips greatly lower the value. Assuming it is under 6" high, I'd guess the value might be in the $75-$125 range. The decorative bowl is another late Victorian decorative piece. It's cased spatter glass, and bowls and baskets in this glass were very popular in the 1890-1910 era. The applied metal band with figures does make it quite unique. It also was probably made in Bohemia. As a rather unique design, I think it might sell today in the $125-$200 range.

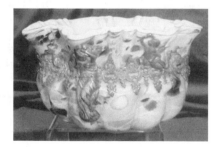

Cased spatter glass bowl

Q. I have a vase that I have wanted information on. It was left to my mother 20 years or so ago by an elderly friend. It is almost 9" tall and very light in weight. The blue is quite beautiful; the pictures show the true color. There are no markings on it. I am not sure where to begin research on this vase. Any ideas to age, maker and worth would be appreciated.

B.W., Timmonsville, SC

A. Your cobalt blue fluted vase with an applied clear foot is very pretty. It is hand-made but I don't believe that it is a Victorian piece. The simple design is too modern and could date it anywhere from the late 1930s through the 1950s. It is possible that it was made in Europe but I haven't seen this form in pieces made in Venice, Germany or Scandinavia during that era. As a pretty, decorative piece I would think it could be valued in the $75-150 range.

Decorative fluted vase

Q. This vase is 10" tall with a woodpecker 4" tall on the side. It looks as though colored glass was blown inside clear glass and it is quite heavy. My husband said the dealer thought it was "Murano." There are no markings at all on it so I am assuming he means "from" Murano, Italy. What do you think?

T.P., Miami, FL

A. Your blown glass vase with the applied bird is the type of novelty ware that has been produced in Murano, Italy, near Venice, for years. Novelty figures of clowns, birds, and fish became especially popular after World War II but I'm sure similar examples are still being made. Old Murano figures, from the 1950s and '60s, are increasing in value. Your vase may be that old or even newer. I would guess that, if perfect, it might be valued in the $50-100 range.

Blown glass vase with applied bird

Q. I am not knowledgeable about antiques. This glass lamp is approximately 21" high and 10-1/2" wide.

B.K., Piscataway, NJ

A. From your photos it is a little difficult to evaluate your glass lamp. It looks like the shade may be cut glass and perhaps the pedestal base is also cut. The form and style of fittings, however, don't quite seem correct for a cut glass lamp from the late 19th or early 20th century. Without any details on its history I hesitate to pin down a date. A great deal of heavily cut Victorian-style glass has been coming out of Eastern Europe in the past 10 to 20 years. If you can trace it back further than that it might date as far back as the 1920s or up into the 1950s.

Cut glass electric lamp

Reader Update

J.K., Minnesota, offered the following information on a cut glass table lamp I covered in an earlier column. These are his comments:

"Dear Mr. Husfloen: I look forward to the reading of your responses in Kyle On Antiques. I thought I would drop a note regarding the cut glass electric lamp, ca 1905-1915. I have collected/restored lighting for some 30-40 years and have seen many marriages. I think this lamp is one—I think the original cut shade was lost or broken and someone found a rather nice acid-etched gas shade, ca. 1890s-1905 that would fit the 5" diameter fitter. I think it is mounted upside down with a brass embossed kerosene-type band for holding the prisms around the base to dress it up. The prisms, however, are incorrect. I think in most cases if these lamps had prisms they were of the spear-point cut variety."

My thanks to this reader for his information. It's hard to evaluate a piece like this lamp from a small photo but his suggestions could certainly help.

Ruby-stained Victorian piece

Q. I have enclosed a picture of what we think is a water carafe. The top has no stopper but has a small lip on one side as a spout. It's ruby red and frosted glass and on the bottom is number 428 in red. The bottom is clear and rough, like it is handblown on the tall part. This came from my husband's grand-mother so we know it is old but wonder about its age and value.

Mrs. M.W., Longview, TX

A. Your interesting ruby-stained piece could have been a carafe but these pieces were also often used in the lady's boudoir to hold eau-de-cologne. The fact that the carafe-style part stacks into the lower section makes it quite unique. There were Victorian "tumble-up" sets, which held water in a carafe, but they usually had a tumbler that was inverted over the neck. The bottom piece here looks a bit too wide and awkward to drink out of. Such pieces were quite often made in Bohemia and exported in large numbers. Perhaps a reader can identify the exact use for this interesting piece. As a decorative late Victorian item I think it could be valued in the $75-150 range or perhaps a bit more to the right collector.

Q. I have a question about the pattern of my set of six glasses and a pitcher. The set belonged to my husband's family (mother) and when she died in 1968, I got the set. I think she had had it for many years before. I always assumed it was carnival glass but never knew the pattern. It seems to be painted on with white paint—big sunflow-ers and leaves and stems. Perhaps you could help

Beverage set in the "Cosmos" pattern

me with the name of the pattern and if it is carnival glass, maybe the age and value. The set is in very good condition—no chips or cracks anywhere. The pitcher is 9-1/2" high and the glasses are 4-1/2" high.

E.M.M., MS

 Your beverage set does have a golden iridescent finish like early Carnival glass but this design was produced long after the early Carnival glass went out of style. This was the last use of this sort of finish until reproductions of old Carnival glass began to appear in the 1960s. Your set in the "Cosmos" pattern was produced by the Jeannette Glass Company of Jeannette, Pa., and it appeared in their 1950 catalog. Kitchen glassware of that era is becoming quite collectible today. This design was probably only made in this water set and some collectors prefer patterns which are available in a wider range of pieces including cups, saucers, bowls and plates. However, I would think your set in perfect condition might be valued in the $75 to $125 range.

Reader Update

Marion Cohen of Albertson, N.Y., wrote:

"After I read your column in June I had to write, for one item brought back fond memories to me.

"When I was a high school senior and college freshman, I had a part time job at an H.L. Green Variety Store in Manhattan, NY. I worked in the housewares department and we sold the very pitcher and glasses set your reader E.M.M. of Mississippi wrote about.

"In those days, the large water pitcher sold for 59 cents and the matching water glasses were 10 or 15 cents, depending on which size you bought. A smaller pitcher for juice was available for 39 cents, and matching small juice glasses were either 5 cents each or two for 15 cents. (I don't recall exactly.) You were right when you said it did not come with plates, cups, bowls, etc. This design was sold by us only in pitchers and matching glasses, which were very fashionable then.

"I cannot believe how the value of this set has risen over the years, for when it was originally sold, you could have both sets for less than $2. Today it would be difficult to find a complete set. I have seen the water pitcher alone on sale in antique shops for anywhere from $35 to $55. If only I had known then what I know now!"

Thanks, Marion, for the fascinating background. Readers will be interested to know that Marion is an expert and author of a book on costume jewelry.
Kyle

Stemmed goblet

Q. I bought these items thinking they were Candle-wick by Imperial Glass. Now I have been told they are not Candlewick and that's why I'm asking for your help. They are 7" tall, hold 12 ounces and they do not have a blue tint—just crystal clear. I have a set of six and they are mint. Can you tell me who made them? When? Range in value?

J.S., Rockford, IL

A. I agree that this stemmed goblet is not Imperial's Candlewick, but I so far haven't been able to match it up with a specific maker of the 1930s era. Duncan & Miller used a triple-knob stem on the Terrace pattern but it doesn't look exactly like this stem and the bowl shape is different. There were some smaller firms during that period and they often did take-offs on popular lines like Candlewick. This may be one of those. Perhaps a reader can pinpoint who made this design and when. Of course, known patterns are more collectible, but I suspect even without knowing the history of these each could be valued in the $15-20 range if perfect.

Reader Update

Reader Peg Liekweg wrote in regarding the goblet shown on page 33 of the November 2002 issue. She believes the design may be from the Seneca Glass Company. A book, *Seneca Glass Company—1891-1983* by Page & Frederiksen (1995) includes a similar design on pages 6 and 63. I didn't have access to that volume, but I checked through *Elegant Seneca—Victorian—Depression—Modern* by Jennifer A. Lindbeck and Jeffrey B. Snyder (Schiffer, 2000). They show a stem No. 1030 with three round knobs in the stem, but I can't really tell if this matches the piece in my column. I found that Bryce Brothers also had a stem with three knobs and I believe there are some similar designs whose makers are not as known. Thanks to Peg for her input.

Q. I've enclosed a picture of two bottles. I'd appreciate any information you could provide as to their age, history and what they might be worth. Many years ago I was offered $100 for the bottle on the right.

S.C., North Las Vegas, NV

A. Your two clear whiskey bottles probably date from the very late 19th century or early 20th century. Although old whiskies are of interest to bottle collectors in general they prefer those that feature embossed lettering on the sides rather than just paper labels. Many of the older bottles came with both the embossed lettering and paper labels but by the 1890s more were made with just paper labels. These labels are interesting and the one on the right is quite decorative; however, I think an offer of $100 was quite generous. I believe in the general bottle market these bottles might be valued in the $25-50 range each at most.

Clear whiskey bottles

Verre de soie mold-blown vase

Q. This item is a glass vase my mother purchased about 35 years ago from an antique dealer in France who called it satin glass. It has no identifying marks. The vase stands about 10-1/2" tall with 6" diameter at the top and a 4-1/2" diameter at the bottom. The top is ruffled and the sides are slightly ribbed. The vase has a nice opalescence. It has small grains of sand embedded in the glass. We thought it was Steuben. The center pontil is clear and smooth so I am not sure it is hand blown.

D.E., Florence, MA

A. Your large mold-blown vase does have a slightly iridescent satiny finish that could be called "verre de soie," French for "glass of silk." Verre de soie was a line of glass produced by Steuben in the early 20th century; however, the fact that this piece has small impurities in the glass makes me feels it wouldn't quite be the quality of Steuben. Also, I checked through *The Glass of Frederick Carder* by Paul V. Gardner, where all the original sketches of Steuben shapes are reprinted. Although quite a few large ovoid optic ribbed vases were made by that company, I didn't see many that featured crimping on the rolled rim as this one does. If you can get better photos of the piece, including the base pontil, I suggest you contact the Corning Museum of Glass in Corning, N.Y. It has an extensive collection of Steuben wares.

Cut and engraved footed beaker

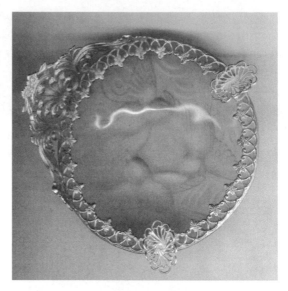

Ashtray with brass filigree trim

Telline perfume flacon

Pierrots covered box

Q. I hope you can help me with these items. They would not photograph well, so I used a color copier. The Telline flacon (1929) is engraved "R. Lalique," but the R. Lalique box and cover with baby Pierrots (1926) is not marked. Could the ashtray with the three birds in a circle be by Lalique circa 1952? It was given to us as a wedding gift in 1952. It looks similar to some other Lalique pieces that we have that were made with only Lalique paper labels. As a young bride, I carefully removed all the paper labels! I have researched this cut glass piece to no avail. It is quite heavy, 6" tall and 3-3/4" wide with a starburst cut in the bottom. The upper band is etched with detailed trees and deer. It is the same pattern as the pattern glass "Deerwood." I assume that it is a spooner as it seems too massive to be a footed tumbler.

R.A.S., Childress, TX

A. You have some lovely pieces of glass. I hope the photos will reproduce here. All older Lalique pieces are sought after, especially those marked "R. Lalique," produced before Rene Lalique's death in 1945. After 1945 Lalique pieces are marked "Lalique—France." The "R" was dropped. The "Telline" perfume flacon (large bottle) was a fairly early design and all

Lalique perfume containers are desirable. However, I couldn't find that this piece was designed for a specific perfume maker and it is those specifically designed containers that seem to have the greatest value today. Also, pieces with more detailed designs, and those with colored stains or in colored glass are much scarcer. I couldn't find a recent sale price for this flacon but I am guessing it might sell in the $1,000 to $3,000 range. The baby Pierrots covered box is charming, but it again appears to be in plain frosted clear glass. Examples with colored stains would sell for more. I am guessing it might be valued in the $600-1,200 range. I don't believe your ashtray is Lalique. The type of brass filigree trim is more typical of wares produced in Czechoslovakia in imitation of Lalique glass. Other imitators included firms such as Verlys, but I'm not familiar with any of their pieces being set in brass frames like this. As a pretty piece of glass I'd guess it might be valued in the $50-75 range. Your handsome cut and engraved footed beaker is most likely a product of Bohemian glasshouse of the second half of the 19th century. The engraved running deer design is typical of many ruby stained and flashed wares produced at that time and the bold, simple cutting was the most popular around the mid-19th century. Your glass is all clear but some fancier examples featured colored staining or enameling or were produced in solid colors such as ruby or green. Although lovely, your clear example isn't quite as dramatic. If it is perfect without any small dings or nicks I believe in today's market it might be valued in the $150-300 range.

Q. This item is an amber glass dog, 7" tall with glass eyes. It is in excellent shape. I appreciate any help you can give.

M.T., Council Bluffs, IA

A. Westmoreland Glass Co. originally produced your amber glass bulldog around 1916 but the mold was also later loaned to the Tiffin Glass Company. Today Summit Art Glass owns the mold. The value will depend on the age and the condition of the piece. You don't give any background on the origins of this example but early ones can sell in the $350-450 range.

Amber glass dog

ABGA Mason Perfect jar

"Red" key jar

Q. I have two fruit jars that I have never found any information on. I would appreciate anything you could tell me.

D.L., Belle Center, OH

A. Thanks for your letter and the nice photos of your fruit jars. I did some research on these two and then contacted Norman Barnett of the Midwest Antique Fruit Jar & Bottle Club in Flat Rock, Ind. Mr. Barnett was kind enough to share the following information: The ABGA Mason Perfect jar was produced in the 1920s by the Ball jar company and was meant mainly for export to Britain and the countries of the British Commonwealth. Today in top condition it can be valued in the $50-75 range. The "Red [key] Mason's Patent 1858" jar is a bit older, dating from about the 1890s; however, it is not as scarce as the ABGA jar. Early examples with ground rims can sell in the $25-35 range while ones with a later, finished rim are valued in the $15-28 range. By the way, the "Red" key jar was actually made in the town of Red Key, Ind. My thanks to Norman Barnett for his help.

Q. Enclosed is a picture of a glass that I believe is a Holly Amber Tumbler. I bought it over 25 years ago from an elderly woman's garage sale in southern Indiana. I know Holly Amber is hard to find and valuable. It's in perfect condition. Could you tell me its value?

V.T., Spencer, IN

Tumbler with Carnival glass finish

A. I wish I could confirm that this is an original "Holly Amber" tumbler produced by the Indiana Tumbler & Goblet Company of Greentown, Ind., but I'm pretty certain it is not. This piece appears to have a definite "Carnival glass" iridescent finish and reproductions of this design in various colors and Carnival finishes were produced by the Joe St. Clair factory in the 1970s. Sometimes they are marked with the initials "SCGC." Although it's not a rare Holly Amber piece, it is still collectible and I think it could be valued in the $15-30 range.

Q. Enclosed are a couple of photos of a glass baby bottle of some type. It pictures an older child (baby) with a long tube it the mouth. On the other side are markings for fluid ounces 1-8. My husband (77 years old) found this stuck in the rafter upstairs at his grandmother's house. We have never seen one anywhere (including museums). What type nipple or sucker was attached? Any information would be interesting. Is there any value?

M.B., Pemberville, OH

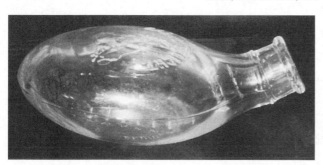

Nursing bottle markings

Nursing bottle with embossed wording and picture

A. Quite a few baby feeding or "nursing" bottles were produced during the late 19ᵗʰ and early 20ᵗʰ century. Some, like yours, had embossed wording and perhaps a picture. Bottle expert Michael Polak has some in his *Antique Trader Bottles Identification and Price Guide* (Krause Publications, 2003). Although many of these old baby bottles have only a modest value, Mr. Polak has listed your "Babys Delight" model, in top condition, at $100 to $130. It was produced around 1890-1900 and would have originally had a rubber nipple. Keep in mind any interior staining or chips and cracks would lower the value considerably.

Q. I have enclosed a photo of a container I pur-chased at a local secondhand store. It is 4-1/2" tall and 6-3/4" wide across the bottom. The glass is beveled and it has felt on the bottom and also on the inside with nailheads visible. It has a lot of detail and has what I think is referred to as paw feet. My first impression was that it was not that old but after more careful examination, I'm not sure. Any information you can give me on age and value will be appreciated.
V.S., Westfield, NJ

Casket with beveled glass sides

A. Your interesting casket does resemble designs produced in Europe in the late 19th and early 20th century. Beveled glass sides were popular at that time as was fancy brass filigree work. I'm not aware that good copies of the detailed old pieces have been made recently so I'm guessing it has good age. Because of its decorative appeal I think it could be valued in the $75-150 range if perfect.

Q. What can you tell me about these glass candleholders?
D.W., Export, PA

A. Your pink glass candleholders with the etched gilt banding are typical of pairs produced in the late 1920s and into the 1930s. They were usually part of a "console set" and would flank a large center console bowl. Many American glass factories produced them so you would need to check through books in elegant glass of that era to pin down which factory made them. Also, other decorating firms sometimes added the gold trim. If perfect I believe the pair could be valued in the $60 to 90 range.

Pink glass candleholders

Q. I would like some help identifying this bowl. I have tried to do some research on my own with no results. It is 8" wide and about 8" tall with the lid. It has yellow inserts of glass and acid-etched floral design that might not be visible in my photo. I would like to know who manufactured the bowl and what value it might have.
V.S., Westfield, IN

Footed large covered bowl

A. You appear to have a footed large covered bowl in the pressed pattern known as "Stars and Bars," which was introduced about 1891 by the Bellaire Goblet Co. of Findlay, Ohio. These larger pieces show up quite frequently with the amber-stained "bars" and engraved border bands. If in perfect condition I believe your piece would be valued in the $75-125 range today.

Q. I have enclosed pictures of a larger bowl and matching smaller ones. I believe them to be a master berry bowl and sauce dishes that were in my grandparents' home as early as 1930-40, as I remember seeing them as a child at that time. Can you please tell me anything about them—what they are called, manufacturer, age, value? Your help is appreciated.

J.R., Topeka, KA

A. Your pressed glass berry set is in the Marsh Fern pattern that was produced in the late 1880s and the early 1890s. It is not often found in green and with the enameled decoration like your set. Most such berry sets come with

Pressed glass berry set with "Marsh Fern" patten

four or six small berry bowls so it would be nice to find some more to fill out your set. As a set of four I would value this group in the $150 to $200 range.

Q. Enclosed are photos of some items belonging to an 87-year-old sister-in-law. They have been in her family for a long time. She believes the cut glass bowl, 3-3/4" in diameter, was brought over from England around 1850, but a neighbor says cut glass in the United States before 1880 was unlikely. The 3" diameter cut glass mustard jar with cover

Round rose bowl in cut glass

Mustard jar

Flattened round heavy glass vase

and sterling silver spoon is from about 1900. The blue vase is hand-blown and Italian, 5-1/2" in diameter.

A. I would agree that the round rose bowl in cut glass would probably date from the 1895-1910 era. If perfect I think it might be valued in the $100-150 range. I can't see the design on the mustard jar very well but it may date from about that same time. If perfect I would value it in the $125-200 range. I have seen similar flattened round heavy glass vases like the blue one you have. They were probably widely produced for export. Unless it has an original sticker or engraved mark showing that it was produced in Murano, Italy, the value would be fairy modest, perhaps $30-60.

Q. This vase is ruby glass with a heavy silver overlay. Our son bought it at an antique store about 35 years ago. It is 11" tall.

R.B., Paxton, IL

A. I checked some references on collectible "Royal Ruby" glass and I believe your vase was made by the Imperial Glass Company around 1950. A different company that specialized in glass decorating probably applied the silver deposit decoration. With the pretty silver deposit decoration combined with the popular ruby color I believe your vase could sell in the $75-125 range.

Imperial "Royal Ruby" glass vase

Jewelry & Costume Accessories

Q. We think this is gold but there are no markings. We know this is at least 85 years old—but we think it could be older. If you open this locket it has a place for a photo on one side. The other side, inside, is the back of the carving. We are wondering what the value of this is and about how old it is. It is 1-1/4" by 1-1/4".

P.W., SD

Locket

A. Your pretty locket is a nice example of commercial Art Nouveau design from around the turn of the 20th century. The sensuous woman was one of the favorite motifs on such pieces. It is most likely gold-filled or gold-plated and set with rhinestones. Most pieces that are 14k gold will be so marked. There is a good demand for such Art Nouveau pieces today and it is nice you know the approximate age since many reproductions of such jewelry items are appearing on today's market, usually in silver. If there is no serious wear to the finish I would guess your locket might be valued in the $75 to $150 range. *See Jewelry Tip #1.

Grooming set

Q. I have been a subscriber for many years, probably a charter member. I have often thought about requesting your assistance but eventually found the answer without bothering you; however, I do now have something that has me stumped. Several years ago at an estate auction, I acquired a lot of 14 pieces of "Sweetheart Beautyware" personal care items. They appear to be made from a brass-like metal, all with their original luster. According to the boxes, it appears a different piece was to be given away each week by the theater. I have no idea as to the period involved, but would guess it to be during the Depression when such giveaways, including dishes, were common as attendance prizes at theaters. I know these are old, as they were in an old-fashioned

Christmas gift box with stripes of poinsettias, which have yellowed with age. I would appreciate it if you can fill me in on the history of these items and their estimated collector value. I always look forward to receiving my monthly magazine and guide and the helpful information it contains!

R.B., St. Louis, MO

A. Your charming grooming set certainly does appear to date from the late 1920s or into the 1930s when such pieces could be used as giveaways at places like theaters. They are some sort of stamped gilt-metal which wasn't supposed to tarnish. Generally such little pieces by themselves don't sell very much, but you are lucky to have the whole group nearly mint with original boxes. Such ladies' accessories are continuing to grow in popularity and your nice set might be valued in the $40-$80 range, I'd think, perhaps more to a specialist collector.

Victorian Revival piece

Q. Enclosed is a picture of a cameo necklace. I don't know how old it is or anything about it, other than it was my mother's. Sorry the picture isn't any clearer. The flowers and circles designs look like fine wire formed into these shapes. The two stones are an aqua blue. The name "Paroo" or something on that order is on the back of two of the circles, shown on the back of the picture. The letters are small so are hard to make out for sure. The cameo stone is a flesh or blush color. I don't know what it is made of. Could you give me more information on it and the value?

R.G., Buffalo, MN

A. Your ornate necklace is a Victorian Revival piece probably dating from the 1930s. The large blue stones are probably faceted glass and the cameo is most likely Bakelite or a related plastic. Without being able to clearly read the marking it's a little difficult to decide on the maker. In searching through jewelry references, however, I found some necklaces with very similar tightly wound circles of wire made by the Napier Co. of New York, so your piece might possibly be from them. Because of its size, style and apparent fine condition, I would say it might sell today in the $75-$150 range.

Q. I would be interested in knowing the age and value of the fan in the attached photos.

G.P., Hyde Park, UT

A. Your interesting fan probably dates from the late 19th century. It's an unusual expandable style with its attached storage. Since it is a simple design I doubt it was used with fancy dress; being solid black, it may have been used during periods of mourning. There are many fan collectors but most seek ornate lace and hand-painted silk fans. I think your fan, if in overall good condition, might be valued in the $50-$100 range.

Fan

Beaded necklace

Q. I have the necklace shown in the enclosed photo. It has three eyes per bead, with various sizes of each eye on each bead. It has a brass chain and clasp (barrel). The beads are glass. Is it from the 1920s? How did they do it? Millefiori? But three different eyes? The eyes do not seem to be applied to the surface. The necklace length is 23-1/2".

C.G., Guthrie, OK

A. Your interesting beaded necklace is a rather unique piece. It is possible that it is as old as the 1920s and could have been made in Venice or perhaps Czechoslovakia, both glassmaking centers. The "eyes" in each bead would be a form of millefiori and consist of a special glass cane that would be inserted into each bead during the hand-manufacturing process. It would have been fairly tricky to do and especially to work the beads so they resemble human eyes. It is possible that the design might have been inspired by the Egyptian design style popular just after the discovery of King Tut's tomb in the early 1920s. A lot of costume jewelry of that time picked up ancient Egyptian motifs such as the "Eye." It's a bit bizarre looking to me but would likely have a good collector value, perhaps in the low to mid-$100s.

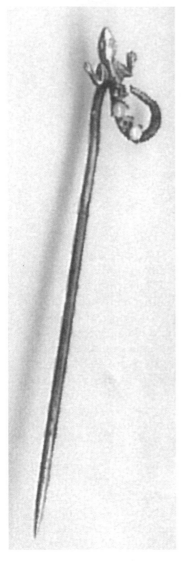

Q. Enclosed is a photocopy of three pins: a cameo stickpin, a mosaic pin with a clamp and "F.A.P." on the back, and an animal stickpin. I know nothing about them except they were my mother's and probably my grandmother's. Please tell me about their history, age and value.

Mrs. N.H., Huron, SD

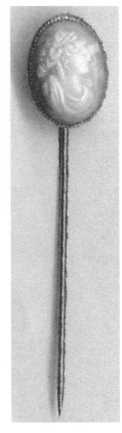

Cameo stickpin

A. The stickpin with the oval cameo at the top features a white classical bust on a rose-colored ground. I can't tell if it is real carved shell, agate or glass and that would help determine the value. A hand-carved cameo piece would be much more collectible. Most likely it dates from the late 19th or early 20th century, which is when I would date all the pieces. Depending on the type of cameo, that stickpin might be valued in the $25-$100 range. The stickpin with the figural lizard or salamander looks like it might be set with seed pearls. It seems to be missing back legs but may not have been made with them. If it is complete and set in gold-filled metal as I suspect, it might be valued in the $25-$45 range. The square brooch features micromosaic floral and scroll designs outlined in twisted wire. The backing appears to be brass. I couldn't find information on the "F.A.P." mark, but it could be for the marker or the retailer. Such mosaic work often came from Italy and I'd guess that's where this piece originated. If there is no damage or missing pieces, I think it might be valued in the $40-$80 range.

Lizard stickpin   *Mosaic stickpin*

Q. This Limoges pin is a lovely piece, but has no signature. How can we tell how old it is? Is it newer? Hope you can help.

M.R., Portland, OR

A. This Limoges pin is marked on the back "Made in France," which indicates it was likely made in the 1925-40 era. A great deal of Victorian Revival

Limoges pin

jewelry was produced then. Again, you need to see if the portrait is hand-painted or a good quality transfer design. I suspect it may be the latter. Depending on that factor it might be in the $40-80 range or several times that if hand-painted.

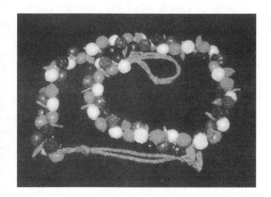

Bakelite or wood?

Victorian hair comb

Q. I always assumed this necklace was wood, but after reading about Bakelite I am wondering if that is what it is. It was given to me by my mother in 1942 for my birthday. The color has faded from the bright red it was. The comb was my grandmother's. She wore it in the late 1800s and early 1900s. She never wore a comb in her hair after 1925. Obviously the "jewels" are not diamonds, but what did they use? Surely rhinestones were later and I never understood what "paste" jewels were. Thank you for your help.

Mrs. W.J. P., Hastings, NE

A. Without examining your necklace first-hand it is difficult to determine for certain whether it is made of Bakelite or painted wood. My first impression is that it is probably Bakelite and that would make it much more desirable than a similar piece with wooden beads. Assuming it is Bakelite it could be valued in the $50-150 range or perhaps more to the right collector. Your late Victorian hair comb is probably made of celluloid, an early synthetic material used to imitate more expensive materials such as ivory and tortoiseshell. The stones trimming the piece would be rhinestones, which are just high-quality faceted glass. Basically that is also what the term "paste" means but this term was used as far back as the 18th century and generally refers to very high quality crystal glass stones made to resemble diamonds. Combs such as this are sought after today and if perfect with all the stones it might be valued in the $40-80 range.

Metalwork box and lid

Q. This item is a small oval
• box. It is 2-1/2" long,
1-1/2" wide and 1-1/2" tall. It
appears to be made of tin and
the top is some kind of marble
or stone. It is smooth and
shiny. There are no markings on any of the items.

J.B., Cumming, GA

A. Since you don't have any real background on the little box it is somewhat
• of a mystery to me also. It could be handmade from thin silver rather than
tin and the stone inset in the top looks like it might be agate. Metalwork of this
type has been produced in India and the Middle East for decades. Dating them is
tricky since such hand-crafted pieces can
still be made there for export. A jeweler
could probably test this to see if it is true
silver. The workmanship is good but not
exceptional. As a little decorative piece I'd
guess it might be valued in the $25-40
range.

Q. I have this sterling silver charm
• bracelet. The tag on each charm
reads "S.S. 925—Limited Edition." The

Charm bracelet

four charms are quite heavy and each has a moving part. Each says "Disney—The Disney Store" on one side and "Disney 925 Lim Ed" on the other side. Can you give me any information on age and value as a collector's item? The charms are a kangaroo with movable baby in pouch; bear with jar of honey; cow or ass or bull; rabbit holding a carrot.

F.G., Pleasant Valley, AZ

A. Your sterling silver charm bracelet features characters from the animated Disney feature "Winnie the Pooh." Since it was marketed through a Disney Store we know that it is quite modern. I guess it would depend on the demand from a Pooh fan, but I think a value in the $30-50 range would be fair.

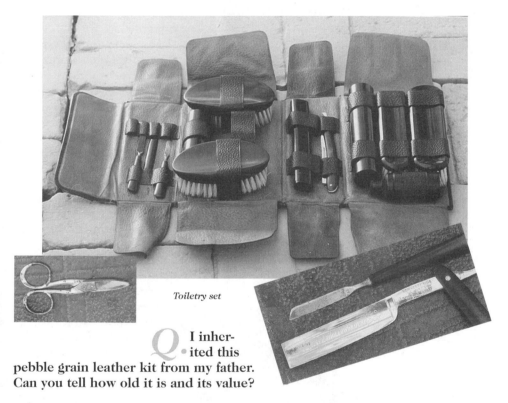

Toiletry set

Q. I inherited this pebble grain leather kit from my father. Can you tell how old it is and its value?

A. You have inherited a nice man's traveling toiletry set that was probably produced in the 1900-1920 era. It appears to be in nearly complete and excellent condition. There are some people interested in such sets, but it is the sets and accessories made for women that are much more in demand. They simply are much more decorative. Since your set is so complete and in nice condition I believe a value in the $40-80 range is appropriate.

REPAIR
SERVICE
WHEN OUT OF ORDER
SEND THIS TIMER TO
REPAIR DEPT.

A. R. & J. E. Meylan
264 W. 40TH ST.
NEW YORK
N. Y.

Q. I am enclosing pictures of two watches in hopes that you can tell me more about them and their value. The first one is a stopwatch that belonged to my father that I can remember playing with when I was a child. My dad owned a tool and die shop during World War II and made parts for the government. Supposedly the watch had some connection to his dealings with the government. The back of the case is stamped "N.R.L. No. 1." He always said the initials stood for "National Research Laboratory," although whether this is true or not, I don't know. The large hand clicks off ten seconds and the small hand (not visible) will time up to five minutes. The first press on the stem brings the big hand back to "0" and the second press will bring the small hand back to "0." The watch is in good working order. Inside the back case is a piece of paper on where to send the watch for repair.

The second watch was found by my father. The

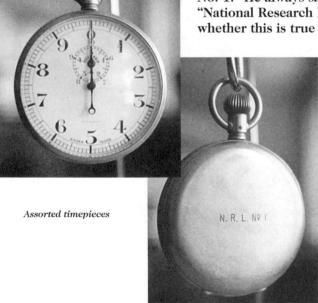

Assorted timepieces

N. R. L. Nº 1

case was in bad condition when he gave it to us. The crystal was missing but the enamel face was in very good condition. The blue numerals are raised and the name in the center says "Regulator." There is a second hand that ticks off one minute on the center bottom of the watch. The date "1793" is scratched inside the back cover and down near the lid hinge, barely visible is "H10500P." There may also be an apostrophe mark after the "P." We had the watch repaired about 30 years ago, as it was in good running condition, and painted the outside of the case black because of its poor condition.

G.W.H., Tucson, AZ

A. You have a couple of interesting timepieces. I've done some checking through the *Complete Price Guide to Watches* by Cooksey Shugart, Tom Engle and Richard E. Gilbert. Unfortunately, I couldn't quickly find background on your pieces. The stopwatch appears to say "Swiss Made" on the dial, so that tells us where it was made. It may be a fine quality instrument purchased by the National Research Laboratory, but I don't believe these devices have quite the collector appeal that pocket watches do. I can only guess that the right collector might offer in the low to mid-$100s. Some of the finest chronometers and related timekeepers, of course, can sell in the thousands. Your other watch does have a lovely enameled dial, but the word "Regulator" doesn't tell me too much. Usually the maker's name would appear here, so this may also have been a special order piece. I don't recognize the "HP" and number mark and I believe the "1793" probably is not a date but perhaps a mark left by an early cleaner/repairer. Pieces like this often have a value determined as much by the quality of the works as the dial and case, so I can't tell you too much about that. Also, I probably would not have painted the case; even a worn original finish is more desirable that something painted over. Perhaps a watch collector can provide further details on your pieces.

Dressing table set

Dressing table set, outside

Q. I am enclosing two pictures, one of the outside of the box and the other inside. It has the original guarantee and was bought in 1942. The manufacturer was Perelin Works, New York, N.Y. The price paid at the time of purchase was $19. This is on the guarantee inside. I have looked at books and cannot find anything on dresser sets. Can you give me some idea of value?

B.S., Pendleton, NJ

A. Your complete portable dressing table set is a great boudoir piece. I can't tell if the exterior of the case is plastic but I suspect it is likely cardboard with a marbleized effect. It appears to be complete and nearly unused, but I doubt the round clear cut class bottle in the front and the framed photos came with it originally. There is a lot of interest in ladies' boudoir items today and complete sets are fairly scarce in top condition. If you found just the right collector I suspect this set might sell in the $100 to $200 range.

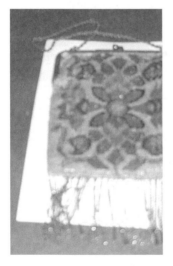

Beaded purse

Q. I am interested in information on the beaded purse: value, date made, etc. It was one of my fortunate garage sale purchases (25 cents).

J.H., Detroit Lakes, MN

A. I wish the photo of your beaded purse was sharper. It is wonderfully colorful and has an abstract design typical of the 1920s and early 1930s. The best purses of that era were sometimes signed inside the metal frame at the top. However, individuals using designs from popular magazines of the era made others. The "signed" examples tend to have the highest values. Condition is also very important so any wear or loose beads will lower the value greatly. Because of its bold, colorful design I feel this piece, even if "home-made," might sell in the $150-300 range.

Lamps & Lighting Devices

Q. We recently purchased this cut glass lamp. It is 40" tall from top of shade to bottom. The shade is 20" tall, and the crystal part of the lamp is 23" tall. Could you give us an estimate of its value? We can find no markings or signature.

W.M., Bella Vista, AZ

A. From the overall style and the way the sections appear to be bolted together, I would guess this piece is not quite an antique. Some nice quality cut glass has been coming out of Eastern Europe in the last 25 years or so and I'd guess this lamp would fall into that category. Some similar examples may be available in better home furnishings shops today so you might check for comparable replacement values.

Cut glass lamp

Art Deco lamp

Q. I am interested in general information on this Art Nouveau lamp. The glass, which seems kind of frosted/vaseline variety, is the original (as far as I know). I found this in my grandfather's attic in Linglestown, Pa., around 1957.

R.C., Ventura, CA

A. Your lamp does have some characteristics of the Art Nouveau style such as the woman's long, flowing hair, but overall the design is more in the Art Deco mode with the angular figure and geometric detailing on the lamp base and mushroom-shaped frosted green glass shade. A number of American companies produced such lamps during their heyday in the 1920s and 1930s and originals in top condition are very sought after. They were not always marked but the Frankart Company was one of the leading manufacturers of such cast metal pieces so double check for any marks under this lamp. Even if it is not a Frankart piece it would be very collectible and might sell in the $500-$1,000 range in the right market if the condition is as good as it appears in the picture. Collectors should be aware, however, that reproductions and knock-offs of originals are on the market today, so shop with care.

Newel post lamp

Q. I value your opinion and look forward to your column in the monthly Collector Magazine. Yours is always the first section I turn to when my issue arrives. In your August 1998 issue you shoed a "newel post" lamp with three Grecian style women as the mid-section. You stated, "Perhaps the top portion has been altered somewhat with a longer post and larger lamp shades," which seemed out of proportion for the base and the owner could check close for any signs of soldering marks. This is such a coincidence, and the very thing that prompted me to write, since I had just two days prior to seeing your column purchased a similar type lamp from a little thrift and collectible shop in Riverside County. Boy, was I shocked when I opened up the issue to your column and there it was, what appears to be a very similar lamp to my new purchase. It is also of a pot metal/bronze-type metal, very heavy and garish looking with ornate openwork metal shades. It appears someone had embellished the finish by painting the women with copper, gold and silver hobby-type paint. The cord appears newer with "Heyco" and "#437-S8" printed on cord washer to base. This base is not flush with the women's feet as you can see in the picture. I'm assuming that portion of the lamp has been changed. My question is, is my lamp also from the turn of the century? Even though some parts may have been replaced? Is it from the 1920s or '30s or a later version? I hope you can tell from my picture though the one-arm, woman and shade are hidden from this angle. There are three women, shades and curling vine metal curved arms. It is 21-1/4" as pictured, the mid-section is 12" and 15" from feet base to top vines and finial. I look forward to hearing your opinion on my newel post-type lamp and any value in it present state.

K.T., Yorba Linda, CA

A. Your lamp does appear to be another nice example of a newel post lamp from around the turn of the century. From your photo it would appear to me that the contrasting painted portions might be original as this was done on some examples of the period. Also, the ornate filigree shades on your piece are more in keeping with the style of the lamp than the large glass shades on the lamp I discussed in the August column. It is certainly possible that the wiring was replaced on this piece at some point but that wouldn't detract from its collector value. Assuming that this piece is all original and from the late 19th or early 20th century I think it could be valued in the $1,500-$2,500 range. A nice find indeed.

Q. My father purchased this lamp at an antiques store in the late 1940s or early 1950s and we have always wanted to know more about it. Being an avid reader of your column, I am sure you can tell me more than I know already. The lamp seems to be constructed of brass filigree with smoky green curved slag glass pieces that were molded for the particular places that they are placed. The only visible markings are molded into the bottom of the base in block letters that read: "PAT APPLIED FOR." It comes apart quite easily into three pieces. We've always thought that a clear glass chimney was probably used to keep it more securely together. The base appears to have all the fittings for an oil lamp, but it was wired for electricity when it was purchased. Someone told my father that it might have been designed for the purchaser to choose whether to use oil or electricity. When we took it apart to have it rewired, the brass holder for the light bulb was dated 1907. I hope the details needed are visible in the photo.

C.V., Murrels Inlet, SC

Unique design

A. Your very interesting lamp is quite an unusual variation of turn-of-the-century lighting fixtures with slag glass shades. I don' believe I've ever seen a tall table lamp with the ornate slag paneled shade as well as slag panels around the font holder base. I would say that it does date within a few years of the 1907 date you found, an era when both kerosene and electricity were used and some fixtures were made to convert. Without a close inspection I can't say for certain if your piece was specifically designed to be converted, but it appears to have been changed at an early date. You didn't give a size but it appears to be quite tall, perhaps of the so-called "banquet" style height. Because of its unique design, it's a bit hard to set a specific value, but I'd say it could be in the $1,200-$2,200 range.

Handel shade

Q. I have in my possession a lampshade (5" tall, 6-1/2" wide) signed "Handel 5529." It had been left hanging over a light bulb by the previous homeowner approximately 40 years ago. Can you give me an idea of its value?

M.S., Rochester, NY

A. Someone left you a real prize when they moved out years ago. The Handel company was one of the best-known makers of reverse-painted shades and lamps and their early 20th century pieces are much in demand. A scenic landscape shade such as yours is especially nice and this form was also produced to fit on small boudoir lamps in the Teens and 1920s. Since Handel also made shades for hanging hall lights, yours may have been original to the home. If it is perfect without any chips or cracks and has nice coloring, a collector might pay in the $800-$1,000 range for this signed example.

Q. **This lamp is one of a pair bought at an estate sale, in good shape. I would love to know if these are of any worth.**

S.S., Osceola, MO

A. Your decorative lamp with the figural bisque porcelain figure on a filagreed gilt-brass base is typical of table and boudoir lamps made in the 1930s through the 1950s. My guess is that this piece might date from the 1930s or late 1940s. The figure is undoubtedly bolted to the base but if marked my guess is that it would indicate Japan as the place of origin, although it's possible it came from Germany. The metal fittings were probably added in this country. You don't give a size but I guess it is a table lamp, and though not antique, is collectible. Value might be in the $150-$250 range if the figure is perfect, a bit more to the right collector.

Table lamp

Q. **I purchased a Gone With The Wind lamp. It has an old burner. The only markings I can find on it are on the flame spreader. On the outer edge of a circle is "Pat APRIL 93," "Sept 9 90," "APRIL 3 95." Inside the circle is "P" with "Royal" underneath it and "A" underneath that. On the wick turner is "Made in US of America." I would like any information and price on this lamp.**

T.N., Houston, TX

A. You have a nice Gone With The Wind table lamp made around 1900. It appears to have a nice decoration of large pink and red roses on a blue ground and features gilt-metal and brass fittings. The markings on the burner indicated they were made by Plumb & Atwood Mfg. Co., who supplied the parts. The glass parts and other metal sections probably came from other companies so it's difficult to say who "made" this piece.

Gone with the Wind lamp

They were popular and sold through catalogs such as Sears and Montgomery Wards when new. You don't say if yours is electrified but it doesn't appear to be. It also appears to need a clear glass chimney for the burner. Overall it appears to be in great shape and might be valued in the $300-$600 range.

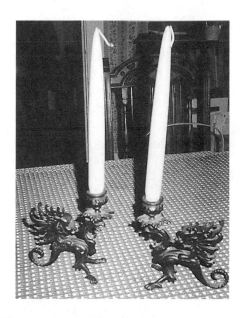

Satsuma lamp

Victorian candleholders

Q. Your section is the best feature of the magazine and I hope you can use one or more of these pictures in the near future. I inherited these items. The lamp was one of a pair of jars. The candleholders are iron.

H.S., Lebanon, NH

A. The lamp on your table appears to be an example of brightly decorated Satsuma pottery of the type widely exported to this county in the first part of the 20th century. The jars may have been drilled at a factory for use as lamps. The pair might be valued in the $200-$400 range. The griffin-form candleholders are probably late Victorian and could sell in the $150-$250 range for the pair.

Q. My mother left me this 19-1/2" tall table lamp, the shade of which seems to be paper, with two globes under shade with pull chain each.

P.C., Charlotte, NC

Table lamp

A. Your table lamp has a paneled waxed paper shade typical of the 1920s and it complements the design on the pottery base. The base has a rather Art Deco look with some Oriental influence also. The base may have been made in China but without a marking it would be hard to know. From the photo it appears that the base has some repairs, which would greatly reduce its collectible value, although it's still an interesting display piece.

Q. **What can you tell me about the age and value of this lamp?**

J.S., Stephenville, TX

A. Your tall elegant "banquet" lamp has a cast and stamped brass base fitted with a section of onyx stone, a high-quality piece. The ruby pigeon blood ball shade would have come from another glass factory and made to fit the base. It's a fine example of a choice type of lamp. I'd value it in the $600-$900 range.

Banquet lamp

Q. **This is a lamp my husband received from his grandmother after her passing. His grandmother was from Germany, but he doesn't know if she brought it over with her or purchased it in America. He said that at one time it burned oil, but was converted to electric. The flowers are hand-painted. All the pieces are in excellent condition. Any information would be greatly appreciated.**

S.H., Brandon, MS

A. Your hanging parlor lamp is typical of the 1890s era and appears to be in nice, original condition. If carefully electrified, I'd say it might be valued in the $450-$650 range.

Parlor lamp

Q. I have read your column for the last few years and have enjoyed it greatly. I hope you can help me with some information on this lamp that I have sent you a picture of. I bought it about 20 years ago at an estate sale. The lamp is very ornate and has glass eyes.

B.S., Oside, NY

A. Your interesting lamp has wonderful detail, with the rearing Oriental dragon holding a large nautilus shell in its mouth to form the lampshade. Your lamp appears to be sitting on a carved wood Chinese stand with a red soapstone insert but I can't be certain if it is of Chinese or Japanese origin. Japanese bronzes from the late 19th and early 20th century appear to be more common on the market today. My guess would be that this piece would date from the early 20th century and, since the quality appears to be excellent, I'd say it might be valued in the $1,200-$2,400 range.

Oriental lamp

Northwood lampshade

Q. I read your article each issue. Perhaps you can help me. I have two "Paneled Poppy" lampshades taken down from my mother's home. They have never been taken down before. They have all the chains and fittings just as bought. We can get no information on these except that they're "scarce." They are made of colored pressed custard glass with nutmeg stain by Harry Northwood. They must be sold soon. We would appreciate any information on who may be interested in buying them, prices, anything.

Mrs. B.W., Ogden UT

A. Your hanging light fixture does look like it is an example of Harry Northwood's "Luna Ivory" glass, which was used in light fixtures in the 1915-20 era. Vintage light fixtures such as this are always in demand and, since it does appear to be a design produced by the Northwood firm, that would add to collector interest. Probably not many such fixtures with original hardware come on the market, so I would say it might be valued in the $800-$1,000 range at least.

Electric kerosene lamp

Q. Enclosed is a photo of an electrified oil lamp. I believe it's brass with an Oriental flavor. It's 14" high and 8" wide. The ring that raises the wick is marked "Pat'd Jan. 17, 1871, May 2, 1875, Feb 27, 1877. H.G. Moehring." I was told that the shade is an antique poolroom fixture. Does this lamp have any value in this condition? The glass is opaque white.

D.P., Far Rockaway, NY

A. Your table lamp appears to be an early electric adaptation of a Victorian kerosene lamp. The wonderful Oriental-inspired Victorian (ca. 1880) font appears to be antiqued brass with a nice patina and fine detailing. The filigree metal base it sits on is quite typical of ones used in the 1920s and 1930s and the slag glass metal-framed shade is also typical of the early electric era, ca. 1910-25. The parts all work quite well together and make an appealing lamp. Because slag glass lamps are very collectible and this is an attractive "marriage," I'd say it might sell today in the $400-$600 range at least.

Q. Enclosed find a photo of a table lamp. The lamp is 22" tall with a six-panel 18" shade. Every other panel has an iced texture with the other panels being smoother. It has one light in the base and two in the top. The scene depicts a small walking bridge over a pond with trees and a house in the background. It is reverse-painted. I cannot find any identifying marks as to manufacturer nor do I have any idea of value. Your reply to shed light on the manufacturer and value would be appreciated.

E.C., Portsmouth, VA

Bent-glass table lamp

A. Your bent-glass paneled table lamp is a style popular from about 1915-30 when the electric lamp was first really the newest thing on the market. Your reverse-painted version was made to compete with the more expensive types produced by firms like Handel and Pairpoint. It could have been made by any number of smaller firms who didn't always mark their pieces. Because it is a colorful Art Deco design with a light in the base and in apparently excellent condition, I think it might be valued today in the $600-$900 range.

Q. Please help. I love your column. When I get my magazine I go straight to your column. I have had this lamp for three years. I found it at a farm sale in Idaho. It is heavy. You can flick the shade and it sounds like crystal. The shade is carnival inside and out and it kind of looks like fine bumps or almost like a sugar glaze outside. I have not seen any names. Please help if you can.

J.K., Hollister, CA

Early electric lamp

A. I wish you had included a size for the shade and overall height. (Readers, please take note: sizes are important.) This table lamp is a nice example of an early electric fixture from 1915-30. The most collectible lamps of that era with domed glass shades such as this were produced by the Handel and Pairpoint companies. Many other firms made less elaborate styles. Your iridized shade has a frosted exterior finish and the cap and base are patinated metal meant to resemble bronze. The value would be much higher if the shade had a reverse-painted decoration. Depending on size, I think it might be valued in the $400-$600 range.

Q. I am including a picture of a possibly pewter and bronze statue, maybe an incense or candleholder, 9-1/4" high. The inscription on base reads "1313 Made in France. Depose." It's also signed "Vantines." I enjoy so much your question-and-answer page in my monthly Collector Magazine.

B.T., La Pine, OR

A. This cast-metal figural piece shows a Medieval troubadour standing by a Gothic-style lamp post. The "Made in France" marking would date it from between the wars. "Depose" is French for "patented" and Vantines was an American importing firm. The piece is interesting, with its painted bronze-style finish. It may have been used as an incense burner since they were popular in the 1920s and 1930s. Again, you don't give a size, but if it is about 8"-12" tall and has no damage, I think it might be valued in the $50-$100 range at least.

Incense burner

*Slag glass
boudoir lamp*

Q. I love your question and answer column. I hope you
can tell me some interesting things about this lamp. It
belonged to my grandmother who died in the '40s. It's ivory
colored with palm trees on the shade. I can't find any name
or marks.

E.H., Waynesboro, VA

A. You appear to have a pretty little slag glass boudoir lamp
that probably dates from the 1920s. The antiqued white
finish on the metal filigree shade and tree trunk base may be
original and the slag glass appears to be pale green which,
when lit, would highlight a tropical seashore landscape. Such
lamps have become very collectible and I'd guess yours might
be valued in the $400-600 range.

Q. Enclosed are pictures of
an old lamp that belongs
to my mother. I have been
unable to find much information about it. I think it was
maybe from the 1920s. It is
made from some type of metal,
possibly bronze. It is quite
heavy, measures 25" tall and is
original except for the cord.
There are no marks that I find.
The shade is very heavy glass. It
measures 18" across the bottom. The top opening measures
3-1/2" across. I have been told
there could be a signature

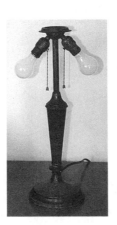 

1920s lamp

hidden in the painting on the shade but I have not found any. The shade is
rather ugly until the light is on and then it is beautiful! The scene in the
painting looks like Austria to me. Any information you can provide would be
appreciated.

J.D., Owensboro, KY

A. You do have a lovely table lamp dating about the 1920s. The shade almost
has the look of layered cameo glass shades from Europe, but I suspect the
effect was achieved by painting the design both on the exterior and interior of
the shade. I've gone through references on three of the major lamp producers of
that era—Handel, Pairpoint and Moe Bridges—but couldn't find a match for your
shade design or the nice antiqued bronze base. It's too bad you can't find any
marking on the shade or base. Maybe one of our readers will recognize it. Just
based on the quality I can see in the photos I wouldn't be surprised if it might
sell in the $2,500 to $4,000 range in the right market.

Q. The French lamp is 26" high and its base is 6" around. It's in perfect condition, with original two bulbs. Markings include a medallion the size of a dime printed with "Made in France" and "Francaise Fabrication" around the medallion on back of the bottom of the statue; and a design in the center of a circle, with "Paris" underneath. A plaque on the base of the statue reads: "Frisson de Mai Par Aug Moreau (Med Ille d'Or)." The reverse-painted lamp is 16" across and 19" high. Markings on the light fixture read "Parker Lamp, 250 Watt, 250 Volt."

J.J.H; No. Riverside, IL

Early electric lamp

A. The tall figural lamp is in the Art Nouveau style and is an early electric fixture. This type, with the leafy vines surrounding the figure and fitted for bulbs, was popular in the early 20th century. It is probably bronze-patinated metal, with the figure being copied from a work by Auguste Moreau, a French bronze artist. Nice examples of these lighting devices are very collectible and can sell in the $1,500-2,000 range. Your table lamp with the reverse-painted shade is typical of the style popular in the 1910-30 era. The Parker Lamp firm is not well known today, and the quality doesn't compare to the examples from firms such as Handel and Pairpoint but, if perfect, it still might be valued in the $800-1,600 range.

Table lamp

Slag glass table lamp and shade

Q. I recently purchased this lamp, and I'm not sure if it is a refinished item or a reproduction. It has a filigree slag glass shade and is marked on the bottom "Enosaic Shade Co., Chicago." Could you tell me anything more about this company, the date of manufacture and approximate value of the lamp? Thank you very much.

N.S., Hartsdale, NY

A. From your photos I would say you do have an original slag glass table lamp from the 1920s. I am not familiar with the name "Enosaic," but there were a number of factories working at that time producing similar lamps. The base appears to be cast metal with a patinated finish. You don't give a size for the lamp or shade, but guessing the shade is about 18" diameter, I think this piece might be valued in the $800-1,200 range.

Pairpoint lamps

Q. I am writing to you in the hope you can give me some information on the Pairpoint lamps pictured. We have had them in the family for the past 50 years. My folks bought them at an estate sale in upper Wisconsin. The photos show them as they were bought (without prisms), but they must have had prisms on the cuff below the light bulb as there are holes there. They are marked with the Pairpoint name along with their mark (P inside a diamond illustrated mark). It also has the mark "Pewter" and name "P3000." About the prisms— we were fortunate enough to find some very old ones when the Elks Club in Manistee, Mich., remodeled its lodge room. They had been there since the lodge was built.

Mrs. D.H., Cadillac MI

A. Your marked Pairpoint candlestick-style lamps are typical of Colonial Revival pieces popular in the 1910-30 period. The bases are made to resemble old pewter candlesticks, with the frosted and engraved shades copying styles of the 1840-60 era. You are right about the prisms, and the ones you found complement them nicely. The most decorative Pairpoint lamps of that era are extremely desirable today, especially the ornate "Puffies." They can sell for many thousands of dollars. Your pieces are very nice, but not in that range. I'd guess that the pair might be valued in the $500-1,000 range.

Q. Enclosed is a picture of a leaded lamp. We believe it to be a Williamson lamp. Height is 24-1/2", leaded shade 14-1/2". Perhaps you can help us identify it and give us an idea of the value.

B.&C.J., Feeding Hills, MA

A. You appear to have a pretty, small leaded glass table lamp probably dating from around the 1920s. I've been trying to research the trademark on the base but without luck. I don't believe it is for the Williamson or Wilkinson lamp company, but there were many other smaller firms producing similar lamps during that era. The leaf and jeweled design on the shade is quite unique and attractive. Even such lamps by lesser-known makers are growing in value. I think one in this size, without any serious damage, might be valued in the $800-1,200 range at least.

Leaded lamp

Q. I have this Tiffany-style lamp with reverse painting of Asian water scenery, given to my parents as a wedding gift in about 1927. It is 23" high with a base 8" in diameter. The shade is 16" in diameter. It appears to have gold paint on cast-metal with a green and red accent spray, similar to air brushing. I cannot find any markings. It has two pull chain sockets. Any information about this would be appreciated.

C.P., River Edge, NJ

Tiffany-style lamp

A. Your paneled and reverse-painted table lamp is a decorative item from the 1920s. Many firms produced such lamps, which were meant to simulate the more expensive ones from firms like Handel and Pairpoint. A decorative one like yours, in top condition, might be valued in the $500-750 range at present.

Q. We have an old hanging fixture with a heavy base, perhaps brass, with five cone-shaped amber glass bulb covers. The bottom also is amber glass with a small bulb inside. We have had these pieces several years and would appreciate any help you could give us on the age and value of them. Thank you.

L.S., Hart, MI

A. Your ceiling light fixture is a great example of Art Deco design. The brass or bronzed metal

Art Deco design fixture

frame and the dramatic conical shades make it a choice example of that design, ca. 1925-35. Depending on the overall size, condition and local market I would think it could be valued in the $1,000-1,500 range. It might sell for more in a major city market.

Lightolier lamp

Q. We have enclosed several pictures of a table lamp we have had in our family for 40 some years. It was purchased from an antiques dealer many years ago who is no longer in business. The lamp is signed "Otto," followed by what looks like two large "X"s and a short space, then an "E" and "H". A road scene goes around the entire shade. The lamp is about 24" tall. I would appreciate any information you could give. Thank you.

D.S., Toledo, OH

A. You have a lovely reverse-painted table lamp dating from the 1920s. It is especially nice that the shade is signed by the artist. It took some looking through references on electric lamps of that era, but the unique blossom-form finial on your lamp helped me identify it as a product of the Lightolier Lamp Co., ca. 1923-25. I didn't see your exact base in the reference I checked, but similar types of lamps from the "After Sunset" line are probably valued today in the $1,500-$2,000 range.

Q. I have written to you in hopes of finding out what I have recently inherited. Enclosed is a photo of a lamp marked on the base "Tiffany Studios," with a shade marked "Quizel."

L.M., Great Neck, NY

A. I appreciate your writing, but I wish you had a little more background history on

Tiffany look-alike

your item. The lamp, although it may be marked on the bottom "Tiffany Studios," looks to me like it may be a modern reproduction. The original balance lamps by Tiffany did come in a style very similar to this but the name should be in two lines reading "Tiffany Studios/New York" and then a style number. The finish on this base has a newer "golden" hue rather than the aged bronze patina of an original. Also, if your shade is actually marked "Quizel" as you noted then we know it is a fake since the actual glass line was "Quezal," a company that competed with Tiffany. Unfortunately, Tiffany lamp fakes have become rampant on the market and I feel quite certain this is one of the newer pieces.

Q. **I am enclosing two pictures of lamps I found in an old trunk in my 93-year-old uncle's basement. They are still working. I have tried to find out a little about them but so far have been unable to get any information. They are about 14" tall and have glass shades painted inside. The label on one says "Handel Lamps." The label is off the other one but the base says "Handel" also. Could you please tell me something about them and if they are auctionable or the value if any. The bases seem to have mold or something on them. Can they be cleaned or restored safely?**

M.M., Mountain View, CA

Handel lamp

A. You have turned up a couple of real treasures in your uncle's basement! The Handel Company of Meriden, Conn., was one of the major producers of early electric lamps during the 1920s and today their pieces are extremely collectible. Your two lamps are called "boudoir" lamps because of their smaller size. It is a treat to find them in such great, original condition. The first one, with the cast forest scene on the bronze base, appears to have a reverse-painted shade featuring goldenrod in a landscape and may be their model No. 6457. The other lamp, also with an original Handel base, has a model No. 6242 Handel shade with a reverse-painted design of pink and yellow blossoms and green leaves. The landscape designs on Handel shades are the most sought after so that lamp might be valued in the $2,500 to $3,500 range. The other with the simpler design might be in the $1,500-2,500 range. Whatever you do, DO NOT CLEAN the bronze bases—they are not moldy but have the original bronze patina. Cleaning that original finish would lower the lamps' values considerably!

Candelabrum

Q. This item is from my private collection, given to me by my mother and father. I have been unable to identify the maker of the candelabra, although it is very much Capo di Monte style. What can you tell me about this piece (signature, history of maker, value)?

P.P., Red Mound, OR

A. I appreciate your letter and photos. The decorative candelabrum (I assume it is a single) appears to have nice molded porcelain floral pieces on a brass framework. A clear drawing of the mark might help track down more history. Such items have been produced for export since the early 20th century, and there are probably some examples still available at better decorating stores. I have seen some ceramic examples that were made in Spain, but this could be Italian-made. I can only guess that, if perfect, it might have a decorator value in the $200-$400 range and might bring more.

Q. I am enclosing a picture of a piano lamp I recently acquired. It is complete with original accessories as an oil lamp. Most importantly, the glass is original. However, it has been wired for electricity. There are four different inscriptions etched on the lamp: (1) "PATD July 3, 1886"; (2) "PAT'D June 18, 1878"; (3) "PATD April 4, 1876"; and (4) "PAT 4309." There are possibly three different metals used on the lamp. I hope the photograph is clear enough for you to identify as much as possible. I would appreciate any information you may be able to give me including a possible value. I am a recent subscriber to Collector Magazine and Price Guide, and enjoy our column enormously.

C.E., Rohnert Park, CA

A. You have an attractive "piano" or "organ" lamp popular in the 1880s and 1890s. It appears that the base may be a combination of brass, iron and perhaps white metal as trim. The frosted lobed shade is also a nice feature and original shades add to the value. Even though it was electrified I feel that in the antique lighting market it should be valued in the $400-800 range.

Piano lamp

Q. I have been receiving Collector Magazine ever since I became aware of it. I really enjoy it and your columns are the best and most informative. I recently renewed my subscription. I have had the enclosed item since 1940— bought from an antique collector. It is a lamp on which I cannot find any markings. It is 30" high, bronze with green grapes and dark green with light below, can use either, or both, lights. It is electrified under feet, and also light under green glass.

J.B., Chicago IL

Hall lamp

A. Your ornate figural lamp is typical of late Victorian pieces that often sat in the entry halls of finer homes and sometimes rested on newel posts. It is probably of cast metal with a bronzed finish but has great details with the woman carrying buckets below the tall vines with grape clusters forming shades. It appears that the base even lights up. It would be a very desirable piece for those who like late Victorian lighting. I suspect it should be valued in the $2,500-$3,500 range.

⌒⌒⌒⌒⌒

Q. I really enjoy your column—it is the first thing I read. Enclosed are pictures of a lamp that has been in our family as long as I can remember. I know very little about it.

C.M., Lusk, WY

A. Thanks for your letter and photos. Your attractive slag glass electric lamp is typical of the many such lamps popular during the 1920s and early 1930s. This piece has a shade with a rather unusual flat-topped form with lighter color slag glass panels there and curved blue slag edge panels covered with classical scrolls and swags. For quite a while these filigree over-laid lamps were not as much in demand as the fine

Slag glass lamp

reverse-painted and leaded glass lamps produced by major makers such as Handel, Pairpoint and Tiffany. More research documents other lamp makers of the era whose pieces are growing tremendously in value. However, a great many of the nice lamps like yours were unmarked and can be difficult to attribute to a specific maker. A series of books called *Electric Lighting of the 20s & 30s* from L-W Books (Indiana) does reproduce various original company catalog pages as well as catalog pages from mass-market sellers such as Sears. The company catalogs can help identify certain lamps, but many of the other ads don't mention any maker. I can say that one company included in these references was the Empire Lamp & Brass Mfg. Co. of Chicago. Some of their pages do show lamps quite similar to yours with elaborate metal overlays on slag glass panels. I didn't see your exact piece, however. Due to its design and condition I feel this lamp might be valued today in the $750-$1,000 range in the right market.

Q. I have always wondered about these candleholder figurines. I can date them in my family to the late 1800s. They have no markings on the hollow bottom. The candleholder is brass, I presume. The two women are really quite lovely. What you think about them will be of interest to me.

J.M.H., York ME

Candleholders

A. You have a very pretty pair of figural candleholders. From what I can tell the seated Classical figures appear to be decorated bisque porcelain and are probably on a painted bisque base. The inserted gilt brass candle sockets are very unusual and it is remarkable that they have remained intact. Such pieces could have been made in Germany or France but I might lean toward a French origin for these. I feel they could date to the 1850-70 period and may well have been used as mantel ornaments. If they are in perfect condition I suspect the pair could be valued in the $450-$850 range in the right market.

Q. This item was left to us by my mother-in-law along with many other very collectible things. Most of them we have managed to find out about but this piece we have searched the Web for with no luck. Can you tell me what this was used for and the value?

Greenfield, MO

A. Your interesting lantern-style lamp features a lovely brass framework enclosing a deep ruby glass shade. One feature that may suggest its origins is the cross-form pendant at the bottom. This suggests to me that this may have originally hung in a church or chapel. The design of the frame is typical of the 1880s and 1890s and it may originally have held a small glass fuel font. It is a very pretty piece and because of its decorative appeal could be valued in the $250-$500 range, perhaps a bit more to the right collector.

Q. I own this silver-colored Aladdin lamp. The "cap" for the kerosene (fuel) well has "Rayo" on it. It's all original. I see no other markings. It is in excellent condition. I have had it over 40 years. A friend gave it to me then. It is 19-1/2" tall. We did replace the clear glass shade inside the white one. I also have a brass Aladdin lamp. We did replace the clear shade and the white hobnail shade. We got this at a garage sale for $3. It had been made into an electric lamp with the cord, plug and switch in the cord. It is 19-1/2" tall. It has "Rayo" on the cap of the fuel tank. I see no other markings. I don't know if it is plated with brass. It doesn't appear to be—it looks like it came in the brass color. The woman said it was her mother's and this woman was 80. Thanks for any help you can give me on value and anything else you can tell me about these pieces.

J.L., Ft. Collins, CO

Rayo nickel-plated lamp

Appealing lantern

A. Your silver lamp is actually nickel-plated and is not a true "Aladdin." The marking "Rayo" indicates that it was made by that lamp maker and it probably dates from the very late 19th century up to around the 1920s. The domed milk glass shade may be original and replacing the clear chimney is not a big problem. If it is not electrified I think it might sell today in the $125-200 range. The brass lamp is also a Rayo of the same era as the silver one. Even though it is electri-

Rayo brass lamp

fied and has a new shade it is still collectible. It is also likely that it was origi-nally nickel-plated and in more recent years was stripped down to the brass since many people like the look of brass. I don't recommend that for original nickel-plate ones in top condition, however, these brass lamps also sell well, this one perhaps in the $125-150 range.

Q. Enclosed is a picture of a lamp base, cloisonné— not marked. It is 25-1/2" high, 24-1/2" in circum-ference at the fullest, has four small marks on bronze between cloisonné and masque and ring handles. Could you please tell me the approximate age (I think turn of the century). When I bought it about 12 years ago it had Chinese marked light bulbs. Also what kind of shade did it have and what is its approximate value?

E.O.K., Norristown, PA

A. Your lamp base is Chinese bronze with bands of cloisonné decoration. It may have started life as a vase, but many such pieces were converted to lamps in the early 20th century. You could fit it with a cloth, heavy waxed or even domed glass shade of the 1915-40 era, either a period one or a modern copy. If there is no damage to the cloisonné this lamp would be valued in the $300-$600 range.

Chinese bronze

Q. Enclosed is a picture of a lamp. The shade is cased glass that shades from deep pink to pale pink with gold spatter. The burner is from E.M. Duplex & Co. It has a double wick. There are four large bees on top of the base in silver. There is an owl, pheasant, rabbit and deer with antlers around the bottom. It is in perfect condition.

M.E.P., Green Valley, AZ

A. You have a lovely late Victorian kerosene table lamp. The shade appears to be a lovely cased and shaded pink example with delicate enameled flowers. The base is a fine piece of ca. 1880s Victorian silver plate. Sometimes these were stamped with a maker's name on the base but there were many American firms

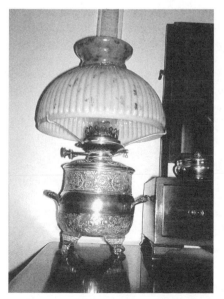

Kerosene lamp

doing such work in the period from the 1870s through 1910 or so. The overall design of this piece leads me to believe it probably dates from the late 1880s or early 1890s. There's a good market for nice early kerosene lamps, especially with original burners. In the right market I would imagine this could sell in the $200-$350 range.

Pittsburgh lamp

Q. I am sending photos and would appreciate any information you can provide, including value. This is a two-socket-lamp. The unusual part of the lamp is the glass shade, which is rough in texture with a pretty snow and mountain scene. Painted on the shade is "Snow in the Alps," but I could find no other marks on the shade or base. The colors in the shade are white, gray, pink and green. It is 21" high, shade is 16" in diameter and the base is 1-1/2" in diameter. It is in perfect condition, working and otherwise, with a natural patina.

G.F., Edgemoor, SC

A. Your table lamp has a reverse-painted domed shade of the type widely produced during the 1920s. Quite a few firms made such lamps, the most famous being Handel and Pairpoint. However, a great many nice quality examples were made by less well-known firms. More information is becoming available on some of those firms and in the book *Better Electric Lamps of the 20s and 30s with Prices* (L-W Book Sales, 1997), I located a color reproduction of 1922 catalog pages of the Pittsburgh Lamp, Brass & Glass Company of Pittsburgh, Pa. One of the models shown, No. S-1388—Electrolier Decoration D, seems to have the same cast-metal base as yours with the stylized Art Nouveau-like leaves and a winter scene shade very similar to yours. I don't find any indication that the company printed the title of the scene on the edge of the shade, but it's possible. Prices for good Pittsburgh lamps, as well as those of other makers, are increasing in value quite sharply. I suspect your lamp would be valued in the $2,000-$2,500 range.

Q. I have enclosed a photograph of my Statue of Liberty. It was given to me by an elderly aunt about 20 years ago. It is brass and stands 19" tall. The bulb still lights and the wind-up clock works perfectly. The book in her left hand reads "4th-July-76." On the front base are the words "Statue of Liberty New York." I can only make out one mark. Can you please help with any information as to history and value?

A. Your interesting early electric table lamp in the form of Lady Liberty was likely produced during the first quarter of the 20th century. It is probably a cast white metal with a bronzed finish. Being a combination lamp and clock adds to its appeal. I don't recognize the mark of the company that cast the metal parts but due to its overall appeal I believe it could be valued in the $250-500 range at least. A Statue of Liberty fan might even offer more.

Lady Liberty

Q. I have enclosed some pictures of an organ/piano lamp that was inherited by our family. The lamp was purchased at an estate auction. It stands 63" tall. We were told the carved base is made from teak wood. It is an electric lamp (in working condition) with the original globes, which are painted with dogwood blossoms. Also shown are the carvings of cherubs and leaves on the base and stand. We are unable to find markings or dates of any kind any-where on the lamp, including on the globes. I would appreciate any information you could give me about the age and value of this lamp.

E.H., Shepherdsville, KY

A. Your floor lamp is a Victorian-style "organ lamp," but I don't believe it is an antique piece. The style of the lamp font and the carved wooden base are not typical of late 19th century originals. I suspect yours is a more modern version most likely produced within the last 30 to 50 years. The base may have been carved in the Far East and then assembled in this country with electric fittings. It is an interesting decorative piece, however, perhaps valued in the low $100s to the right person.

Newer organ lamp

Toys, Dolls and Games

Andy Gump figures

Q. I have enclosed a photo of some figurines I have and would like to know their value. The figures are of the Andy Gump family from the Andy Gump cartoons, which ran in newspapers until the late 1930s or early 1940s, I believe. The tallest figure is about 4" and they are in excellent condition. I inherited them from my mother (I am 89 years old) when she died in 1964. I don't know when she acquired them, but I well remember the ongoing story of Andy and Minerva and Chester and their Uncle Bim, who was infatuated with a widow whom he finally married. The maid, Tilly, also played an important part in their lives. I'd appreciate any information you can provide as to age and value.

A.F., OK

A. You have a nice complete set of character bisque figures from the early Andy Gump comic strip. Not many folks may remember this comic today, but they were very popular in the 1920s and 1930s. Your set was probably produced in Japan in the early 1930s and a complete set does add to their rarity. The only thing scarcer would be to have them in their original box. Today, the better known comic characters would probably have a somewhat higher collector value and some of your pieces show signs of paint wear and maybe some slight chipping. These are also important factors in valuing the pieces. In very good condition, with only slight wear and no damage, each figure might be valued in the $15-$25 range. Perhaps a 10 percent premium could be added because of the complete set.

Q. Help save a 26-year marriage, which is about to end over this '57 Chevy Bel Air Model Car. I got it from a yard sale for $7. I've been getting offers from friends who collect model cars who will give $100 for it. My wife thinks it's worth much more. Help us. The car was put out in 1996. It is called the

Ready to Rumble

"Ready to Rumble" style. Information under the base of the car: "1/18 **57 Chevrolet Bel Air. Licensed by GM Corp. Ertl 0497 GA.**" The engine starts, lights come on inside and out, horn blows, doors open, hood comes off. It's metal, 12-1/2" long, 4-1/2" wide, with two doors. Trash or treasure?

A.P ., CA

A. Gee, I hope I'm not too late to save your marriage! Since the Ertl Company is well known for its die-cast vehicles, I got in touch with Doug Kelly, author of *Antique Trader Books Die Cast Price Guide, Post-War: 1946-Present.* Doug was familiar with this series but hadn't seen too many on the market right now. Most of the 1/18th scale Ertl models that are fairly new and still on the market can sell in the $15-$30 range, but yours, with its electric features, would bring more and Doug noted that "hot rod" die-casts are a field of growing interest with collectors. Even with its special features and overall good condition he felt, however, that $100 was a very generous offer. Hope it's still open.

Q. A friend has this child's horse and wagon, 30" long. The cart and horse are wood, the horse rides off the ground on a center wheel. "Danger" is on back of wagon, "Heavy Teaming" on the side, with no other marks. Can you tell me anything about this? My friend knows nothing about its origin, only that it came from an old house where it had probably been in the attic for years.

M.D., NJ

Push cart

A. Your unique riding toy is a bit of a puzzler to me. It is not a pedal vehicle but actually a type of push cart, powered by the legs of the young rider who sat on the box at the back and guided the wheeled horse with the upright handlebar. Wooden toys are much tougher to track than metal ones and I've looked all through toy guides, including *Riding Toys (No Pedal Cars)*, put out a few years ago by L-W Book Sales. Dozens of wagons, push and pull vehicles from the turn of the century through the 1950s are illustrated in this volume, but nothing quite like your piece. Smaller companies were turning out quality wooden toys and I'd guess this toy might date between about 1915 and 1935. It appears to be in wonderful original condition with good paint and original horse tail. Because of the demand for such toy vehicles it might well sell in the mid- to upper hundreds to the right collector.

Q. I have enclosed pictures of two dolls, front and back. Could you please tell me the names of the dolls, what year they are from and their value?

B.R., Shavertown, PA

1930s doll

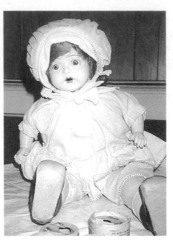

1920s doll

A. Your doll photos are quite good, but you give almost no information on these two dolls such as markings and size. The one in the blue flowered dress with molded hair does resemble the Effanbee Doll Company's "Patsy" or "Patsy Ann" doll made of composition and popular in the 1930s. There was a whole "family" of Patsy dolls produced then and Patsy was about 14" tall while Patsy Ann was about 19". Her dress appears to be a homemade replacement for the original outfit, which would have included shoes and socks. If the body and head are in good condition without any serious crazing or damage, the doll, if it is an Effanbee, might be valued in the $150-$250 range. The doll with the bonnet and pink outfit is a talking doll also made of composition and probably dating from the 1920s. She somewhat resembles the Georgene Averill (Madame Hendon) "Dolly Record" made in the 1920s, but that doll had an open mouth with two teeth. Perhaps the teeth in yours are missing. Value depends on the maker, size and condition. If this is the original "Dolly Record" in her original costume and with the mechanism working, she could be valued in the $400-$600 range.

Q. I was given this Shirley Temple doll at Christmas 1935. She is 15" tall, marked "Shirley Temple" on back of head. Also on head are these marks: "COP IDEAL N & TC." Across the upper back is "Shirley Temple/16." Written in pencil is "e/pM295." She has a composition head with hazel sleep eyes with real lashes, painted lower lashes, single stroke brows, open mouth with six upper teeth, original curly blonde mohair wig, original set, five-piece jointed composition body wearing original clothes, as shown, that have never been off

Shirley Temple doll set

the doll. She's been in the original box 64 years. The picture in the photo came with the doll. On the back of the picture is a lovely 8" by 10" photograph of Shirley signed by her after she became famous. I would like to know the value of this beautiful doll. I look forward to reading "Kyle on Antiques" each month.

S.T., Buffalo, SC

A. What a wonderful Shirley Temple doll set you have! These original Shirleys from the 1930s are always in demand and to have a large-sized one nearly "mint in box" is very rare. In such pristine condition, with the original box and advertising photo, I wouldn't be surprised if a serious doll collector might not pay in the $650-$850 range or a bit more should you decide to part with her. Perhaps you have a family member who would treasure her.

Q. I have not been able to find any information on this miniature commode. It is made of porcelain and has "Tootsietoy" on the bottom. I cannot find it in the Tootsietoy books. I have had it for 60+ years. I do not believe it is a toy. Any information, such as value, would be appreciated.

R.S., Mt. Vernon, OH

A. Your interesting little enameled metal commode marked "Tootsietoy" was most likely produced for use in a dollhouse. That brand name was used on a large line of die-cast vehicles beginning in the 1930s, but they may also have had pieces such as this produced for little girls of the era. Your little piece has nice detailing. If it is a good quality dollhouse accessory, I would guess the value might be in the $20-40 range.

Dollhouse commode

Metal game board

Q. This game is approximately 12-1/2" in diameter. I bought it at a flea market for 25 cents. Under "Checkers" there are two banners. I've written as close a copy of what is written on it: "Another Pixie Game by Steven, St. Louis, Mo." The other side is a checkerboard. I would like some information and an approximate worth before I try to clean it.

A. Your two-sided colorful metal game board probably dates from the 1950s or so. It is probably worth more than you paid but I detect some rusting and that would be hard to remove without damaging the finish further, and it does lower the value to collectors.

1960s doll

1950s doll

Q. Enclosed are pictures of two dolls I have which I'm having difficulty finding any information on. I hope you can help me. The first doll is about 20" tall with a talking string on her right hip. Her tag states she is a 1966 Mattel "Little Sister Look 'N Say." When the string is pulled, her eyes and mouth both move while she talks. Her body is soft material and her hands and face are of a pliable (plastic?) material. She's in very good condition and her speech is quite clear. She says a variety of sentences. You would think with all this information that I could find something on her, but to no avail. The second doll is approximately 15" tall and has "American Character Doll No. 2.675.644" on the back of her head. Her body is also of a pliable material but her head is of a hard substance. She "cries" when you squeeze her chest. She also has a small hole in her mouth for a make-believe bottle and has sleep eyes. Could you please tell me the current value of the talking doll and the value and actual age of the other doll? Please keep writing your column, as it is very interesting and of great help.

V.B., East Brunswick, NJ

A. You have two collectible dolls. The 1966 Mattel "Little Sister Look 'N Say" was one of a number of "talking" dolls that came out in the 1960s. Her flowered short skirt reminds one of the "flower children" of that era. She appears to be in good, clean condition and if she works and her vinyl is in top shape, she might be valued in the $25-$50 range. Your American Character baby doll was one of a large line of dolls turned out by that firm in the early to late 1950s. She may be vinyl, although a soft rubber material, which does not hold up well, was used in the earlier. I'm not sure if this baby originally had a specific name but her dress does not appear to be original and her hair doesn't appear to be in the original set, which affect value. I'd guess she might sell in the $15-$30 range.

Q. Pictured is a copy of an old game that I've had for a long time. I got it from a pre-Civil War house that was being demolished. I couldn't take a photo of it as the glass covering it caused a glare. It's quite colorful with the man wearing a yellow hat, red coat, blue tie, with red lips, etc. There are four holes in the hat band with four tiny marbles you can see on the left

Skill game

side. The object of the game is to get the marbles in the holes of the hat band. It's 1/4" thick with a metal band and the opposite side is a mirror. I can't find any information on it and hope you can help me with an approximate value. I have someone who wants to purchase it from me but I don't want to over- or under-charge him, therefore I'm writing to you for help. I enjoy your column and anticipate getting the *Antique Trader's Collector Magazine* every month.

V.B., East Brunswick, NJ

A. I wish we had a good color photo of your disk-form skill game because it is a fascinating piece of black Americana. This piece, which features a rather grotesque caricature of a black man dressed up like a dandy, probably dates from the late 19th or early 20th century when such black comic themes were popular. Your piece is quite a scarce survivor since it is small and could easily have been damaged. If it doesn't have any staining or wear and the colors are good, I would say it might be valued in the $50-$100 range today.

Q. What can you tell be about this doll?

V.D.J., AR

A. I asked doll expert Patricia Smith to help me out with some background on your doll. Pat replied that this doll was made about 1950 by the Artisan Novelty Co. and made from quality hard plastic with sleep eyes. It is a walker doll with the head moving when the legs "walk" and she was called "Miss Gadabout." There is a non-walking version of the same doll called simply "Raving Beauty." These dolls by Artisan were only made about three years and were expensive in their day, priced around $20 then. This example appears to be clean and only needs clothes and a hair restyling. As is, her value would be around $115. Thanks, Pat, for your expert help.

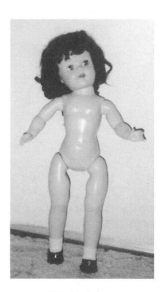

Miss Gadabout

Toy stove

Q. I have enclosed pictures of a child's stove, which is 9" high by 14" wide including shelf to the left. It has a little handle for shaking out ashes. The color is as shown.

J.McC., Sedan KS

A. Your child's toy stove is a nice piece and dates from the early 20th century. A couple of years ago *The Antique Trader Antiques & Collectibles Price Guide* listed a "Baby" model much like yours, including the accessories, for about $700.

Answers To Questions About Antiques & Collectibles

Stuffed animals

Q. I find your column useful and fun. I have these small animals, probably from an Ark set. They vary in size from 2-1/2" to 5" high, have glass eyes and great character. I would like to know their origin and age and maker, if possible. Thank you for any help you can give.

G.S., Fallbrook, CA

A. You have a charming group of early stuffed animals, probably dating from around 1900-1920. They have great character and detail. The Steiff firm of Germany, is, of course, the most famous maker of such items, but I can't say for certain that they produced these. Value would depend on condition and the rarity of the animal, with the lion, elephant and tiger being especially desirable. I can only guess that each might be valued in the $40-200 range and perhaps more as a collection.

Q. This toy is a Wyandotte. The box states it is "Made of Brilliant Litho-graphed Metal. One No. 850 Wyandotte Mechanical Toy—'The Three Little Ducky Ducklings.'"

L.&H.P., Quincy IL

A. Your windup tin toy is a nice example from a well-known toy maker, Wyandotte. That firm is especially noted for its metal trucks and vehicles. Your duck toy appears to be in near-perfect condition and with the original box would be quite desirable today. It could date from the late 1930s before World War II, but some tin windups also came out in the 1950s. You didn't note an age so I'll assume it is of

Wyandotte toy

earlier vintage. I think to the right toy collector it might be valued, with the box, in the $100-$250 range.

Pin the Tail on the Donkey game

Q. I am renewing my subscription to *Collector Magazine* for the umpteenth time primarily because of your most interesting and informative articles. In 1998 I asked you for help in identifying and pricing a couple of articles. Your response to my request was thorough and saved me from selling them for considerably less than their worth, for which I am deeply grateful. I am again asking for your assistance! I am enclosing snapshots of an old (copyright 1887) "Donkey" game and would appreciate an estimate of its current value. On the back it says "Copyrighted in 1887 by Charles Zimmerling." Original price sticker shows "Schwerdimimann's St. Louis—25 cents." It is on a thin 26" x 30" type of oil cloth. It was never used.

R.G.B., St. Louis, MO

A. Your donkey cloth game is an early version of "Pin the Tail on the Donkey," still a popular party game for kids. You don't mention if you have the original box or not and that would make a difference in the collector value. Without any box, but in nice clean condition I'd guess it might be valued in the $30-60 range.

Battery-operated bear

Q. This bear is 10" high. It holds two batteries and pours and drinks. I've had him for many years. He was made in Japan.

L.W., Cando, ND

A. I own a similar drinking bear, which I received as a gift in the early 1960s. Most of these battery-operated action toys were made in Japan and have become quite collectible. The highest prices are paid for those that are nearly mint with their original boxes. Bear toys are fairly common but some others, like monster toys and those featuring Santa Claus, are much scarcer. If your fellow is still in good working order and as nice and clean as he appears I'd guess even without a box he might be valued in the $50-100 range.

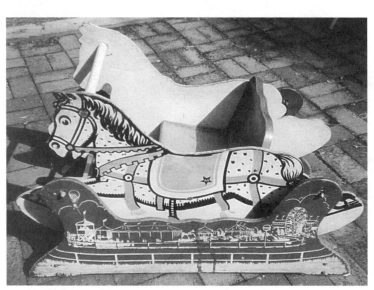

Mengel Elephant Playthings horse glider

Q. Enclosed are a few photographs of a child's horse glider, which is in great condition—apparently well used by a child for many happy hours. On the back of the seat the logo is "Mengel Elephant Playthings" with an "M" in a circle. The side of the glider also has a scene of a circus. Is this foreign or American made? Age and value would also be appreciated.

J.L., Norwich, CT

A. Your charming rocking seat toy most likely dates from the 1940-55 period but I haven't been able to locate any information on the maker, Mengel

Elephant Playthings. There were a number of small firms during that time and some produced wooden toys, especially during the metal shortages of World War II. Perhaps a reader will provide some background on the company. Since your rocker-glider appears to be in excellent condition I would value it in the $50-100 range.

Raggedy Ann   *Raggedy Andy*   *Pinocchio*

Q. I have a Dale Evans watch that I got as a child and I will be 60 this year. I could not get a good picture of it, but it has Dale's picture on it and her name and "Made in U.S.A."

My daughter-in-law has toys that she got as a child. A Pinocchio doll made of wood is printed on the back "op. WDP. & Iden." She also has a pair of dolls, Raggedy Ann and Andy made by Knickerbocker. Ann is about three feet tall and Andy is a little smaller.

D.K., Upper Black Eddy, PA

A. There were several models of the Dale Evans watch produced by Ingraham in the late 1940s and early 1950s. Value depends a great deal on condition. An all-original one with its original box will sell for much more than one without the box or one with a replaced wristband. If it is badly worn and doesn't work the value would be very low. Values can range from $50 for a good working one without box to over $200 for a mint-in-box example.

Since you note the Pinocchio jointed figure and the Raggedy Ann and Andy dolls belonged to your daughter-in-law I would assume they date about the 1950s-1970s. An early Pinocchio jointed figure by Ideal dating from the time the movie was first released, ca. 1939, will have a much higher value than a later version. This one also appears to have some general wear so I'd guess it might be valued in the $25-75 range. In recent decades the Knickerbocker Company has had these Raggedy dolls produced in Taiwan but because of their large size they are still collectible. The value would be highest if they had their original boxes and hangtags. In nice clean, played-with condition I believe the pair might still sell in the $75-150 range to the right collector.

Howdy Doody characters

Q. I have had these cake decorations since I was a child. They still have chocolate icing on their feet. Clarabell had a balloon attached to the right hand. The other four characters have moveable mouths. What is the value of my set?

C.W., Midland, TX

A. Howdy Doody items are very popular with Baby Boomer collectors. I checked one guide to Howdy items, but didn't locate these cake decorations. Were they meant to hold the small cake candles? They are made of hard plastic and would date from the early 1950s. Although they are a little worn overall they are in good condition and the working mouths add to their appeal. Such items vary in value depending on their condition. A set like this in "mint" condition in the original packaging would be much rarer than a gently used set such as this. I would guess that your pieces could be valued in the $10-25 range each. Who knows, the right Howdy Doody fan might even offer more.

Q. Enclosed are some photos of a game I've had for years, which has never been played with. Included with the game are the three packaged feathered darts, instructions and a reorder sheet plus a metal stand for tabletop use. It was made by the American Doll Carriage and Toy Co. of Beverly, Mass. Could you give me some idea of its value, plus when it was made?

C.P., Tacoma, WA

Dart games

A. Your photos are not too clear but from
what I can see of the box and dart boards
I would guess this set dates from the late
1930s, perhaps just before World War II.
During and after the war it was less common to
have the metal dart boards. Many dart games
are not terribly sought after, but yours with the
baseball tie-in would have added appeal,
especially in top condition in the original box. I
would guess it has a value in the $75-100
range, but the right collector might offer more.

Toy stove

Q. Recently I received an unexpected
treasure that has been in storage
for a good many years. My mother was
born in Belle Plain, Iowa, in 1880 and
was given the stove shown in the picture. It is of cast iron, 6-1/2" high, 6" x
8-3/4", with the name "Bird" on the
oven door, which is hinged, as is the fuel
door. On the left side is a removable
shelf. The top surface has four stove
lids, each removable, with a combination lid lifter and ash shaker. A separate
plate covers the water reservoir. The
miniature utensils are a coal scuttle, fry
pan, cooking pan and teakettle with separate lid. A 5" high stovepipe completes
the unit. Several dealers cannot identify it further. I would appreciate any information you might furnish.

R.S. Bremerton, WA

A. These Victorian cast-iron kitchen ranges with their accessories are very collectible today. A surprising number of them survived, however, since they were quite durable. Quite a variety of "names" are found on them. In some markets sets such as this can sell in the $500-$700 range but especially nice, clean and complete sets could go for more to the right collector.

Mechanical banks

Q. I have two pieces I would like some information and value on. They are heavy cast-iron mechanical banks. One is Uncle Sam with box that says "Not for Resale" from Paul Sebastian Inc. of Ocean, N.J. It is 11" long, 4-3/4" wide and 3-3/4" deep. The other is a trick dog that is 7-7/8" long, 7" high and 2-1/2" deep. Both banks are in excellent condition and work very well.

J.F., Pittsburgh, PA

A. Your two metal mechanical banks are reproductions of the Victorian originals known as the "Trick Dog" and "Uncle Sam" banks. I don't have specific information on the Paul Sebastian firm but they may have commissioned these. I suspect they date about the 1970s. As novelty pieces they might each have a value in the $35 area. Collectors should also be on the lookout for some earlier reproductions of cast-iron mechanical banks that are clearly marked on the bottom "Book of Knowledge." I believe these came out in the early 1960s and they are now becoming collectibles also.